CORPORATE CRIME

Selected Titles in ABC-CLIO's
CONTEMPORARY
WORLD ISSUES
Series

For a complete list of titles in this series, please visit
www.abc-clio.com.

Books in the Contemporary World Issues series address vital issues in today's society, such as genetic engineering, pollution, and biodiversity. Written by professional writers, scholars, and nonacademic experts, these books are authoritative, clearly written, up-to-date, and objective. They provide a good starting point for research by high school and college students, scholars, and general readers as well as by legislators, businesspeople, activists, and others.

Each book, carefully organized and easy to use, contains an overview of the subject, a detailed chronology, biographical sketches, facts and data and/or documents and other primary-source material, a directory of organizations and agencies, annotated lists of print and nonprint resources, and an index.

Readers of books in the Contemporary World Issues series will find the information they need in order to have a better understanding of the social, political, environmental, and economic issues facing the world today.

CORPORATE CRIME

A Reference Handbook

Richard D. Hartley

CONTEMPORARY WORLD ISSUES

A B C · C L I O

Santa Barbara, California
Denver, Colorado
Oxford, England

Copyright © 2008 by ABC-CLIO, Inc.

Library of Congress Cataloging-in-Publication Data

Hartley, Richard D.
    Corporate crime : a reference handbook / Richard D. Hartley.
        p. cm.—(Contemporary world issues series)
    Includes bibliographical references and index.
    ISBN 978-1-59884-085-8 (hard copy : alk. paper)—
    ISBN 978-1-59884-086-5 (ebook)   1. White collar crimes.
2. Commercial crimes.   3. Corporations—Corrupt practices.   I. Title.

HV6768.H37 2008
364.16'8—dc22

                                                        2007048174

12   11   10   09   08   1 2 3 4 5 6 7 8 9 10

ABC-CLIO, Inc.
130 Cremona Drive, P.O. Box 1911
Santa Barbara, California 93116–1911

This book is also available on the World Wide Web as an ebook.
Visit www.abc-clio.com for details.

This book is printed on acid-free paper. ∞

Manufactured in the United States of America.

Contents

Preface

Corporate and white-collar crime have gained increased attention in recent years from both government and law enforcement officials as well as the general public. Corporate malfeasance and scandal broke in the early part of the 21st century with several corporations collapsing in accounting and fraud scandals, forcing thousands of people to lose their jobs and thousands more to watch their investments and retirement funds dwindle to nothing. Prior to these events, most of the public probably did not think of corporations and businesses—and their presidents, CEOs, and management—as criminals. After these events, however, there has been an increased awareness of the type and extent of white-collar and corporate crime that occurs in the business world. Although corporate offending still does not receive the attention from the media and law enforcement that conventional street crime does, it is nonetheless as pervasive and harmful.

Numerous laws and regulations have been enacted and implemented in attempts to curb incidents of corporate offending, but with increased globalization and decreased government funding to combat corporate crime, little progress is being made. Business experts and scholars alike have suggested that prevention must originate within the corporations themselves and with the business culture and behaviors that for-profit big business breeds. Although some corporations caught violating laws are charged, prosecuted, convicted, and punished, others seem to have internalized into their business ethos that paying fines for violations is simply part of the cost of doing business. Moreover, critics argue that legislation enacted against corporate offending is merely symbolic, and that because those with political power are in bed with corporate America, no concerted effort will ever be made to control corporate offending.

Indeed, corporations benefit society in many ways. They create new technologies, produce better and cheaper products, spur economic growth, and provide employment opportunities. Conservative estimates of the cost of corporate crime to taxpayers, however, are in the hundreds of billions of dollars annually. Corporations have existed since Roman times and continue to thrive and flourish today, and corporate wrongdoing has existed for as long. The question is, however, whether the benefits of corporations outweigh the costs incurred because of them. If the benefits do not outweigh the costs, what is the best method for holding corporations responsible? Can a balance be achieved? Finally, which types of punishments are necessary to deter corporations from future offending? This book is an attempt to look into these queries and provide information about the causes and cures of corporate crime.

Chapter 1 provides an introduction into the background and history of corporations and corporate crime. It traces the growth and development of corporations throughout history. It also outlines the different typologies of corporate and white-collar crime, and looks at the extant research on white-collar crime. Finally, it discusses some important laws and statutes and the legal origins of corporations and corporate offending.

Chapter 2 looks at various problems, issues, and controversies concerning corporate crime. It provides a discussion of the definitional issues surrounding what constitutes corporate and white-collar offending. It also looks at the consequences of corporate offending, and at philosophical issues regarding whether corporations should be held socially and legally responsible for the actions of their employees. In addition, this chapter outlines methods of detection, prosecution, and punishment of corporate offending. Finally, it offers insight into the nature and scope of the data that exist on corporate offenders and offending, including federal-, state-, and local-level data. Some collections are better than others, none are absolutely accurate, and no systematic methods exist for collection and classification of corporate and white-collar crime.

Chapter 3 offers a worldwide perspective. Corporate crime is ubiquitous. It reaches every corner of the globe; developed and developing nations, capitalistic and socialistic societies, no place on earth is safe from the reaches of corporate crime. Chapter 3 also discusses multinational corporations, which tend to be the worst offenders in today's global economy. It looks at corruption as a form of white-collar crime. Politicians and government leaders and their corrupt practices have bankrupted countries, caused destruction, and hindered development. Their actions have even caused countless injuries and loss of human lives around the globe. War and conflict, reconstruction and development, and provisions of health care to the poor and suffering all provide ample opportunities for corporations and those in positions of power to embezzle, to commit fraud and bribery, and to profit at the expense of the underprivileged and powerless. The chapter finishes with some ideas about what can be done to curb corporate and white-collar offending on a global scale.

Chapter 4 is a chronology of key events in the history of corporate and white-collar crime. Chapter 5 provides biographical sketches of important persons on all sides of corporate crime. Chapter 6 gives facts, statistics, and important government documents and data on criminal justice outcomes, as well as excerpts from speeches, memos, and quotes. Chapter 7 is a selected list of organizations, associations, and agencies, including a brief description of each, as well as Web site information if available. Chapter 8 provides a list of resources and important references for anyone interested in further investigation of a particular topic related to corporate and white-collar offending. These include both print and nonprint resources. A glossary of key terms regarding corporate crime is also provided.

Overall, the purpose of this book is to provide an up-to-date and comprehensive discussion of the nature and extent of corporate criminality, the laws against corporate criminal offending, the extant research, and government and law enforcement responses to corporate crime. It is my hope that this work assists, informs, and also influences students, researchers, and practitioners alike.

I would like to thank the many people who directly and indirectly helped in the completion of this book. First and foremost, I am grateful to Criss for her love, patience, and self-sacrificing support, without which none of my academic aspirations could be realized. Debts of gratitude are also owed to my family, friends, and colleagues whose support is a constant source of motivation and determination. Special thanks to Dean Champion for his academic tutelage, and Roberto Heredia for his scholarly wisdom. I am also indebted to Dayle Dermatis and Mim Vasan, who diligently guided this book into fruition.

> *Only after the last tree has been cut down;*
> *Only after the last fish has been caught;*
> *Only after the last river has been poisoned;*
> *Only then will you realize that money cannot be eaten.*
>
> — Cree Indian Prophecy

1

Background and History

This chapter provides a historical background for the study of corporate crime in the United States. Although there are numerous instances of crime occurring in the course of an occupation throughout history, the focus on, study of, and prosecution for corporate crime is a relatively new phenomenon—a phenomenon that has recently gained the public's interest. For criminologists, "corporate crime" refers to acts in violation of the law that are committed by businesses, corporations, or individuals within those entities. Corporate crime is also closely associated with white-collar crime, organized crime, and state-corporate crime. Although most of us do not think of businesses, corporations, or presidents and CEOs of companies when we think of criminals, corporate and white-collar offenses actually cause more deaths, physical injury, and property loss than the Uniform Crime Report's eight serious index offenses together (Kappeler, Blumberg, and Potter 2000).

While the main focus of the criminal justice system is still toward detection and apprehension of serious street crime and criminals, corporate wrongdoing and malfeasance by such corporations as Enron and WorldCom have brought white-collar and corporate crimes to the attention of justice officials. The mass media has also played an important role in pushing for increased accountability for violators of these types of crimes. The steady reporting of insider trading, embezzlement, corruption, consumer fraud, and tax evasion by the media has helped bring to light the frequency of occurrence, and monetary loss associated with, corporate offending. As a result, concerns about controlling these acts have moved to the forefront of the American justice system.

Corporate and
White-Collar Crime Defined

The official history of corporate or white-collar crime dates back to 1939. Edwin H. Sutherland first coined the term in his address to the American Sociological Society in Philadelphia in an effort to distinguish between these types of crime and street crime. Sutherland sought to spur research on crime in the upper classes. Before his seminal speech, few studies looked for an empirical relationship between crime and higher socio-economic classes. Most research and criminological theories showed that crime was related to, and had a high incidence within, lower socio-economic classes. This speech was also an attempt by Sutherland to gain support for the idea that both types of criminality could be explained by his "differential association theory." Sutherland (1940) believed that the "white collar criminal" was not much different from the street criminal. He stated "that a description of white collar criminality in general terms will also be a description of the criminality of the lower class" (7). Sutherland believed that the only difference between white-collar and lower-class criminals was in the "implementation of the criminal law which segregates white-collar criminals administratively from other criminals" (1940, 12).

Throughout his works on white-collar criminality, Sutherland gave several varying definitions of the term; however, the most frequently cited is from his book *White Collar Crime*, in which he conceptualizes white-collar crime "approximately as a crime committed by a person of respectability and high social status in the course of his occupation" (1949, 9). Since this initial formal definition by Sutherland, there has been much debate about the meaning, definition, and application of the term white-collar crime. With these debates stemming from definitional and conceptual concerns, as well as lack of data, white-collar crime research failed to generate the interest that Sutherland was trying to stimulate. Although today the general public is more concerned than ever before about the quality of life that we live, the water we drink, the air we breathe, the safety of the products we use, and even the security of our savings and stock portfolios for retirement, we remain more fearful of being the victim of a heinous predatory act. Public outcry, political agendas, and therefore the thrust of our criminal justice system focuses more on detection, apprehension, and correction of those engaged in "crime on the streets" rather than those engaged in "crime in the suites."

A large part of the problem in the progress of the study of corporate and white-collar crime stems from the real meaning and appropriate application of the label white-collar criminal. Many scholars of white-collar and corporate crime have written on numerous occasions about definitional and conceptual difficulties (see Geis 1974, Geis and Meier 1977, Wheeler 1983, Meier 1986). What constitutes white-collar and corporate offending? That depends on whom you ask. Part of the problem in defining white-collar and corporate offending stems from the larger, more fundamental issue of what constitutes a crime. One could argue, for instance, that there would be no crime if there was no law. This may seem at first to be a little ridiculous; however, from this viewpoint, a crime by definition becomes any act that violates the law. If the powers that be do not decide that a behavior is morally wrong or hurtful, they will not make a law against that behavior, and it will not be defined as a crime.

If the law defines what crime is, then it follows that two things can be inferred about crime in the United States: "No behavior is automatically a crime unless it is defined by the government as a crime" and "any behavior can be made a crime" (Robinson 2005, 51). Crimes have been categorized as either *mala in se* (inherently wrong or intrinsically evil) or *mala prohibita* (offenses defined by legislatures as crimes) (Champion 2001). Some argue that this distinction should not be made—that no act is wrong in and of itself, but rather acts become wrong when the government says they are wrong. As proof of this, consider the fact that "no behavior . . . has been considered wrong in every society at all times in history" (Robinson 2005, 8).

Crime, then, is socially constructed and is whatever a society says it is. Different societies define crime differently. Similarly, defining white-collar and corporate crime has proved divisive. Foremost, numerous terms have been employed to describe corporate crime: commercial crime, elite crime, political crime, economic crime, governmental crime, white-collar crime, and occupational crime to name a few. The confusion comes in the notion that these various terms are often used to describe diverse behaviors or, conversely, that they have all been used to describe the exact same behaviors. Someone studying corporate crime can find it very difficult to determine which behaviors fall under corporate crime's guise, or if they can even refer to the behaviors they are studying as corporate crime.

Because of this, there have been some efforts at reaching an agreement on what constitutes white-collar and corporate crime. These efforts, however, have not been fruitful. Definitions of corporate and white-collar offending vary both across and within disciplines. The struggle has been to form a universal meaning. Scholars have been unable to find a generally accepted definition; most attempts to date have proven insufficient (Green 2004). Besides Sutherland's initial definition, the ideas others have proffered have tried to delineate the various crimes by type. The following list provides some of those delineations.

> **Corporate Crime:** "Offenses committed by corporate officials for their corporation and the offenses of the corporation itself" (Clinard and Quinney 1986, 188).
>
> **Elite Crime:** "A violation of the law committed by a person or group of persons in the course of an otherwise respected and legitimate occupation or financial activity" (Coleman 1985, 5).
>
> **Elite Deviance:** "Acts by elites and/or the organizations that they head that result in . . . physical harms . . . financial harms . . . moral harms" (Simon 2006, 35).
>
> **Occupational Crime:** "Violation of the law in the course of activity in a legitimate occupation" (Clinard and Quinney 1986, 188).
>
> **Organizational Crime:** "Illegal acts of omission or commission of an individual or a group of individuals in a legitimate formal organization in accordance with the operative goals of the organization, which have serious physical or economic impact on employees, consumers or the general public" (Shrager and Short 1978, 411–12).
>
> **Political Crime:** "Crimes committed by (or on behalf) of the government . . . motivated by the desire for financial gain . . . [involving] violation of a public trust" (Friedrichs 1996, 122–23).

In order to bring some clarity and progression to the confusion, scholars have begun to formulate strategies for consensus on the conceptual issues. They have stressed using either deductive or inductive strategies in order to arrive at definitions or identify a conception of white-collar crime (Meier 1996). The deductive approach would start with a formal definition and then uncover actions or behaviors that are in line with that definition. The inductive method would seek to categorize commonalities in the meaning of white-collar crime and come up with a definition from these. These methods may, however, evade conceptualization. A third method would get rid of definitions and seek to conceptualize white-collar crime to incorporate several definitions.

Scholars of white-collar crime are in contention about which elements of crime should be included in a definition. Friedrichs (1996) poses some questions: Should definitions be narrow and operational or broad and ambiguous? Should definitions be limited to behaviors that the state says are criminal, or include behaviors based on harm and misuse or abuse? Should criminologists pursue these questions for the sake of science, or awakening political awareness, or in order to focus on the offenses and offenders? Generally, some scholars have proposed that our definitions should be developed concurrent to our purpose. If this is done, Friedrichs (1996) believes white-collar crime becomes a multidimensional phenomenon.

Corporate Crime Typologies

According to Geis (1982), in order to come up with definitions or conceptions of corporate and white-collar crime, several things should be considered. One is the existing law; other factors include a determination of forms of harm, categories of offender traits, modus operandi, and types of victims the offenses were committed against. White-collar crime, therefore, can and does incorporate many under-arching activities. White-collar offenses are those "socially injurious and blameworthy acts committed by individuals or groups of individuals who occupy decision-making positions in corporations and businesses, and which are committed for their own personal gain against the business, and corporations that employ them" (Frank and Lynch 1992, 17). Corporate crimes, on the other hand, are those "socially injurious and blameworthy acts, legal or illegal, that cause financial, physical, or environmental harm, committed by corporations and businesses against their workers, the general public, the environment, other corporations and businesses, the government, or other countries" (Frank and Lynch 1992, 17).

Addressing white-collar crime and its definitional issues is beyond the scope of this book. As such, a separation of these definitions is important in order to concentrate more fully on the issue of corporate crime. Corporate crime, at least for the purpose of this book, encompasses those acts that are beneficial not for the individuals inside the corporation but instead for the corporation itself. Some overlap with white-collar offenses does exist, considering that the individuals who engage in these behaviors and represent the corporations are usually of a high social class. Likewise, the line between organizational crime and corporate crime is indistinct, since criminals can often start corporations with the intention of committing crime or laundering their earnings from crime. This book will maintain a focus on the corporations themselves, and will provide more limited coverage of the individuals in the corporations.

History of Corporate Entities and Corporate Offending

Corporations have been in existence since the time of the Romans (Geis 1988). During this time, corporations existed in order to set up and control such legal entities as universities, churches, and associations. The king, in other words, gave corporate status to these entities, essentially granting them the ability to have legislative and judicial powers over themselves (Clinard and Yeager 1980). The East India Company is probably the first entity with such recognized corporate powers. Established in 1602, it is said to have been the first multinational corporation that issued stocks (Mason 1968). In the four centuries following the genesis of the East India Company, the development of the corporation and its characteristics took shape. Legally speaking, a corporation had the following characteristics: "it was a body chartered or recognized by the state; it had the right to hold property for a common purpose; it had the right to sue and be sued in a common name; and its existence extended beyond the life of its members" (Clinard and Yeager 1980, 22). Seventeenth- and eighteenth-century corporations engaged in many egregious acts. Using and trading African Americans as slaves and destroying the Native American culture provide glaring examples of this (Sale 1990).

The Industrial Revolution and expanding enterprise in the eighteenth and early nineteenth centuries produced very wealthy and influential capitalist corporations. These corporations effectively avoided regulation and control even though they engaged in such activities as fraud, price gouging, labor exploitation, manipulation of stocks, and keeping unsafe work environments (Myers 1907; Clinard and Yeager 1980). The genesis of corporations in America was similar; such entities as towns, churches, associations, and universities became trusts with certain legal powers and authority. Colonial America disliked many of the British corporations that were ruling the American colonies. The Revolutionary War was fought in part to rid the colonies of British monopolistic rule. After the signing of the Declaration of Independence, Adam Smith ([1776] 1998) stated that the idea that corporations were needed for the betterment of government was unfounded. For the next 100 years, corporate charters, and therefore control over corporations and trusts, was rigid. Public opposition was fierce, and very few charters were approved; even when they were approved, legislatures limited the number of years they could last. At the expiration date, the corporation would be terminated, and its shareholders would enjoy the division of assets. The colonists wanted to be free from the exploitation they suffered under British rule. After the Revolutionary War, the founding fathers were nervous about the power of corporations. Through various legal means, they limited the role of corporations in society solely for business purposes. Corporations could not interfere in other aspects of society. Several conditions were set forth regarding the establishment and activities of corporations: Corporate charters (licenses to exist) were granted for a limited time and could be revoked promptly for violating laws. Corporations could engage only in activities necessary to fulfill their chartered purpose. Corporations could not own stock in other corporations nor own any property that was not essential to fulfilling their chartered purpose. Corporations were often terminated if they exceeded their authority or caused public harm. Owners and managers were responsible for criminal acts committed on the job. Corporations could not make any political or charitable contributions or spend money to influence lawmaking (Reclaim Democracy 2004).

The nature of corporations changed in Britain in 1844 with the passage of the UK Joint Stock Companies Act, which essentially allowed a corporation to define itself and its purpose. Investors in a corporation could now collect funds for a specified purpose. Control over corporations at this point moved from being a governmental responsibility to one of the courts. Limited liability was awarded to shareholders in 1855, meaning that the assets of individuals in the corporation would be protected from any bad behavior that the corporation engaged in. A landmark U.S. court decision in 1866 in the case of *Santa Clara County v. Southern Pac. R. Co.* (118 U.S. 394 [1886]) granted corporate personhood, which meant that corporations could now enjoy many of the rights and responsibilities of individuals. These rights included ownership of property, signing of binding contracts, and payment of taxes. This case used the Fourteenth Amendment in defense of corporations, citing the same clause that was used to emancipate slaves in the South:

> No state shall make or enforce any law which shall abridge the privileges or immunities of citizens of the United States; nor shall any state deprive any person of life, liberty, or property, without due process of law; nor deny to any person within its jurisdiction the equal protection of the laws. (The Constitution of the United States, Amendment 14, Section 1)

Corporations were not well liked by people living in the original colonies. The entities remaining after the American Revolution were mostly colleges and nonprofit corporations. The Constitution of 1788 made no mention of corporations and so left their existence to the states. Corporations were chartered by states but not without opposition and objection from the public. Thomas Jefferson, believing in a decentralized government for the United States, stated of corporations: "I hope we shall crush in its birth the aristocracy of our moneyed corporations which dare already to challenge our government in a trial of strength, and bid defiance to the laws of our country" (Hartmann 2002). Jefferson is also quoted as having said: "History has informed us that bodies of men, as well as individuals, are susceptible of the spirit of tyranny" (Hartmann 2002). Several court cases would come to shape the idea of the corporation in the early formation of the republic. In the case of *The Rev. John Bracken v. the Visitors of*

William and Mary College, the central issue was whether or not the charter grant of William and Mary College could be altered. The court decided that the corporation (the college) could indeed make changes—in other words, reorganize the curriculum and faculty—and that this would not violate the original charter. John Marshall, who was representing the visitors of William and Mary College, said this of the charter in his arguments during the case:

> The Visitors or Governors have power to make such laws for the government of the College, from time to time, according to their various occasion and circumstances, as to them should seem most fit and expedient. The restraining clause annexed, serves to shew the extent of the grant: Their power of legislation, then, extended to the modification of the schools, in any manner they should deem proper, provided they did not depart from the great outlines marked in the charter; which are divinity, philosophy, and the languages. It was proper, that this discretion should be given to the Visitors, because a particular branch of science, which at one period of time would be deemed all important, might at another, be thought not worth acquiring. In institutions, therefore, which are to be durable, only great leading and general principles, ought to be immutable. If, then, the Visitors have only legislated on a subject upon which they had a right to legislate, it is not for this Court to enquire, whether they have legislated wisely, or not, and if the change should even be considered as not being for the better, still it is a change; still the grammar school is lawfully put down; and there can be no mandamus to restore a man to an office, which no longer exists. One of the statutes, enacted by the trustees themselves, authorises the Visitors to change even those very statutes, one of which creates the grammar school. (7 Va. 573; 1790 Supreme Court of Virginia)

The U.S. Supreme Court heard arguments on a similar matter in 1818. In the case of *Dartmouth College v. Woodward*, Supreme Court Chief Justice John Marshall, the very same man who had argued in favor of the changes to the charter of William and

Mary College, had to decide whether or not the state of New Hampshire could rewrite the charter of Dartmouth College, thereby intervening in its academic operations. Chief Justice Marshall wrote:

> This court can be insensible neither to the magnitude nor delicacy of this question. The validity of a legislative act is to be examined; and the opinion of the highest law tribunal of a State is to be revised—an opinion which carries with it intrinsic evidence of the diligence, of the ability, and the integrity, with which it was formed. On more than one occasion, this Court has expressed the cautious circumspection with which it approaches the consideration of such questions, and has declared that in no doubtful case would it pronounce a legislative act to be contrary to the Constitution. But the American people have said in the Constitution of the United States that "no State shall pass any bill of attainder, ex post facto law, or law impairing the obligation of contracts." In the same instrument, they have also said, "that the judicial power shall extend to all cases in law and equity arising under the Constitution." On the judges of this Court, then, is imposed the high and solemn duty of protecting, from even legislative violation, those contracts which the Constitution of our country has placed beyond legislative control; and however irksome the task may be, this is a duty from which we dare not shrink. (17 U.S. 518 [1819])

This decision did not please state legislatures. State courts protested that governments of the state maintain the right to amend or repeal a corporate charter (Grossman and Adams 1993). Less than 10 years later, the Supreme Court decision in the case of *Society for the Propagation of the Gospel in Foreign Parts v. Town of Pawlet* (29 U.S. 480 [1830]) expanded the rights of corporations to be similar to those of natural persons.

During the Industrial Revolution, the United States was rapidly expanding both economically and geographically. Production and manufacturing swelled, as did international trade. In order to protect themselves from competition, large manufacturing businesses became corporations. These corporations began to take over not only the business world but U.S. courts, politicians, and society (Brown 2003). Corporations soon tried to unchain the fetters that controlled their business dealings. It should not come as a surprise that corporations were granted personhood through the rulings of many of these court cases: the justices of the Supreme Court had loyalty in the propertied class. This is apparent in Chief Justice Waite's opinion in the case of *Santa Clara County v. Southern Pac. R. Co.*: "The court does not wish to hear argument on the question whether the provision in the Fourteenth Amendment to the Constitution, which forbids a State to deny to any person within its jurisdiction the equal protection of the laws, applies to these corporations. We are all of opinion that it does" (118 U.S. 398 [1886]). Legal status of corporations therefore is similar to that of persons. United States law recognizes that under corporate personhood, the corporation is viewed as a legal person, giving it certain inalienable rights. Arthur Miller, author of *The Modern Corporate State* (1976), believes that because corporations enjoy personhood under the guise of the Fourteenth Amendment, they should also be willing to adhere to due process of law:

> The corporate community . . . should be held to minimum standards of decent treatment of individuals it directly affects. . . . The corporate community should take cognizance of the overall interests of the American people when making basic decisions, such as those affecting wages and prices; in other words, it should take public interest into account.

A corporation is a legal entity comprised of persons, but one that in some ways exists apart from those persons. It is this separation that gives corporations distinctive authority and control over its practices. The most important aspects of incorporation include the ideas of limited liability and perpetual lifetime. Limited liability gives members of a corporation limited personal liability for the debts and actions of the corporation. The key benefits of limited liability include the following:

1. A corporation has separate legal entity and distinction from its shareholders and directors, which means that both the directors and the company have completely separate rights and existences.
2. The liability of shareholders is limited to the amount unpaid on any shares issued to them.

3. Shareholders cannot be personally liable for the debts of the company.
4. Creditors can look to the company for payment, which can only be settled out of the company's assets; thus generally, the personal assets of the shareholders and directors are protected.
5. The company's name is protected by law; no one else is allowed to use it in that jurisdiction.
6. Suppliers and customers can have a sense of confidence in a business. (Benefits of a Limited Company 2006)

Perpetual lifetime is also important to a corporation because it means that the structure and assets of a corporation are permitted to exist past the lifetime of its members. These features give corporations tremendous power and ability in the business world. Individuals who own shares of stock in a corporation are called shareholders; nonprofit organizations do not have shareholders. Usually, a corporation will have a board of directors overseeing operations for the shareholders and administering the interests of the corporation. If a corporation were to dissolve, the members would share in its assets, but only those assets that remained after creditors were paid. Again though, through limited liability, members can only be held responsible for the amount of shares they had in the corporation.

The Corporation Today

Corporations today are looked at in both a positive and negative light. They are seen as the heart of capitalist and free-market economies and an outgrowth of the entrepreneurial nature of U.S. society. However, they are also seen as the mechanism by which exploitation of the people in the labor market exists. David O. Friedrichs (1996) best describes what corporations mean for society today.

Many people hold corporations in high esteem. Millions of people are employed by corporations and regard them as their providers. Many young people aspire to become corporate employees. Corporations produce the seemingly endless range of products we purchase and consume, and they sponsor many of the forms of entertainment (especially television) we enjoy. They are also principal sponsors of pioneering research in many fields and a crucial element in national defense. Corporations are important benefactors of a large number of charities, public events, institutions of higher learning, and scientific enterprises. And of course the major corporations in particular, with their large resources, are quite adept at reminding us of their positive contributions to our way of life. (67)

Indeed, the corporation of the twenty-first century has its interests in profits and growth. The large corporations of today are vast and have enormous wealth. Yearly profits from U.S. corporations have been estimated at around $500 billion per year (Korten 1999). The cost of industry to U.S. taxpayers, however, is over $2.5 trillion annually (Estes 1996). Corporate exploitation of the citizenry and the workforce in society is not a shock, given the fact that profits are the main objective of the corporation. Stockholders and managers alike have a general interest in maximizing profits at the expense of others. Since corporate management usually holds a hefty share of the company's stock, managers tend to proceed with their own interests in mind, thereby augmenting their own wealth while common stockholders and workers consume the costs (Friedrichs 1996).

Corporate America is also well positioned to advance its interests through political corruption. Because of their abundant resources, corporations can have enormous influence on the polity and the outlining of public policy. The people at the top of corporations, the government, and the military all have connections to one another that allow them to advance common interests (Simon and Eitzen 1990; Friedrichs 1996). If it is hard to believe that the American political system could be bought, consider that corporate donations to both political parties account for over 70 percent of their fundraising contributions (Greidner 1991). Corporations have also been able to hide most of the political influence they enjoy and remain free from liability due to the fact that the government has deregulated control over many of the industries these corporations control.

The corporations of today have also been able to gain increasing control over key economic and political institutions because of mergers. The large corporations are conglomerates, meaning that they have gobbled up smaller companies and multiple industries, becoming producers of a wide array of products. These mergers and takeovers have led to corporations being able to cross-subsidize, meaning they can sustain one business with the profits from another (Clinard and Yeager 1980). Conglomerates have increased in size, number, and market share due to multibillion-dollar mergers occurring in the 1980s (Curran and Renzetti 1999). An outcome of these mergers has been the ability of these companies to expand their business geographically to the point where they now compete in the global marketplace and have widespread foreign and domestic assets. Clinard and Yeager (1980) report of current corporate activity that "through mergers, foreign subsidiaries, and other growth, today's multinational corporations represent the largest accumulation of wealth ever seen in the world" (38). The increasing globalization of the world marketplace has allowed corporations to further violate laws in the name of profit without taking responsibility for their actions. By becoming multinational, corporations "in the conduct of international business, can obey, for example, the antitrust laws of their own country and yet violate with impunity the antitrust laws of other countries in which they do business." (40)

Although Third World countries and the citizens who inhabit them do enjoy some advantages from globalized economic business, they too pay a penalty in terms of workforce abuses. These transnational abuses will be outlined further in chapter 3. As the global marketplace expands, the wrongdoings of these multinational corporations are likely to become more pronounced. (Friedrichs 1996)

Laws and Legal Origins of Corporate Crime

Although images of crime and criminals today have increasingly included the actions of business executives and members of the upper class, this has not always been the case. Corporations historically have been able to avoid prosecution because of the limited liability they have written into their charters. It has also been difficult to bring charges against an entity because of a lack of a body to punish, and because the populace finds it difficult to grasp the idea that corporations, which are not persons, could offend. Nevertheless, there has been a rapid rise in the criminal liability that corporations can be accountable for under various laws concerning securities, antitrust violations, and the environment. Charges against corporate offending are normally levied against individuals in the corporation; however, the corporation itself could be held responsible and be sanctioned for certain offenses. At both the federal and state level, legislation has been promulgated against corporate criminal offenses. The U.S. Constitution, under its commerce clause, allows the control of corporate offenses by the federal government. Numerous federal agencies also play a part in enforcing this legislation. Such agencies as the Internal Revenue Service, the Environmental Protection Agency, the Federal Bureau of Investigation, the Secret Service, the Securities and Exchange Commission, and others attempt to control and regulate corporate activity.

Early notions of liability held that a corporation could not have criminal charges applied to it. Holding a corporation liable was difficult for a number of reasons (Khanna 1996). First, corporations are fictional entities, not individuals. Second, there are moral problems in proving that a corporation is capable of formulating criminal intent. Third, courts had trouble making corporations criminally responsible for acts not listed in their charters. Finally, difficulty stemmed from criminal procedural rules that the accused be brought into court. In the United States, two doctrines have been of primary use in holding corporations criminally responsible: the Model Penal Code, section 2.07, which makes the corporation responsible for the behaviors of leaders in the organization, and *respondiat superior*, which holds the employer responsible for the criminal acts of its employees. Even though these two doctrines are in place, many prosecutors fail to act against corporations because the shareholders, not the corporate elite, will suffer most from any punishment a corporation receives.

The Supreme Court applied the *respondiat superior* doctrine initially in the case of *New York Central & Hudson River Railroad v. United States*, where the company was not applying mandated shipping rates to all customers equally. The Supreme Court decided that this action violated the Elkins Act, and the corporation was subject to penalties under that act. Justice Day, writing for the court, stated that under the Elkins Act:

> anything done or omitted to be done by a corporation common carrier subject to the act to regulate commerce, and the acts amendatory thereof, which, if done

or omitted to be done by any director or officer thereof, or any receiver, trustee, lessee, agent or person acting for or employed by such corporation, would constitute a misdemeanor under said acts . . . and upon conviction thereof it shall be subject to like penalties as are prescribed in said acts, or by this act. . . . In construing and enforcing the provisions of this section, the act, omission or failure of any officer, agent or other person acting for or employed by any common carrier, acting within the scope of his employment shall, in every case, be also deemed to be the act, omission or failure of such carrier, as well as that of the person. (212 U.S. 481 [1909])

Other courts have also made similar rulings under the *respondiat superior* doctrine; however, critics have pointed out that the doctrine is better suited for civil torts than criminal liability. Section 2.01 of the Model Penal Code ameliorates this criticism because it enforces liability for the actions of corporate employees. Today, there are only two instances when corporations cannot be held liable for criminal actions: if the corporation is incapable of committing the crime (these would involve such acts as arson), or where there is no fine attached as punishment for the action. The Model Penal Code outlines three categories of corporate offenses. The first requires *mens rea*, or a guilty mind, and is traditionally individual offenses, including embezzlement and fraud. Corporations may be charged in these cases if "the offense was authorized, requested, commanded, performed or recklessly tolerated by the board of directors or by a high managerial agent acting in behalf of the corporation within the scope of his office or employment" (Model Penal Code § 2.07 [1] [c]). The second category of offenses includes such acts as collusion that call for *mens rea* and can be committed by corporations. Corporations can be punished for these offenses if, during the scope of employment, an agent acted to benefit the corporation. Under section 2.07 (5) of the Model Penal Code, however, the corporation may not be punished if "the defendant proves by a preponderance of evidence that the high managerial agent having supervisory responsibility over the subject matter of the offense employed due diligence to prevent its commission." The third category covers the strict liability crimes. Under the Model Penal Code, and on the basis of the *respondeat superior* rule, corporations can be held liable consistent with strict liability principles; in other words, there is no need to show intent to benefit a corporation.

The case of *New York Central & Hudson River Railroad v. United States* provides the framework for the idea that a corporation can be held liable for the deeds of agents acting in the capacity of their jobs. The notion of agents acting within their employment capacity is important in charging liability to the corporation. Other components to imputing liability are that employees have the authority to carry out the behavior in question. This authority "attaches when a corporation knowingly and intentionally authorizes an employee to act on its behalf" (Viano and Arnold 2006, 314). The government also has to show that the individual whose actions are in question does indeed have a relationship to the agency (*United States v. Bainbridge Management*, No. 01 CR 469–1, 6 [2002]). The concept of acting within the scope of an agent's authority has generally been determined in different ways with regard to federal and state control. Federally, corporate criminal liability can be imputed based on the responsibilities of the agent, not his or her rank (*In re Hellenic*, 252 F.3d 391 [2001]). The goal of the government is to impute liability on the corporation through an action of an employee. This has been done via the Model Penal Code, section 2.07, (1–6), which states the following:

(1) A corporation may be convicted of the commission of an offense if:
  (a) The offense is a violation or the offense is defined by a statute other than the Code in which a legislative purpose to impose liability on corporations plainly appears and the conduct is performed by an agent of the corporation acting in behalf of the corporation within the scope of his office or employment, except that if the law defining the offense designates the agents for whose conduct the corporation is accountable or the circumstances under which it is accountable, such provisions shall apply; or
  (b) The offense consists of an omission to discharge a specific duty of affirmative performance imposed on corporations by law; or
  (c) The commission of the offense was authorized, requested, commanded, performed or recklessly

tolerated by the board of directors or by a high managerial agent acting in behalf of the corporation within the scope of his office or employment.

(2) When absolute liability is imposed for the commission of an offense, a legislative purpose to impose liability on a corporation shall be assumed, unless the contrary plainly appears.

(3) An unincorporated association may be convicted of the commission of an offense if:

(a) The offense is defined by a statute other than the Code that expressly provides for the liability of such an association and the conduct is performed by an agent of the association acting in behalf of the association within the scope of his office or employment, except that if the law defining the offense designates the agents for whose conduct the association is accountable or the circumstances under which it is accountable, such provisions shall apply; or

(b) The offense consists of an omission to discharge a specific duty of affirmative performance imposed on associations by law.

(4) As used in this Section:

(a) "Corporation" does not include an entity organized as or by a governmental agency for the execution of a governmental program;

(b) "Agent" means any director, officer, servant, employee or other person authorized to act in behalf of the corporation or association and, in the case of an unincorporated association, a member of such association;

(c) "High managerial agent" means an officer of a corporation or an unincorporated association, or, in the case of a partnership, a partner, or any other agent of a corporation or association having duties of such responsibility that his conduct may fairly be assumed to represent the policy of the corporation or association.

(5) In any prosecution of a corporation or an unincorporated association for the commission of an offense included within the terms of Subsection (1)(a) or Subsection (3)(a) of this Section, other than an offense for which absolute liability has been imposed, it shall be a defense if the defendant proves by a preponderance of

evidence that the high managerial agent having supervisory responsibility over the subject matter of the offense employed due diligence to prevent its commission. This paragraph shall not apply if it is plainly inconsistent with the legislative purpose in defining the particular offense.

(6) (a) A person is legally accountable for any conduct he performs or causes to be performed in the name of the corporation or an unincorporated association or in its behalf to the same extent as if it were performed in his own name or behalf.

(b) Whenever a duty to act is imposed by law upon a corporation or an unincorporated association, any agent of the corporation or association having primary responsibility for the discharge of the duty is legally accountable for a reckless omission to perform the required act to the same extent as if the duty were imposed by law directly upon himself.

(c) When a person is convicted of an offense by reason of his legal accountability for the conduct of a corporation or an unincorporated association, he is subject to the sentence authorized by law when a natural person is convicted of an offense of the grade and the degree involved.

At the state level, some states have limited assigning criminal liability only to those in a high managerial position. For instance, 18 Pa. C.S.A. § 307 states that liability may be imputed if "the commission of the offense was authorized, requested, commanded, performed or recklessly tolerated by the board of directors or by a high managerial agent acting in behalf of the corporation within the scope of his office or employment." Other states have applied liability through judicial precedent (*North Dakota v. Smokey's Steakhouse, Inc.* 478 N.W. 2d 361 [1991]). Further, others have been able to impute liability in cases even where high-level management disapproved of the employee's actions (*New Hampshire v. Zeta Chi Fraternity* 696 A.2d 530 [1997]; *Ohio v. Black on Black Crime, Inc.* 736 N.E. 2d 962 [1999]). However, corporate criminal liability will not be imposed unless the actor behaved in a manner deliberate to benefiting the corporation. This can be the case even if, for instance, the corporation did not actually benefit. The corporation would not be criminally liable where the employee's behaviors were counter to the benefit of the corporation (*Standard Oil Company of Texas v. United States* 307 F. 2d 120 [1962]).

Recent Legislation

Sarbanes-Oxley Act

The Sarbanes-Oxley Act of 2002, also called the Public Company Accounting Reform and Investor Protection Act of 2002, was enacted in response to a number of questionable business practices by major corporations (Sarbanes-Oxley Act of 2002, Pub. L. No. 107–204, 116 Stat. 804 [2002])—specifically, the Enron, WorldCom, and Tyco debacles that caused deterioration in the trust of the accounting and reporting practices of these companies. Included in this legislation were increases in punishments under the White Collar Crime Penalty Enhancement Act. The penalty increases included longer prison sentences for those found guilty of certain Employee Retirement Income Security Act (ERISA) infractions. In addition, falsely certifying Securities and Exchange Commission (SEC) reports became criminal under the Sarbanes-Oxley Act. In all, nearly a dozen sections are included in the act obligating certain accountabilities of corporate officials and mandating penalties for their violation. The act also set up the Public Company Accounting Oversight Board, whose charge it is to regulate, inspect, and discipline accounting firms. Major provisions of the Sarbanes-Oxley Act include:

1. Obligation for public companies to assess and give details of the efficiency of their fiscal reporting.
2. Requirement that CEOs and CFOs certify their fiscal reports.
3. Increased penalties, both civil and criminal, for security law infringement.
4. Stipulation that no personal loans can be given to any executive officer.
5. Requirement of independent auditing committees for companies registered on stock exchanges.
6. Guarantee of back pay and compensatory damages, and protection of employees who act as whistleblowers.

Criminal Antitrust Penalty Enhancement and Reform Act

Legislation against antitrust violations is not new. The Sherman Antitrust Act was promulgated in 1890 to place a limit on monopolistic practices. Although this act was, for the most part, unenforced for the last 100 years, President George W. Bush signed the Criminal Antitrust Penalty Enhancement and Reform Act in 2004. This act essentially raised the upper limit penalties in cases of corporate crime to $1 million and 10 years imprisonment for convicted individuals, and $100 million fines for corporations found guilty of antitrust violations. Corporations and their agents may now face severe penalties if convicted.

Types of Corporate Crime

As stated earlier in this chapter, corporate crime involves injurious acts that result in physical, environmental, and financial harms, committed by entities for their own benefit (Frank and Lynch 1992). Although there is overlap with white-collar crime, occupational crime, and other types of crime, corporate crime encompasses those behaviors that are engaged in by a corporation for its benefit. Corporate crime can result in political and economic consequences, as well as physical harm, injury, and death to persons. Friedrichs (1996) sets forth a comprehensive list of corporate offenses that includes fraud, tax evasion, price fixing, price gouging, false advertising, unfair labor practices, theft, monopolistic practices, toxic waste dumping, pollution, unsafe working conditions, and death.

Fraud, Tax Evasion, and Economic Exploitation

Fraud, tax evasion, and economic exploitation have serious consequences for society and the citizenry because they allow corporations to raise their profits, lessen their tax burdens, and at the same time underpay their employees. Fraud covers violations of the Internal Revenue Code and involves corporations defrauding the government and taxpayers, usually through contractual agreements they hold with the government. The U.S.

government contracts with numerous companies every year to carry out certain services. The large number of contracts the government holds with companies sometimes makes it difficult to track whether the money is being used for the purpose the government authorized.

The war in Iraq that began in 2003 has provided numerous instances of companies overcharging the U.S. government—and ultimately taxpayers—for services rendered in an attempt to make a larger profit. A recent report by Congress shows that the Department of Defense has 149 contracts in Iraq with 77 different companies that are worth approximately $42 billion; this report also shows that, according to government auditors, Halliburton, the largest contractor in Iraq, and its subsidiaries, namely Kellogg, Brown, and Root, have submitted questionable bills in the amount of $1.4 billion (U.S. Senate Democratic Policy Committee 2005). Halliburton is reimbursed for the costs it incurs in provision of services, and it also receives supplementary payments based on those costs. Therefore, Halliburton has monetary incentives in billing the U.S. government as much as possible. The congressional report found that Halliburton greatly exaggerated its costs, made invoices for unnecessary equipment, and submitted receipts for duplicate costs. Testimony from former Halliburton employees revealed that the company charged the U.S. government $45 for cases of soda, $100 to clean 15-pound bags of laundry, and $1,000 for video players, and torched and abandoned numerous $85,000 trucks instead of making the minor repairs the trucks needed. The company has also been accused of overcharging for fuel that it supplied to the U.S. Army; in one case, they charged the army $27 million to transport $82,000 worth of fuel from Kuwait to Iraq (Giraldi 2005). So far, one Halliburton official has been indicted for fraud against the U.S. government. The indictment alleges that the Halliburton official billed $5.5 million for work that cost approximately $685,000.

Recent efforts to clean up the damage to the Gulf Coast of the United States caused by Hurricane Katrina have also been fraught with waste of taxpayer dollars. According to a report to the U.S. House of Representatives, as of June 30, 2006, roughly $10.6 billion had been given to private contractors, with only about 30 percent awarded in an open and competitive bidding process (U.S. House of Representatives 2006). This report also identifies 19 contracts worth about $8.75 billion that have overcharged, wasted, or otherwise mismanaged the money they received from the government.

The health care industry is another one of the biggest defrauders of U.S. tax dollars, according to Taxpayers against Fraud (2006). In July 2006, Tenet Healthcare agreed to pay back $900 million to the federal government for violations of Medicare billing, although they are alleged to have stolen $1.9 billion. Tenet, which is the largest for-profit U.S. hospital chain, pleaded guilty to criminal charges in 2000 and agreed to pay $840 million in fines for unlawful billing practices. The same company also paid $631 million in civil penalties and damages from false claims submitted to Medicare, and $250 million as an administrative settlement to Medicare and Medicaid services. Combined, the government has recovered $1.7 billion from this company for health care fraud. In October 2005, Serono, a company that manufactures a human growth hormone that helps fight AIDS, agreed to pay $704 million to settle a fraud case. Serono was charged with giving kickbacks to doctors who prescribed, and pharmacies who recommended, their drug, as well as using diagnostic equipment that was not approved by the U.S. Food and Drug Administration in the hopes of stimulating prescription sales (Taxpayers against Fraud 2006). The list of health care providers that have committed some type of fraud against the government goes on and on; as of September 30, 2006, a total of 94 cases were settled in which the accused company had to pay back monies procured under false claims (Taxpayers against Fraud 2006).

Religious leaders in the last few decades have also been prosecuted and convicted of defrauding the citizenry of millions of dollars. Probably the most well-known case is that of Jim and Tammy Faye Bakker and their corporation Praise the Lord (PTL) Club ministries. Jim Bakker had influence over millions of people in the 1980s with his religious preachings and evangelical television program. The Bakkers, through their PTL ministries, were able to raise unprecedented amounts of charity dollars in the name of religion; however, in the late 1980s, the PTL empire came crashing down because of Jim Bakker's extravagant lifestyle, an extramarital affair, and a money scandal. The Bakkers were said to be living as lavishly as many of the corporate CEOs caught up in scandal in the early 2000s. They supposedly had an air-conditioned tree house for their children and even an air-conditioned dog house (Pfeifer 2000). Bakker was eventually charged with 15 counts of wire fraud, eight counts of mail fraud, and conspiracy (*United States v. Bakker*, 925 F.2d 728, 740 [4th Cir. 1991]). He allegedly raised $150 million from his worshipers under the guise of partnerships in a vacation park. Instead, the monies were used for his family home and to travel in limousines and on private jets. Bakker was sentenced to 45 years in prison and fined $500,000. On appeal, the sentence was reduced to eight years, of which he eventually served five.

Corporations like the ones listed above cost taxpayers billions of dollars a year by defrauding the government and dodging their share of the tax burden. Corporate tax rates have been declining slowly, and many corporations with profits in the hundreds of millions of dollars pay almost nothing in taxes because their lobbyists have been able to convince legislators to approve laws that are helpful to corporations (Friedrichs 1996). Corporations have also found numerous ways to evade paying taxes owed to the federal government, which results in augmentation of our national debt and eventually more taxes to be paid by the citizens.

Price Fixing, Price Gouging, and False Advertising

At the heart of a capitalistic society is competition. Competition is good in the sense that it allows consumers to get high quality products at the lowest price possible. The idea is that if companies want to stay in business, they will have to improve quality and decrease the costs for their products. Consumers lose out, however, when corporations together fix prices at certain levels, thereby prohibiting any benefit to the customer. Price fixing is also referred to as parallel pricing, because companies that are supposed to be competitors manipulate the cost of items, keeping them artificially high, thereby maximizing profits (Friedrichs 1996; Simon 2006). Archer Daniels Midland (ADM), among other companies, was convicted of price fixing commodities used in common processed foods. They paid a $100 million antitrust fine. Similarly, Hoffman-La Roche, a vitamin company, was fined $500 million for attempting to fix the price of some vitamins worldwide, and several music industry firms have been accused of fleecing consumers to the tune of $480 million in CD overpricing (Simon 2006).

Price gouging involves taking advantage of consumers who are at risk, raising prices during times of scarcity of products, or charging the highest price possible because of monopolies, manipulating the market, or biases in the law (Simon 2006). U.S. corporations have long been accused of taking advantage of the poor. "Many food chains find that it costs 2 or 3 percent more to operate in poor neighborhoods, yet low-income consumers pay between 5 and 10 percent more for their groceries than those living in middle-income areas" (Simon 2006, 12). During times of scarcity of products, price gouging is frequent. In 2004, the southeastern coast of the United States was hit by a number of hurricanes. In the aftermath of the storms, the Florida Department of Agriculture and Consumer Services received over 3,000 complaints of price gouging by hotels, gas stations, and other retail service providers (Simon 2006). The oil company Exxon paid a $2 billion fine in the late 1980s because of charges of price gouging for oil products between the years of 1973 and 1981; other oil companies were also levied fines in excess of $5 billion (Friedrichs 1996).

False advertising is nothing new, either. Consumers in the United States have been deceived into purchasing billions of dollars of products or services that never lived up to their claims. Food products giving false nutritional values and products claiming certain utility through false demonstrations are examples of false or deceptive advertising. All advertising in some sense is deceptive in that it tries to influence us to purchase the product. Some examples of charges of false advertising include: labeling products as cholesterol free or sugar free when they contain saturated fats and ingredients similar to sugar; advertising products at inflated dimensions, such as a quarter-pound hamburger that isn't a quarter of a pound; advertising performance claims, as in high octane fuel and enhancement effects for your vehicle when there are none; and advertising low costs in bold print and hiding additional payments and contradictory information in small print, as in calculations of the monthly payments for an automobile (Simon 2006).

Corporate Theft, Exploitation, and Unfair Labor Practices

A typical scenario of white-collar offending involves employees stealing from their employers, but the opposite is sometimes also true. Examples are companies that bilk employees out of proper overtime pay, violate minimum wage laws, fail to make Social Security payments, or use employee pension funds improperly (Friedrichs 1996). Economic exploitation is also prevalent in that companies drive down wages by decreasing union positions, using foreign parts in domestic products, outsourcing jobs, and hiring more part-time employees. Friedrichs (1996) notes that in the United States, many profitable manufacturing plants have been shut down by corporations, leading to economic hardships for those employed there. Not allowing labor to unionize, strike, or collectively bargain are three examples of unfair labor practices. The result is a loss of millions of dollars by employees who cannot negotiate or who are passed over for promotions on the basis of race, ethnicity, gender, or age. One of the largest alleged exploiters of labor in the United States is Wal-Mart. The allegations of wrongdoing against Wal-Mart are numerous and varied (Buckley and Daniel 2003). Charges of unfair labor practices make up most of the charges filed against the company. Wal-Mart's supposed violations of labor laws range from illegally firing those attempting to organize unions to illegal surveillance to threatening and intimidating employees who protest. Many lawsuits that have been filed against the company have been won or are still in the courts (Lee 2005). These labor law violations were known by Wal-Mart officials, but they did not take the necessary steps to alleviate the problems. In 2000, 25,000 employees alerted Wal-Mart officials to potential violations, and an audit found 60,767 missed breaks, 15,705 lost meal times, and 1,371 instances of minors working too late or during school hours (Greenhouse 2004).

There have also been reports of violations of health coverage among Wal-Mart employees. In January 2006, the retailer reported 43 percent of its employees were covered by health insurance, compared to the national average for large companies who cover about 66 percent of their employees. To get to the average coverage rate, Wal-Mart would have to cover an additional 318,000 employees (Bernhardt, Chaddha and McGrath 2005). Studies have also shown that Wal-Mart stores reduce earnings in counties where they are located by 5 percent per person (U.S. House of Representatives 2004). Additionally, in an ongoing lawsuit, six female workers sued Wal-Mart in California, claiming the company discriminates against women by paying them less than men and denying them promotions. The original lawsuit (*Dukes v. Wal-Mart*) has expanded into the largest class action lawsuit ever and, as of 2007, included more than 1.6 million current and former female employees. The lawsuit claims that although more than two-thirds of Wal-Mart's hourly employees are female, women occupied only one-third of managerial positions and less than 15 percent of store management positions. These statistics belie the fact that females on average had more seniority and higher merit ratings than their male counterparts. Finally, Wal-Mart has been accused of violating child labor laws and has paid fines in many states for minors working during school hours, working too late, and working too many hours in a day. Although much of this wrongdoing has been uncovered and fines have been levied, for many companies, Wal-Mart included, it is more cost-effective to continue to violate the law—and pay the fines—than it would be to provide health care, to allow unions to form, to promote and increase the pay for females, and to follow child labor laws.

Violent Corporate Offenses

Corporate executives are not usually thought to be associated with violent offenses; however, corporations do engage in acts with violent outcomes. The belief that corporate crime is less harmful than street crime is a myth (Kappeler and Potter 2004). The loss of life and injuries that result from corporate wrongdoing far outweighs those from street crime (Reiman 2007). Reiman argues that these corporate deaths and injuries are as much out of the control of the victims as being murdered is beyond the control of a homicide victim. Just because many of the deaths and injuries result from the recklessness or negligence of corporations does not mean they should be ignored (Robinson 2005). We do not pay as much attention to these acts because they are perceived as somehow being different. For instance, Friedrichs (1996) notes that the violence seems indirect, as the victims are not directly assaulted by a corporate official. The fact that a corporation causes the injury or death means that a collective group is to blame, not one, or a few, individuals. Corporate violence is also unintended in the sense that in the pursuit of maximizing profits, death and injury are consequential rather than intentional. The criminal justice system, in turn, has not responded to this violence in the same way they have taken action against street violence. Reiman (2007), however, argues that corporations and their employees are just as responsible as street criminals because the injuries and deaths are caused either purposely, knowingly, recklessly, or negligently, and our laws allow for persons to be held culpable in these instances.

Unsafe Environmental Practices

The most prevalent form of corporate violence may be pollution. Corporations account for a large share of environmental violations. As of 2007, corporations were manufacturing more toxic waste than ever, about 600 pounds per person annually, and improper disposal of this deadly waste occurs in about 90 percent of cases (Friedrichs 1996). The detrimental consequences of this is obvious: about 25 percent of U.S. residents will get cancer in their lifetime, and a study by Cornell University finds that roughly 40 percent of deaths worldwide can be attributed to environmental pollutants (Segelken 2006). Pollution has also been linked to health problems other than cancer—things like birth defects, heart and lung disease, and sterility (Brownstein 1981). The Exxon Valdez oil spill in 1989 is probably the worst case of pollution of the environment in world history. A thorough investigation of this case revealed that the captain of the ship may have been intoxicated when the tanker ran aground in Prince William Sound, Alaska. In 1991, Exxon pleaded guilty to criminal charges and paid a $100 million fine, followed three years later by payment of $5 billion in punitive damages (Friedrichs 1996). Emissions from automobiles also account for a considerable amount of pollution in the air, and many cities' air quality is harmful year-round, yet the automobile industry is still reluctant to manufacture vehicles with lower carbon monoxide discharges because of the costs their companies would incur.

Unsafe Consumer Products

Again, corporations may not intend to harm consumers, but their desires to maximize profits often lead them to cut corners when it comes to product safety. Everything from the food we eat, to the medicines we take, to the vehicles we drive, to any of the products we use on a daily basis can be dangerous to our health and well-being. According to the U.S. Consumer Product Safety Commission (2003), whose charge it is to protect the public from unreasonable risks of serious injury or death, injuries, deaths, and property damage from consumer product incidents cost us more than $700 billion annually. Deaths occurring from unsafe products or product-related accidents are alleged to number 70,000 annually (Consumer Product Safety Commission 2003). Although the FDA promulgates the regulation and proper labeling of food products, corporations seem to lure us into eating unhealthy and mislabeled foods that may, because of processing, lead to many preventable diseases.

Consumer products that are imported into the United States from foreign companies have fueled recent safety warnings. With changing economics, foodstuffs have become a commodity in the global market. In 1998, food imports into the United States were $32 billion, and imports exceeded exports in that same year by $2.6 billion (Cohn 2001). This has prompted the Food and Drug Administration to be involved in issues of foreign trade now more than ever and has led to better established standards for food that is being imported from foreign countries; however, because of the sheer volume of the imports, they cannot be assured that everything that enters the country is safe. According to Schmidt (2007) roughly 25,000 shipments of food arrive in the United States each day from over 100 countries; the FDA inspects about 1 percent of these imported foods, down from 8 percent in 1992. The U.S. Department of Agriculture, on the other hand, inspects about 16 percent of imported meats and poultry, but about 80 percent of the U.S. food supply is the responsibility of the FDA (Schmidt 2007).

Ensuring the health of U.S. citizens is the number one concern when the FDA inspects imported foods from all over the world, but it is also an enormous task. Currently, most food takes only minutes to be cleared by FDA inspectors after reviewing the information that importers have presented with the shipment. In 2003, green onions imported from Mexico and carrying the hepatitis A virus caused three deaths and made more than 600 persons sick. But many illnesses caused by food are never reported. The Centers for Disease Control and Prevention (CDC) estimates that there are 5,000 deaths and 76 million illnesses caused by unsafe food in the United States annually (Schmidt 2007). Funding for FDA food safety has increased in recent years, but it is still not adequate; there are over 126,000 FDA food facilities in the United States, and inspections have dropped 19 percent since 2004 (Schmidt 2007).

Recently, the pharmaceutical industry has been one of the main culprits in much of the unsafe manufacture and distribution of products that have a variety of adverse consequences for users, one of which is death. The pharmaceutical industry had profits of $35.9 billion in 2002, which accounted for half of the profits of all the Fortune 500 companies in that same year (Public Citizen's Congress Watch 2003). Despite these profits, and the exorbitant salaries of the CEOs of these companies, the nation is less healthy and less wealthy because of the behaviors of some corporations in this industry. Babies born with defects due to pregnant women's use of the drug thalidomide, which is now being used as an experimental cancer treatment drug, in the 1960s was an early example of the harmful effects that unregulated and untested drugs can have on the body. The company that manufactured the drug eventually took it off the market, and criminal charges were dropped after the company agreed to pay $31 million in fines (Friedrichs 1996). Dow Corning provides another example of a corporation that did not conduct adequate testing or divulge the potential harmful effects of their product, silicone breast implants, before putting them on the market (Friedrichs 1996). The implants caused adverse health effects and, in some cases, even death to the women who received them.

Americans have an obsession with new and improved products, even though unsafe products have been the cause of many injuries and deaths in the nation. The automobile industry has always been scrutinized for not doing enough to make its automobiles safer. The case of the Ford Pinto's exploding gas tank and the hundreds of thousands of automobile recalls each year give credence to the idea that car manufacturers often take shortcuts to save money.

The Consumer Product Safety Commission (2003) is responsible for overseeing over 15,000 products for the public's protection. More than 800 persons die annually from materials that are not protected against flammability, and another 800 perish and 18,000 are injured from unsafe equipment (Consumer Product Safety Commission 2003). The bottom line is that these corporations are more worried about their profits than the health and safety of the consumers purchasing their products. Even with tougher laws, increased prosecution, heftier fines, and negative publicity, these companies have been unaffected and continue to be the most profitable corporations in the nation.

Unsafe Working Conditions

In 2003, the Bureau of Labor Statistics, a division of the U.S. Department of Labor, reported 4.4 million work-related illnesses and injuries (Reiman 2007). Indeed, work-related accidents and illnesses may be the leading cause of death and disability in the nation. The 1972 *President's Report on Occupational Safety and Health* reported the number of deaths from industrial disease at around 100,000 annually (Department of Health, Education and Welfare 1972). Since this report, several pieces of research have documented the high incidence of death and injury in the workplace. According to Reiman (2007), these studies also report "that much or most of this carnage is the consequence of the refusal of management to pay for safety measures, of government to enforce safety, and sometimes of management's willful defiance of existing law" (82). Although accurate statistics are hard to come by, deaths caused by inhalation of asbestos, and the fatalities from unsafe conditions in the chemical, mining, and textile industries throughout our history, speak volumes about the numbers of persons who have died prematurely due to unsafe work environments.

Universities and Colleges as Corporate Offenders

The idea that universities and colleges can engage in corporate wrongdoing may seem absurd; however, many of the nation's colleges and universities are run like corporations. Although many of these institutions are run as nonprofit organizations, some have been accused of misusing federal research grant monies and misappropriating funds in general. Many have also been accused of failing to provide to students the quality education that they guarantee, or unnecessarily creating administrative positions to maintain their bureaucratic structure. Increasingly, universities are worried about their bottom line, and thus emphasizing quantity over quality. Universities have been charged with price fixing of tuition and faculty salaries, exploiting part-time faculty, and defrauding the federal government through waste and loan defaults (Friedrichs 1996).

In the summer of 2007, many internal investigations at universities around the country uncovered wrongdoing by financial-aid directors and other administration officials. In a congressional report by Senator Ted Kennedy, who is the chairman of the education committee, numerous instances of wrongdoing by school officials were brought to light. The report states that illegal payments and improper inducements were common practices for several educational institutions and loan lenders both small and large. Kennedy further claims that university administrators across the country have accepted gifts from lenders to steer students toward their loan companies. Gifts ranged from pens and wine to vacations and stock options in the companies. The most high-profile case involved the financial aid director from the University of Texas at Austin. Investigations showed that the director of financial aid at the institution used lenders who were generous with personal gifts more often than those who had the best interest rates and payment options for students. The UT financial aid director was eventually fired because he held stock in a parent company of the student loan agency that was the preferred lender of the university (Field 2007b). A congressional investigation indicated that the UT administrator regularly accepted gifts of tequila, wine, and tickets for sporting events. He also accepted free golf packages and birthday parties for members of his family (Basken 2007).

The University of Texas, however, is not the only culprit. Kennedy's report names numerous lending institutions and the universities they served. For example, Citizen's Bank spent $43,000 dollars on a three-day golf and spa trip to Arizona for the administrators of one college, and JP Morgan Chase Bank spent $45,000 on a three-day trip to San Diego for university administrators that included $18,000 dollars in drink costs alone (Basken 2007). The attorney general of New York, Andrew Cuomo, has also investigated many institutions, their administrations, and their lending practices. Cuomo sent out over 400 letters to colleges and universities around the United States detailing the wrongdoing that his investigation uncovered (Field 2007a). Although the investigation is ongoing, some executives at lending institutions have been placed on leave, and universities throughout the country are conducting internal investigations of their own to ensure that university rules have not been violated. Meanwhile, students seeking funding for education are on alert about whether their respective universities indeed have their best interests in mind when referring them to a lending provider.

Importance of Studying Corporate and White-Collar Crime

Why is it important to study corporate crime? The primary reasons for increasing the study of corporate crime are as follows:

1. There is still debate about whether current research and theorizing about crime can extend to white-collar and corporate criminals.
2. There has been a lack of focus on enforcement of these crimes.
3. With an increase in globalization of companies, there will be more opportunities to offend unless laws against corporate criminal liability are further formalized.
4. Despite increased pressure to punish corporate criminals, little funding has been allocated, compared with street crime, for the control and prevention of white-collar and corporate offending.
5. Because many large corporations have made headlines due to engaging in egregious behavior, the public has showed a renewed interest in the subject of corporate crime.
6. The impact of corporate offending regarding death and monetary loss amounts to a far greater detriment on society than all eight UCR index offenses added together.
7. If we can increase the view of the seriousness of corporate offending to the public, the result may be increased pressure on the legislature and criminal justice system to give higher priority to the enforcement of laws against these offenses.

Conclusion

The history of corporate offending is long and storied. Since their beginnings in Roman times, corporations have nearly been outlawed, have expanded rapidly, have gained and lost legal rights and responsibilities, and have engaged in behavior both beneficial and harmful to society. Through court decisions and government statutes, corporations have grown into the multinational, enormous conglomerates that we see today. Corporations are viewed as the center of capitalism and the free-market economy of the United States. Many students aspire to work in the corporate world. Corporate America provides countless products that citizens consume daily, as well as grants in sponsorship of many events, charities, scientific foundations, and educational institutions. Corporations, however, are also seen increasingly as greedy, corrupt, and exploitative entities that cost U.S. citizens huge losses in terms of both lives and taxpayer dollars.

Legally, corporations are comprised of persons but also exist apart from employees and shareholders. This feature has allowed them to be distinct entities with authority and control over their own practices. The fact that a corporation is essentially a distinct and separate legal entity from its shareholders means that no one is responsible for the wrongdoing of the corporation. For a time, this allowed some corporations to proceed in increasing profits at any cost without any repercussions for corporate management or shareholders. Recent legislation and Supreme Court rulings have attempted to hold management and shareholders liable and responsible for any wrongdoing by the entity, and the criminal justice system in the United States has given increasing priority to the detection and apprehension of serious corporate offenders.

Types of corporate crime include everything from tax evasion and economic exploitation to price fixing and false advertising to such violent corporate offenses as promoting unsafe practices and unsafe working environments. Countless lives and billions of dollars a year are lost because of behaviors that corporations knowingly engage in. Recent offending by big-name corporations like Enron, Tyco, and WorldCom has increased public awareness of the malfeasance that is occurring. But the focus of the criminal justice system on white-collar crimes lags far behind the attention given to street crimes. Whether this is due to the ability of corporations to lobby lawmakers, or to the disinterest in corporate wrongdoing by the people, or to the media's ability to concentrate our attention on street crime are questions that remain unanswered.

What is known is that scholars and lawmakers continue to struggle with a universal, all-encompassing, agreed-upon definition of corporate criminals and corporate criminal offending. What is settled, however, is that the importance of continuing to study corporate and white-collar crime is of the utmost importance. There remains a lack of focus on enforcement of these crimes, and little funding has been allocated to apprehend and punish these offenders. In addition, increasing globalization of the economy provides more opportunities for offending while at the same time increases the difficulty of detecting these behaviors. For these reasons, the debate and debacle that currently surround corporations and corporate behavior and offending will continue.

References

Basken, Paul. 2007. "Abuses in Lenders' Relationships with Colleges Were Widespread, Senator's Report Finds." *Chronicle of Higher Education*, June 15. Benefits of a Limited Company Web site. 2006. fletcherkennedy.com/benefits_of_a_limited_company.html.

Bernhardt, Annette, Anmol Chaddha, and Siobhán McGrath. 2005. "What Do We Know About Wal-Mart? An Overview of Facts and Studies for New Yorkers." *Brennan Center for Justice*, August.

Brown, Bruce. 2003. *The History of the Corporation*. Sumas, WA: BF Communications.

Brownstein, R. 1981. "The Toxic Tragedy." In *Who's Poisoning America—Corporate Polluters and Their Victims in the Chemical Age,* edited by R. Nader, R. Brownstein, and J. Richard, 1–59. San Francisco: Sierra Club Books.

Buckley, Neil, and Caroline Daniel. 2003. "Wal-Mart vs. the Workers: Labour Grievances Are Stacking Up Against the World's Biggest Company." *Financial Times*, November 20.

Champion, Dean J. 2001. *The American Dictionary of Criminal Justice*. Los Angeles: Roxbury.

Clinard, Marshall B., and Peter Yeager. 1980. *Corporate Crime*. New York: Free Press.

Clinard, Marshall B., and Richard Quinney. 1986. *Criminal Behavior Systems: A Typology*. Cincinnati: Anderson.

Cohn, Jeffrey. 2001. "The International Flow of Food: FDA Takes on Growing Responsibilities for Imported Food Safety." *FDA Magazine*, January/February.

Coleman, James. 1985. *The Criminal Elite*. New York: St. Martin's Press.

The Constitution of the United States, Amendment 14, Section 1.

Consumer Product Safety Commission. *2003 Annual Report*. www.cpsc.gov/cpscpub/pubs/reports/2003rpt.pdf.

Curran, Daniel J., and Claire Renzetti. 1999. *Social Problems: Society in Crisis*. Needham Heights, MA: Allyn and Bacon.

Dartmouth College v. Woodward, 17 U.S. 518 (1819).

Department of Health, Education, and Welfare. 1972. *The President's Report on Occupational Safety and Health*. Department of Labor, Washington, DC.

Dukes et al. v. Wal-Mart Stores, Inc., No. C 01-02252 (N.D. Cal. June 21, 2004).

Estes, Ralph. 1996. *Tyranny of the Bottom Line*. San Francisco: Berrett-Koehler.

Field, Kelly. 2007a. "New York Attorney General Cites 'Deceptive Practices' Uncovered in Inquiry into Student-Loan Industry." *Chronicle of Higher Education*, March 16.

Field, Kelly. 2007b. "U. of Texas at Austin Fires Financial-Aid Director Implicated in Student-Loan Scandal." *Chronicle of Higher Education*, May 15.

Frank, Nancy K., and Michael J. Lynch. 1992. *Corporate Crime, Corporate Violence: A Primer*. Albany, NY: Harrow and Heston.

Friedrichs, David O. 1996. *Trusted Criminals: White Collar Crime in Contemporary Society*. Belmont, CA: Wadsworth.

Geis, Gilbert. 1974. "Avocational Crime." In *Handbook of Criminology*, ed. D. Glaser, 272. New York: Rand McNally.

Geis, Gilbert. 1988. "From Deuteronomy to Deniability: A Historical Perlustration on White-Collar Crime." *Justice Quarterly* 5: 7–32.

Geis, Gilbert. 1982. "A Research and Action Agenda with Respect to White-Collar Crime." In *White Collar Crime: An Agenda for Research*, ed. Herbert Edelhertz and Thomas D. Overcast. Lexington, MA: Lexington Books.

Geis, Gilbert, and Robert F. Meier. 1977. *White-Collar Crime*. New York: Free Press.

Giraldi, Philip. 2005. "Money for Nothing." *The American Conservative*, October.

Green, Stuart P. 2004. "The Concept of White-Collar Crime in Law and Legal Theory." *Buffalo Criminal Law Review* 8: 1–34.

Greenhouse, Steven. 2004. "In-House Audit Says Wal-Mart Violated Labor Laws." *New York Times*, January 13.

Greidner, William. 1991. "Who Will Tell the People: Betrayal of American Democracy." *Washington Post*, September 30.

Grossman, Richard L., and Frank T. Adams. 1993. *Taking Care of Business: Citizenship and the Charter of Incorporation*. Cambridge: Charter Ink.

Hartmann, Thom. 2002. *Unequal Protection: The Rise of Corporate Dominance and the Theft of Human Rights*. New York: Rodale Press.

In re Hellenic, 252 F.3d 391 (2001).

Kappeler, V., M. Blumberg, and G. Potter. 2000. *The Mythology of Crime and Criminal Justice*. Prospect Heights, IL: Waveland Press.

Kappeler, Victor, and Gary Potter. 2004. *The Mythology of Crime and Criminal Justice*. Prospect Heights, IL: Waveland Press.

Khanna, V. S. 1996. "Corporate Criminal Liability: What Purpose Does It Serve?" *Harvard Law Review* 109: 1479.

Korten, David. 1999. *The Post-Corporate World*. San Francisco: Berrett-Koehler.

Lee, Henry. 2005. "Wal-Mart Loses Suit over Lunch Breaks: Oakland Jury Orders Giant Retailer to Pay Workers $172 Million." *San Francisco Chronicle*, December 23.

Mason, Edward S. 1968. "Corporation." In Vol. 3 of *International Encyclopedia of the Social Sciences*, ed. David L. Sills and Robert K. Merton. New York: Macmillan and Free Press.

Meier, Robert. 1986. "Review Essay: White Collar Crime Books." *Criminology* 24: 415.

Meier, Robert F. 1996. "Understanding the Context of White-Collar Crime: A Sutherland Approbation." In *Definitional Dilemma: Can and Should There Be a Universal Definition of White Collar Crime? Proceedings of the Academic Workshop*, ed. James Helmkamp, Richard Ball, and Kitty Townsend, 205. Morgantown, WV: National White Collar Crime Center.

Miller, Arthur. 1976. *The Modern Corporate State*. Westport, CT: Greenwood.

Model Penal Code § 2.07 (1–6).

Myers, Gustavus. 1907. *History of the Great American Fortunes*. New York: Modern Library.

New Hampshire v. Zeta Chi Fraternity, 696 A.2d 530 (1997).

New York Central & Hudson River Railroad v. United States, 212 U.S. 481 (1909).

North Dakota v. Smokey's Steakhouse, Inc., 478 N.W. 2d 361 (1991).

Ohio v. Black on Black Crime, Inc., 736 N.E. 2d 962 (1999).

Pfeifer, Paul E. 2000. "Jim Bakker's Federal Court Appeal." www.sconet .state.oh.us/Justices/pfeifer/column/2000/jp041200.htm.

Public Citizen's Congress Watch. 2003. "2002 Drug Industry Profits." www.citizen.org/documents/Pharma_Report.pdf.

Reclaim Democracy. 2004. *Our Hidden History of Corporations in the United States*. www.reclaimdemocracy.org/.

Reiman, Jeffrey. 2007. *The Rich Get Richer and the Poor Get Prison: Ideology, Class, and Criminal Justice*. 8th ed. Boston: Allyn and Bacon.

The Rev. John Bracken v. the Visitors of William and Mary College, 7 Va. 573 (1790 Supreme Court of Virginia).

Robinson, Matthew B. 2005. *Justice Blind? Ideals and Realities of American Criminal Justice*. Upper Saddle River, NJ: Prentice Hall.

Sale, Kirkpatrick. 1990. *The Conquest of Paradise*. New York: Knopf.

Santa Clara County v. Southern Pac. R. Co., 118 U.S. 394 (1886).

Sarbanes-Oxley Act of 2002, Public Law 107–204, 116 Stat. 804.

Schmidt, Julie. 2007. "U.S. Food Imports Outrun FDA Resources." *USA Today*, March 18.

Segelken, Roger. 1998. "Environmental Pollution and Degradation Causes 40 Percent of Deaths Worldwide, Cornell Study Finds." *Cornell News*, September 30, www.news.cornell.edu/releases/Sept98/ecodisease.hrs.html (accessed September 19, 2007).

Shrager, Laura S., and James F. Short, Jr. 1978. "Toward a Sociology of Organizational Crime." *Social Problems* 25: 411–12.

Smith, Adam. [1776] 1998. *An Inquiry into the Nature and Causes of the Wealth of Nations*. New York: Oxford University Press.

The Society for the Propagation of the Gospel in Foreign Parts v. Town of Pawlet, 29 U.S. 480 (1830).

Standard Oil Company of Texas v. United States, 307 F. 2d 120 (1962).

Sutherland, Edwin H. 1940. "White-Collar Criminality." *American Sociological Review* 5: 12.

Sutherland, Edwin H. 1949. *White Collar Crime*. New York: Dryden Press.

Simon, David R. 1996. *Elite Deviance*. Boston: Allyn and Bacon.

Simon, David R. 2006. *Elite Deviance*. Boston: Pearson/Allyn and Bacon.

Simon, David R., and D. Stanley Eitzen. 1990. *Elite Deviance*. Needham Heights, MA: Allyn and Bacon.

Taxpayers against Fraud. "FY 2006 False Claims Act Settlements." www.taf.org.

United States v. Bainbridge Management, No. 01 CR 469–1, 6 (2002).

United States v. Bakker, 925 F.2d 728, 740 [4th Cir. 1991]).

U.S. House of Representatives. 2004. "Everyday Low Wages: The Hidden Price We All Pay for Wal-Mart." Committee on Education and the Workforce, Democratic Staff, February 16.

U.S. House of Representatives. 2006. *Waste, Fraud, and Abuse in Hurricane Katrina Contracts*. United States House of Representatives Committee on Government Reform.

U.S. Senate Democratic Policy Committee. 2005. *Halliburton's Questioned and Unsupported Costs in Iraq Exceed $1.4 Billion.* United States House of Representatives Committee on Government Reform.

Viano, Michael, and Jenny Arnold. "Corporate Criminal Liability." *American Criminal Law Review*, March 22, 2006.

Wheeler, Stanton. 1983. "White-Collar Crime: History of an Idea." In *Encyclopedia of Crime and Justice*, ed. S. Kadish, 1652–56. New York: Macmillan and Free Press.

2

Problems, Controversies, and Solutions

Types of Corporate Crime and Definitional Problems

Many typologies for characterizing corporate crime have been proffered by a number of scholars. What is the preferred method of labeling behaviors that encompass corporate crime? One method focuses on the principal victims. For example, victims may be the employees of the offending corporation, other corporations, consumers, or the general public. Another method centers on the dimension of the corporation. Crimes are committed by small local companies as well as by nationally based corporations and even transnational companies. A third method categorizes corporate crime based on the industry to which the corporation belongs, such as the oil and gas industry, pharmaceutical companies, the automotive industry, banking and accounting institutions, and providers of health care. Yet another method looks at the type of crime in which the corporation is engaging. Is the corporation involved in deceit, fraud, corruption, or violence? None of these methods has been accepted as ideal. One could even look at the types of personnel involved and the means by which they enter into criminal activity, although most corporate criminal activity involves employees at all levels and stems from existing circumstances in the corporation. This chapter will explain the various types of corporate crimes and provide examples of each one. It will also discuss measurement issues as well as the debate about the detection and apprehension of corporate crime and criminals.

Due to recent well-publicized scandals, the general public has an increased awareness of the amount of corporate malfeasance that occurs in the conduct of doing business. Managers and those in upper-level positions, as well as shareholders, are now giving added attention to the business practices in which their companies engage. They are also paying attention to the diligence with which the records of all things fiscal in the organization are completed and kept.

Since the beginning of the 21st century, we have observed unparalleled levels of corporate malfeasance and financial wrongdoing. The bankruptcies of WorldCom and Enron have raised public ire about the legitimacy of reported corporate profits. Recent examples include such companies as Xerox, which doctored its books to show $1.4 billion more in profits than was actually true, and WorldCom, which overstated its profits to the tune of $3.8 billion ("Corporate America's Woes, Continued" 2002). The top-level officers in these companies have also been accused and convicted of wrongdoing. Some top executives have enjoyed the rewards of the sales of their companies' stocks prior to filing for bankruptcy and have been charged with fraud in the process. Scott Sullivan of WorldCom made $35 million this way; Kenny Harrison and Kenneth Lay of Enron made $75 million and $220 million, respectively, from the sales of company shares; and Gary Winnik of Global Crossing made $500 million in the two years before his company went bankrupt ("Corporate America's Woes, Continued" 2002). The accounting firms that were in charge of these companies' books were also implicated in many of the scandals. Three accounting firms—Arthur Andersen LLP, KPMG, and Ernst and Young—were all charged with violations, and Andersen was forced out of business because of it. Andersen's fall was partly due to its practice of providing consulting services and auditing services for the same company. In 2000, Andersen charged Enron $25 million to audit their books and in the same year billed them $27 million for providing consulting services. In 2002, approximately 250 American companies were ordered by the U.S. government to conduct further investigations and check their accounting methods again, compared with the 92 companies asked to do this in 1997 and only 3 companies in 1983 ("Corporate America's Woes, Continued" 2002).

Companies and their employees have traditionally been able to safeguard themselves from government inquiries, the media, and shareholders because of the authority and influence they have over the information they release about company transactions. These companies are complex organizations to the extent that they can engage in shady business dealings while at the same time keep some employees inside the corporation, and many shareholders outside of the corporation, blind to this devious corporate conduct (Simon 2006). Criminal actions of this nature continue because of the benefits the corporations enjoy and the minimal risks of being caught and punished for wrongdoing (Gray, Frieder, and Clark 2005). Others, however, have suffered some punishment; former Tyco CEO Dennis Kozlowski was sentenced to 8 to 25 years for misappropriating $400 million of the company's money. John and Tim Rigas are currently serving 15 and 20 years respectively for fraud and conspiracy related to their company Adelphia. Ex-Enron CFO Andrew Fastow received a 6–year prison term for his role in the company's wrongdoing. Even Martha Stewart served 5 months in prison for obstructing justice in the investigation of her selling ImClone stock.

The costs of corporate crime are beyond compare, totaling more than the combined price of all other crime *plus* the cost of operating the criminal justice system (Simon 2006). Actual costs are hard to gauge; however, research undertaken by Congress estimates the price of corporate crime at roughly $200 billion annually (Coleman 1985). Couple this with the fact that penalties are rarely imposed (or, if they are imposed, are not severe enough to guarantee compliance in the future), and it becomes obvious why corporate malfeasance continues. David R. Simon (2006, 39) has articulated some of the consequences of corporate crime:

1. Estimates are that roughly five times as many persons are killed annually from job-related injuries and illnesses than are murdered by street criminals.
2. Public confidence in corporate management and political leaders in the United States has dropped, and researchers believe that corporate and political offending may actually cause others (nonelites) to engage in monetary crimes.
3. The role played by political leaders and corporate America in constructing and implementing criminal law leaves

us questioning the belief that crimes are typically associated with poverty and minority status.

4. The rate of inflation is said to be affected by the monetary costs of corporate offending.

5. Corporate criminal offending perpetuates the continuation of organized crime in the United States.

Should Corporations Be Held Socially Responsible?

In general, the past notion that corporations cannot and should not be responsible for the actions of their employees has disappeared. Critics maintain that prosecutors today are still gun-shy when it comes to holding corporations criminally liable, but some attorneys have successfully secured severe fines and lengthy prison terms for those convicted of wrongdoing. This is a welcome change for those in charge of regulating the activities of these corporations, as well as for the public. In the 1980s, corporate malfeasance resulted in punishments that could be measured in months, not years. So, what is the best way to go about punishing corporations? If the corporation itself is punished, and hefty fines are imposed, innocent shareholders will be punished alongside those in high-level positions. Punishing corporate executives could result in the same fate for the company and shareholders. If nothing is done, however, what will deter corporations from continuing to engage in criminal behavior? Also, consider that other entities in society—political bodies and armies, for instance, who may be more powerful than corporations—are not subject to sanctions (Geis and Di-Mento 1995). Who should be punished—the corporation or the employees who engaged in the illegal behaviors? Is it easier to place blame and impose fines on the corporation and its shareholders than it is to prove the culpability of individual employees? Should punishing corporations remain the realm of civil law and courts? What is the utility of holding corporations criminally responsible? What does the conviction and punishment of corporations do to the larger American economy? These are all questions that arise in the debate about whether or not corporations should be held criminally liable for the actions of their employees.

Gilbert Geis and Joseph DiMento (1995) offer some important arguments in favor of holding corporations criminally liable:

1. A corporate body is distinctive from the sum of those persons who make up the organization: therefore, it is more reasonable to pursue the collectivity rather than the individuals who separately fall short of satisfactorily representing the culpable entity.
2. Punishing individuals rather than the corporate body is not an effective strategy, since the risks associated with potential criminal liability for employees will generally be less compelling than those related to failure to meet organizational demands.
3. The shame associated with criminal conviction will be a stronger deterrent to a corporation than to individual malefactors within it.
4. Corporations can be redesigned by court sanctions more readily than individuals.
5. It is much easier for prosecutors to establish corporate criminal guilt than it is to discover and prosecute guilty individuals.
6. Since the corporation almost invariably possesses far greater assets than the individuals who work for it, the opportunity for satisfactory redress of the harm inflicted will be enhanced if the corporate resources can be attacked instead of those of its employees. (76–77)

Indeed, there have been rules and regulations in place since the time of the Industrial Revolution to keep corporations in check and to protect the public from the harms involved in corporate wrongdoing. As noted earlier, however, corporations in the past were rarely held liable, and in the cases where they were, the punishments were paltry. This may have had more to do with society's general view, prior to recent scandals, that corporations benefited society rather than with a lack of legislation in place for them to be held responsible. The aforementioned arguments are influential in recognizing that holding corporations criminally liable may have some benefits for increased regulation and prevention.

However, some arguments can also be made against holding corporations criminally liable, the most prominent one being that holding corporations responsible conflicts with the doctrine of criminal law. Imputing liability onto a corporation is contrary to the criminal law ideal that an agent is responsible only for its own actions and intentions. In other words, fictional entities (corporations) do not have intent and are therefore not appropriate for criminal prosecution. Furthermore, corporations cannot be imprisoned, and imprisonment is an essential element of the criminal law. Another argument against criminal liability for corporations rests on the belief that the process harms the entity. This line of thought holds that corporate malfeasance should be the realm of administrative regulatory agencies and not criminal prosecution; the amount of money corporations now spend to internally monitor their behaviors greatly diminishes their competitiveness in a global economy. Another argument offered is whether or not corporate liability is a true deterrent to these behaviors. Some observers have argued that the threat of criminal prosecution may actually induce corporations to cover up any illegal actions they are engaged in. Finally, holding corporations criminally responsible harms the innocent (shareholders and employees who are not responsible) more than it punishes the actual corporation. Shares will lose value, some employees may lose their jobs despite not being a part of, or even privy to, the wrongdoing of the corporation, and even the community served by the corporation may suffer consequences. It is because of these arguments against criminal liability that we must now turn to the prosecution of corporations. How do prosecutors know when to hold corporations criminally liable, and which, if any, of the employees are to be included in holding the corporation liable?

Prosecution of Corporations

As stated in chapter 1, prosecutors have at their disposal legislation that supports charging corporations and holding them criminally liable for wrongdoings.

The federal government has the authority to police white-collar and corporate offenses through the commerce clause of the U.S. Constitution. Indeed, Article I, Section 8 of the Constitution states that the legislative branch of government has the power to "regulate commerce with foreign nations, and among the several states, and with the Indian tribes." Several agencies of the federal government are an integral part of the enforcement of federal laws pertaining to corporate and white-collar offending. State agencies are also involved in policing these types of offenses, but only at the state level. Federal agencies such as the Internal Revenue Service (IRS), U.S. Customs, the Environmental Protection Agency (EPA), the Federal Bureau of Investigation (FBI), the Securities and Exchange Commission (SEC), and the Secret Service all have agents employed to combat white-collar crime.

Most federal statutes in place for use against white-collar and corporate offending are part of the United States Code. Titles 15 and 18 of the U.S. Code contain the laws regulating trade and financial transactions. The laws most widely used to charge individuals and corporations with corporate offenses are contained in Title 18 and include: §201 Bribery, §371 Conspiracy, §470–514 Counterfeiting and Forgery, §641–649 Embezzlement and Theft, §1001–1036 Fraud and False Statements, §1334 Bank Fraud, §1341 Mail Fraud, §1343 Wire Fraud, §1347 Health Care Fraud, §1501–1518 Obstruction of Justice, §1831–1839 Economic Espionage, §1956 Money Laundering, §1961–1964 Racketeering, and §2325–2327 Telemarketing Fraud. Among the most frequently used laws under Title 15 of the U.S. Code are: §1 Antitrust Violations, §45 Making False Statements in Commercial Trade, §77 Securities Fraud, and §78 Foreign Corrupt Practices. In recent years, many government officials have stressed the importance of prosecution of these offenses under these statutes.

The following is an excerpt from a memorandum sent by former deputy attorney general of the United States, Eric Holder, to component heads and U.S. attorneys on June 16, 1999:

> Corporations should not be treated leniently because of their artificial nature nor should they be subject to harsher treatment. Vigorous enforcement of the criminal laws against corporate wrongdoers, where appropriate, results in great benefits for law enforcement and the public, particularly in the area of white collar crime. Indicting corporations for wrongdoing enables the government to address and be a force for positive change of corporate culture, alter corporate behavior, and prevent, discover, and punish white collar crime. . . .
>
> Generally, prosecutors should apply the same factors in determining whether to charge a corporation as they do with respect to individuals. . . . Thus, the prosecutor should weigh all of the factors normally considered in

the sound exercise of prosecutorial judgment: the suffi-
ciency of the evidence; the likelihood of success at trial;
the probable deterrent, rehabilitative, and other consequences of conviction; and the adequacy of non-criminal approaches. . . . However, due to the nature of the
corporate "person," some additional factors are present. In conducting an investigation, determining
whether to bring charges, and negotiating plea agreements, prosecutors should consider the following factors in reaching a decision as to the proper treatment of
a corporate target:

1. The nature and seriousness of the offense, including the risk of harm to the public, and applicable
   policies and priorities, if any, governing the prosecution of corporations for particular categories of
   crime.
2. The pervasiveness of wrongdoing within the corporation, including the complicity in, or condona-
   tion of, the wrongdoing by corporate management.
3. The corporation's history of similar conduct, including prior criminal, civil, and regulatory enforcement actions against it.
4. The corporation's timely and voluntary disclosure
   of wrongdoing and its willingness to cooperate in
   the investigation of its agents, including, if necessary, the waiver of the corporate attorney-client
   and work product privileges.
5. The existence and adequacy of the corporation's
   compliance program.
6. The corporation's remedial actions, including any
   efforts to implement an effective corporate compliance program or to improve an existing one, to re-
   place responsible management, to discipline or
   terminate wrongdoers, to pay restitution, and to
   cooperate with the relevant government agencies.
7. Collateral consequences, including disproportionate harm to shareholders and employees not
   proven personally culpable.
8. The adequacy of non-criminal remedies, such as
   civil or regulatory enforcement actions. (Holder
   1999)

Corporate criminal cases present prosecutors with many complex factors to consider and weigh when deciding to go ahead with charges against a corporation. Prosecutors do have a number of options at their disposal, including indictment of the corporation, plea agreements, deferred prosecution, civil resolutions, or simply refusing to prosecute (Christie and Hanna 2006). Using the Holder memorandum in a decision of how best to proceed gives some uniformity and a systematic method for prosecutors to follow in these investigations. This memo assists prosecutors in estimating the extent of wrongdoing by the corporation, its directors, and its employees.

Some options available to prosecutors are to hold corporations criminally liable if the senior management of the corporation has created an atmosphere of criminal wrongdoing. However, if employees other than senior officials have engaged in conduct that the upper management has not condoned, prosecuting only those individuals responsible may be the best method. Finally, if unable to prove criminal conduct, a prosecutor could proceed with civil action against the corporation. Prosecutors must consider all options available to them and conduct thorough investigations to uncover the facts. Obviously the more egregious the actions by the corporation, the more harsh the penalties against the corporation should be. Another avenue is a deferred prosecution agreement, which allows the corporation to work with authorities to fix the issues and begin a life of compliance. According to Christopher J. Christie and Robert M. Hanna (2006), deferred prosecution also allows the government "to achieve more than we could through court imposed fines or restitution alone," including the realization of the goals of "general and specific deterrence . . . , carefully targeted reform of a corrupted criminal culture, and restitution to victim shareholders" (1043–44).

The Holder memorandum (1999) also outlines several general guidelines for charging a corporation. A wide range of possible offenses exist, so commonsense discretion must be used in any evaluation of a corporation's actions. For instance, a corporation may be charged for minor misconduct if it appears that many employees within the corporation, or all employees in one department, have engaged in the activity. On the other hand, a prosecutor may not want to impose liability on a corporation for the behavior of only one employee, especially if the corporation has safeguarded against the activity, but the employee acted independently. The role of management in the corporation is an important factor to consider as well; a corporation's management is responsible for generating an atmosphere where criminality is either promoted or frowned upon.

Prosecutors should also consider a corporation's past history. Like individuals, corporations are supposed to be deterred from wrongdoing, especially if they have been reprimanded in the past. Prosecution of those already subjected to sanctions and warnings should be seriously considered. There are other principles used in determining whether or not to press charges against a corporation: one is an assessment of the willingness of the corporation to divulge the nature of its actions and work together with an investigation; another is whether corporate management is trying to protect culpable employees or trying to hinder the government's investigation (Holder 1999). However, cooperation by a corporation should not mean an entitlement of leniency or exemption from prosecution.

The consequences of a conviction for a corporation must be considered as well. There are alternatives such as regulatory sanctions that are not criminal in nature. Sanctions, however, may punish employees who played no part in the wrongdoing or had no knowledge of it; therefore, such action should be given serious thought before being pursued. There also may be nonpenal sanctions that are attached to a criminal conviction that should be explored. In some cases, the corporation, if convicted, will be ineligible for government contracts and federal funding. In considering noncriminal alternatives, though, a prosecutor must balance such issues with the ability of the less severe sanctions to be a deterrent to further wrongdoing (Holder 1999). As the primary goals of prosecuting and punishing a corporation are deterrence, retribution, and rehabilitation, a noncriminal alternative may not be the proper course of action.

Prosecutors can also, where appropriate, enter into plea agreements with corporations. The Holder memorandum sets forth some principles for negotiating plea agreements with corporations. Prosecutors should try to get the corporation to plead to the most serious offense charged. The agreement should be drawn up with the goals of deterrence, rehabilitation, and compliance in mind, and prosecutors should not accept a plea of guilty from a corporation in exchange for dismissal of the charges or nonprosecution. Certain factors should be used in negotiating a plea—the guideline sentencing range for the specific charge, whether the penalty is proportional to the harm caused by the corporation's actions, and whether the corporation understands that entering into the plea agreement is an admission of guilt.

Problems with Criminal Justice System Control

At the outset, one must recognize that the criminal justice system as a whole is not very effective at deterring any type of crime. Since the late 1990s, the United States has become increasingly more crime control oriented. The implementation of harsher punishments, mandatory minimum punishments, habitual offender statutes, and increased law enforcement presence has not done much to prevent criminal activity. The indisputable result is that more and more persons are going to prison for longer periods. In mid-2007, the FBI revealed in its preliminary Uniform Crime Reports (UCR) for 2006 that violent crime was again increasing throughout the nation (FBI 2007). These statistics offer compelling evidence that increasing law enforcement does not necessarily decrease or prevent crime. In fact, having more police may increase arrest rates and thus inflate crime rates. It is also erroneous to equate increases in incarceration with decreases in crime; research shows that there are numerous factors that are related to engaging in crime, and citing that one factor (increased incarceration) can result in large reductions in crime is flawed.

The UCR statistics represent arrest rates and therefore must be viewed with caution. The reports vastly underestimate the amount of crime occurring in the country; experts believe that only 40 to 50 percent of crimes are reported to the police (Bachman and Schutt 2007). The UCR are probably more a measure of police behavior than offender behavior. Not all criminal behavior comes to the attention of police, citizens are reluctant to report criminal activity to authorities, and the political climate of the time often influences these measures (Mosher, Miethe, and Philips 2002).

The formal institutions of social control (law enforcement) rely heavily on informal institutions to regulate behavior. Early in life, people learn the difference between right and wrong from their families, schools, churches, and peer groups. The less successful these informal social controls are, the more the authoritative and formal social control institutions will need to be invoked. Peter Grabowsky (2001) believes controlling corporate behavior is no different. He contends that without informal social controls on corporate behavior, attempts by governmental law enforcement agencies to control corporate offending are futile: "Just as the effective control of conventional street crime requires something more than increased risk of arrest, conviction, and imprisonment, so too does control of corporate crime require a more comprehensive approach, based on a wider array of institutions" (137).

Even before the passage of so-called harsher legislation against corporate offending, there were over 300,000 criminal offenses with which a corporation could be convicted federally (Khanna 2004). New legislation has been called purely symbolic—an attempt by politicians to make it look like they are getting tough on corporate crime (Geis 2007; Khanna 2004). The gap between the richest and poorest in the United States continues to grow every year. Most citizens doubt that government officials will ever really punish corporate wrongdoers the way they do street offenders. Throughout U.S. history this has been the case. Marshall B. Clinard and Peter Yeager (1980) believe this is the nature of capitalistic societies like the United States. They state:

> Radical or Marxist criminologists believe that government regulatory agencies are virtually powerless to control the illegal actions of corporations because corporate power in a capitalistic society is so great. Since the economic elite, they argue, controls lawmaking as well as enforcement, the nature and application of criminal laws will coincide with their interests. (1980, 75)

Gilbert Geis (2007) used the Sarbanes-Oxley Act of 2002 to illustrate Clinard and Yeager's point. The Sarbanes-Oxley Act is designed to protect investors by requiring corporations to make important financial disclosures. The act called for the creation of a board to oversee corporate accounting standards. The first appointee to chair this new oversight board had to resign before he was confirmed due to his connections with corporate America. In addition, at the first meeting of the board, its members voted an annual salary of $500,000 to its chair and, to themselves, an annual salary of $432,000. If the public wasn't cynical enough about this new legislation, these exorbitant salaries seemed to assure them that the new board was not in place as a service to the public (Geis 2007). As an aside, the first person prosecuted under the Sarbanes-Oxley Act was acquitted of all 36 counts against him, including charges of $2.7 billion in fraudulent accounting.

Jeffrey Reiman, in his book *The Rich Get Richer and the Poor Get Prison: Ideology, Class, and Criminal Justice* (2007), outlines what he calls a Pyrrhic Defeat Theory, which states that the failure of the criminal justice system to reduce and prevent crime amounts to a victory for the wealthy and powerful in the country. A brief look at the demographics of the current prison population shows that our prisons are filled with the poorest and most undereducated persons in our society as well as a disproportionate number of ethnic and racial minorities. Reiman attributes the overall crime reduction failure to three synergistic criminal justice system failures: the criminal justice system not putting into practice policies that will result in crime reduction, the criminal justice system not categorizing damaging acts of the wealthy as crimes, and the socio-economic prejudice of the criminal justice system (Reiman 2007). The benefits to the rich and powerful are that the public often believes members of the lowest socio-economic statuses pose the greatest criminal threat—not those in the upper class—and that poverty is not society's fault but the result of a moral defect in the lower classes. This failure then "leads Americans to ignore the ways in which they are injured and robbed by the acts of the affluent . . . and leads them to demand harsher doses of 'law and order' aimed mainly at the lower classes" (Reiman 2007, 170).

Consider the following examples:

Millionaire American businessman Ken Lay (1942–2006) claimed that he had no idea of the accounting or wire fraud that was occurring at Enron, and his assets were not frozen by the government; meanwhile, he cashed out $103 million in personal Enron stock and borrowed $19 million from the company, which he paid back in Enron shares (Reiman and Leighton 2005). Yet, routinely in the war on drugs, officials seize houses of those charged with narcotics offenses even if one of the parties (say, the wife of the accused) is not aware of the criminal activity but also owns the house. Likewise, in prostitution stings, if a man is caught soliciting a prostitute and is driving his girlfriend's car, the car can be seized even if the girlfriend has no knowledge of his actions (Reiman and Leighton 2005).

In California, "three strikes" laws have sent many persons convicted of multiple felonies to prison for lengthy periods. Two examples are Gary Ewing, who stole $1,200 golf clubs and was sentenced to 25 years in prison, and Leandro Andrade, who stole $153 of videotapes and was sentenced to 50 years in prison (Drutman 2003). These two minor criminals are now costing California taxpayers roughly $25,000 dollars a year in incarceration expenses. Yet, in 2000 and 2001, a number of energy companies in California cost taxpayers $9 billion by conspiring to manipulate energy prices. Many of the persons involved in the conspiracy were never indicted, even though they stole millions of dollars, and of those who were arrested, prosecuted, and sent to prison, none received the 25 and 50 years that Ewing and Andrade received. California wants the energy companies to pay back the $9 billion they stole, but the U.S. Federal Energy Regulatory Commission has only seen around $85 million returned. It is doubtful that California taxpayers will ever recoup the money stolen from them. The larger point here is that shoplifters, for example, do not enjoy the luxury of simply paying back the dollar amount of what they stole, even though the monies lost pale in comparison to the losses by corporate offending. In fact, the $9 billion lost in the California energy scandal is over twice as much as the $3.8 billion that the FBI estimates street crime costs *the entire country* each year (Drutman 2003).

Grabowsky (2001) has proffered that what is needed is a wider conception of corporate crime control. Other institutions need to be involved in the same informal preventative efforts that families, schools, and churches perform for traditional criminal offending. These suggestions for increased control will be discussed in a later section on improving current methods of crime control. The U.S. government also needs to play an important role, by setting examples of transparent and fair awarding of contracts and impartial and objective decision making.

Government Officials and Politicians as Corporate Offenders

Corporations that violate federal or regulatory standards often continue to do so because the fear of getting caught and the severity of punishment are relatively low compared with the high stakes and potential for profitability of getting a competitive edge. In essence, corporations have created a business culture that rationalizes violation in the name of profit and sees paying criminal fines for violations as simply part of the cost of doing business. Critics of federal enforcement efforts argue that legislation passed to thwart corporate offending is merely symbolic, because political power is inextricably linked with corporate power. Large, powerful corporations continue to lobby government to make decisions in their best interests. Numerous politicians have been caught accepting bribes and kickbacks for enacting laws and making decisions in the best interest of corporate America. Many political leaders and even ex-military officials have some connections with private corporations. They may have sat on boards before coming into office, or they may secure positions in the private sector after retiring from public office. U.S. vice president Dick Cheney used to be the CEO of Halliburton. Cheney has spent most of his life in public office, but after he took the helm of Halliburton, its contracts with the government doubled. Now that he is back in public office as vice president, Halliburton continues to receive billion-dollar noncompetitive government contracts. Critics believe that because corporate and political America are so intertwined, no real attempts will ever be made to control corporate offending.

Furthermore, George Bush in July 2007 commuted the sentence of former White House aide I. Lewis Libby, Jr. (better known as "Scooter" Libby). Libby was convicted of perjury and obstruction of justice in the leak of a CIA agent's identity. This commutation sends a message to the country that government officials are above the law, and that obstruction of justice, perjury, and other offenses are not enforced against those in positions of power or those with close ties to the government.

Consider who contributed to George W. Bush's presidential campaign, and it becomes easy to see why this president is so supportive of big business. Julian Borger (2001) reported on some of the business corporations that donated to the president's campaign and the favorable decisions Bush made in return. Tobacco giant Philip Morris, for instance, donated $2.8 million to the Republican Party and Bush's inauguration. In fact, the tobacco industry donated a total of $7 million to Bush and other Republican candidates. In return, some of the federal lawsuits against the company have gone away. Although a federal judge found the industry guilty of deceiving the public about the dangers of smoking as well as marketing their products to children, she did not impose the millions in damages but instead issued a ruling requiring stricter labeling of cigarette packages. The logging industry gave $3.2 million, and in return restrictions on the use of logging roads were lifted. The oil and gas industry gave over $25 million in return for favorable decisions on carbon dioxide emissions, the Kyoto treaty, and drilling in places where it was before restricted. Enron also gave generously to the Bush campaign. Finally, the pharmaceutical industry donated over $17 million to Republican campaigns in hopes that caps would not be put on the prices of prescription medicine. Incidentally, Bush's appointee to head the White House Office of Management and Budget was the former senior vice president of drugmaker Eli Lilly. Borger (2001) says the list of business alumni that Bush has appointed to government positions is quite long. Indeed, Bush's election campaign was one of the most expensive in history, and Borger believes that with the big donations from big business, "corporate America bought itself a president" (2001, 1).

Other presidents have been accused of similar wrongdoing, and numerous state senators and government representatives have been caught accepting bribes and kickbacks for government appointments or contracts. But the United States is not the only country where political contributions will buy favors and where politicians are often accused of these types of corrupt practices. Chapter 3 further discusses worldwide corruption in government. Whether in procurement of contracts or in individual kickbacks, corrupt government officials and political leaders account for most of the corporate and white-collar offending in other parts of the world.

Punishment of Corporate Crime

Punishment for corporations convicted of criminal offenses can be harsh and is established under the sentencing of organizations section of the *United States Sentencing Guidelines Manual*. The manual defines an organization as "a person other than an individual" and "includes corporations, partnerships, associations, joint-stock companies, unions, trusts, pension funds, unincorporated organizations, governments and political subdivisions thereof, and non-profit organizations" (*United States Sentencing*

Guidelines Manual §8A1.1 [2005]). Although the recent case of *United States v. Booker* has made the guidelines only advisory in nature, judges are to consult them when meting out sentences (543 U.S. 220 [2005]). Sentences are directed by four general principles found in chapter 8 of the *United States Sentencing Guidelines Manual* (2005). First, a court must order an organization to remedy any harm caused by its actions. Second, organizations run with a primarily criminal purpose should have fines levied that serve to deplete all the assets of the business. Third, organizations not run with a criminal purpose should have fines levied that are proportional to the seriousness of the offense and the culpability of the organization. Last, an organization may receive probation if this will accomplish conformity with sanctions and deter future offending. This final guideline is used regularly in sentencing corporations. In 2005, for instance, roughly 65 percent of organizations sentenced had some sort of probation ordered as part of their sentence (U.S. Sentencing Commission's *Sourcebook of Federal Sentencing Statistics* 2005, Table 53).

The goals of federal sentencing guidelines—enhanced penalties for organizations and newly enacted legislation against corporations—are to deter corporations from offending, make it easier to prosecute corporations, and ensure proportionality in their punishment. In other words, corporations that cause harm and a great deal of monetary loss are supposed to be levied with hefty fines, and the individuals involved are to suffer severe punishment for their behavior. The statistics from the U.S. Sentencing Commission's (USSC) *Sourcebook of Federal Sentencing Statistics* from 2005 break the data into pre- and post-*Booker* convictions. Out of the 45 corporations sentenced in the pre-*Booker* era (October 1, 2004, to January 11, 2005), only 5 did not have any fines or restitution attached as part of their sentence (USSC *Sourcebook* 2005, Table 51). Of those that received fines and restitution, the mean fine was $8,980,039 and the mean amount of restitution was $3,371,659 (2005, Table 52). In the post-*Booker* era (January 12, 2005, to September 30, 2005), only 12 of the 142 organizations convicted did not have any fines or restitution attached as part of their sentence (2005, Table 51); the mean fine was $3,870,330, while the mean restitution ordered was $569,042 (Table 52). These statistics show that the mean amount of monetary damages ordered for corporations has declined dramatically since the *Booker* decision. It should also be noted that in 48 percent of the pre-*Booker* cases and 31 percent of the post-*Booker* cases, the fines imposed were reduced because of the organizations' inability to pay all or part of the fine (2005, Table 53).

Remedies for Harm Done

The *United States Sentencing Guidelines Manual* provides methods for organizations to remedy the harms they have caused. These include restitution, community service, notifying victims, and remedial measures (2005, §8A1.2 [a]). Restitution is required where there is an identifiable victim (§8B1.1 [a]). Community service is essentially an indirect monetary sanction where the service provided is intended to fix the harm caused by the offense (§8B1.3). Notification of victims under the guidelines is an attempt to comply with §5F1.4 of title 18 U.S.C. §3555 (§8B1.4). Remedial measures—for instance, product recalls or environmental spill cleanups—are actions that are intended to eliminate risk of future harm (§8B1.2 [a–b]).

Determining Fines

The organizational guidelines state that fines are imposed primarily "to deter and punish illegal conduct; require full payment of remedial costs to compensate victims for any harm and the disgorgement of illegal gains; regulate probationary sentences; and implement other statutory penalties such as forfeiture and the assessment of prosecution costs" (USSC's *2005 Annual Report* 2006, 35). These guidelines apply to federal felonies and Class A misdemeanors, but the conditions for fining organizations are directed for offenses: where economic loss can be quantified (tax offenses, fraud, theft); where there are instances of other offenses (antitrust violations, bribery); and where specific formulas exist to calculate fine amounts. There are, however, no directives for imposing fines for offenses involving matters of food, drugs, environment, consumer and agricultural products, civil rights violations, or issues of national defense (USSC's *2005 Annual Report* 2006).

Probationary Sentences

Under the organizational guidelines, a sentence of probation may be given to convicted entities (*United States Sentencing Guidelines Manual* 2005, §8D1.1). Probationary sentences may be imposed for purposes of securing payment of restitution, ensuring an organization will maintain the ability to make payments, prevention and detection of future violations, ensuring that an organization makes essential modifications to be in compliance with the law, and achieving the objective of sentencing (§8D1.1 [a 1–8]). When probation is imposed for a felony, judges must ensure that the probationary term is at least one year but no more than five years (§8D1.2). Finally, conditions attached to probationary sentences include that the organization not engage in any other criminal wrongdoing during the probationary period, and that the organization make restitution, notify victims, and maintain residence in a specified place (§8D1.3). Judges can also attach other conditions to the terms of probation (§8D1.4). These include ordering the corporation to publicize the offense that brought its conviction, to provide details of the punishment received, and to offer a plan to prevent future wrongdoing. Conditions may also include that periodic financial statements be submitted to the court; that the corporation submit to random examinations of its records; and that the corporation notify the court of any change in its financial condition, the start of any bankruptcy proceedings, major civil litigation or other criminal or administrative proceedings against it, and/or periodic payments for restitution, fines, or other monetary sanctions (§8D1.4).

As the information above shows, there are several mandates from government officials and numerous laws in place for detection, apprehension, prosecution, and punishment of corporate offenders, but for those corporations and individual agents within organizations who are charged, prosecuted, and convicted, the mandated punishments are rarely imposed. However, the number of corporate prosecutions and punishments has increased, probably due to the fact that consumer rights activists and other environmental and citizen rights groups are demanding them, rather than due to increased legislation. Still, corporate criminals are not prosecuted with the vigor or punished with the severity that traditional criminals are. This may have to do with the idea that punishing corporations harms innocent persons (shareholders) or with Marxist views that the rich and powerful in society use the law to maintain the status quo. Indeed, a few lengthy sentences have been handed out to select CEOs and CFOs of large corporations, but individuals charged with corporate offenses more often than not receive sentences drastically below that which is mandated and nowhere near as lengthy as those convicted of other federal offenses.

Deferred Prosecutions

Increasingly—despite added legislation in place to punish corporations more harshly—both federal and state prosecutors are entering into special agreements with corporations charged with wrongdoing instead of enforcing the law. In research prepared by the *Corporate Crime Reporter* (2005), statistics reveal that since 2003, the U.S. Department of Justice has put into practice a policy of not convicting or sentencing corporations charged with serious offenses. The report states that no major corporation charged with accounting or securities fraud has been convicted since Arthur Andersen's conviction in 2002. These agreements result in deferred prosecution and even nonprosecution in exchange for promises that the corporation will pay fines and increase monitoring of business activities. Again, we see a contradiction between what those charged with enforcing the law promise they are going to do and what they actually do. These deferred prosecutions are the very reason skeptics consider tougher legislation against corporations and sentencing guidelines for organizations merely symbolic. Clearly, there is a difference between the ideals and the realities of the criminal justice system.

Consider an excerpt from former Deputy Attorney General Larry D. Thompson's remarks to the American Bar Association's Criminal Justice Section in Washington, D.C., on August 10, 2002:

> Corporations are economic and cultural facts in our society. Employees act on the corporation's behalf and take on the corporation's identity. Large corporations, develop their own methods and culture that guide employees' thoughts and actions. That culture is a web of attitudes and practices that tend to replicate and perpetuate itself beyond the tenure of any individual manager. That culture may instill respect for the law or breed contempt and malfeasance. The organization itself must be held accountable for the culture and the conduct it promotes. Without this tool, the public would have no adequate deterrent to corporate criminal conduct because the culture that condoned, or at least

acquiesced in, that behavior would be beyond the criminal law's power to correct. Only by clearly preserving the possibility of prosecuting the corporation itself can we ensure systemic reform. . . .

Without corporate criminal liability, there would be no effective deterrent to a corporate culture that—expressly or tacitly—condones criminal conduct. Instead, corporations could merely appoint a "vice president in charge of going to jail" who would serve as a whipping boy for the collective acts of the organization. It should go without saying that the criminal law seeks to punish individuals who commit crimes. But the criminal law wisely seeks to punish and reform the corporation that fosters or condones its employees' criminal behavior.

When asked why he robbed banks, Willie Sutton famously responded, "Because that's where the money is." So, too, is the money in the corporation. In order to change corporate cultures that foster criminal conduct, it is sometimes necessary to punish the corporation itself through substantial fines and the associated collateral consequences of criminal convictions that not only have a direct impact on the bottom line, but also spur reforms in the way the business makes money.

I believe we are on the right track at the Department of Justice. But we will not be complacent. As Will Rogers, the famous American philosopher, once said, "Even if you are on the right track, if you just sit there and do nothing, you will eventually get run over." (Thompson 2002)

This excerpt makes it clear that, under current laws, criminal liability can be imputed on corporations, and that corporations need to be prosecuted for serious violations. Yet, since Thompson's remarks (2002) and the 2002 Sarbanes-Oxley Act, both mandating harsher punishment for corporations, prosecutors have negotiated twice as many nonprosecution and deferred prosecution agreements as they did in the previous 10 years: there were 23 agreements between 2002 and 2005, but only 11 agreements of this type between 1992 and 2001 (Corporate Crime Reporter 2005). It appears as if the U.S. Department of Justice, in the words of Will Rogers, is "get[ting] run over" by corporate America.

Even in cases where a corporation confesses to violating federal law, the result may not be a criminal conviction. A perfect example of this is the 2005 case against the professional services firm KPMG. KPMG confessed to accounting fraud in which they falsely reported $11 billion in tax losses, resulting in evasion of taxes to the U.S. government to the tune of roughly $2.5 billion. Even the former attorney general of the United States, Alberto Gonzales, stated that the case involving KPMG was the largest case of tax fraud in U.S. history. David Kelley, then the U.S. attorney general in New York, tried to convene a grand jury and indict KPMG for fraud and obstruction of justice but was advised by the deputy attorney general at the time, James Comey, to enter into a deferred prosecution with the company. Unnamed sources say that KPMG itself contacted Comey and struck a deal, much to the objection of Kelley (Corporate Crime Reporter 2005). Many have questioned whether the U.S. Department of Justice can have any authority and deterrent effect over corporate criminal offending if the corporation that confesses to the largest-ever case of criminal fraud and tax evasion does not get convicted and punished.

Measuring Corporate Crime

Although to date it appears that the detection, reporting, and prosecution of corporate criminality is greater than ever, we are still not certain if corporate participation in criminal activity is decreasing. Obviously, the citizenry, and as a result the polity, is making corporate crime one of the main concerns of society today. It seems, however, that the changing nature of the economy and the increasing globalization of the marketplace may be providing more opportunity for corporations to engage in illegal activity. Consider the fact that the U.S. government in 2007 was appropriating more money to health care, defense, and antiterrorist agencies. More federal funding to these areas means more contracts with more agencies, which makes it more likely that these monies are at risk of being misappropriated.

Corporate crime measurement is a very difficult matter because it involves organizations, individuals, and the associations between them (Simpson, Harris, and Mattson 1995). Official statistics on corporate offending are not well kept. The traditional summary reporting format makes only a limited amount of information available (Barnett 2006). Police statistics do include information on negligent homicide, some regulatory violations, forgery, bribery, and fraud, but the problem becomes investigating whether in fact a corporation—or an employee of the corporation—was the offender, and who benefited most from the illegal behavior (Simpson, Harris, and Mattson 1995). For these reasons, data at the state and local level are not adequate for getting information on corporate offending.

The public's knowledge of corporate offending has risen considerably. It remains unclear whether this is because corporations are increasingly engaging in corporate wrongdoing, especially because of today's global marketplace, or because we are getting better at detecting and formally charging these organizations for criminal behaviors. What is clear, however, is that we need to devise better methods for obtaining and maintaining data on corporate offending.

Sources of Data

Federal Sources

Various sources of data exist for measuring the extent of corporate offending; some are better than others, but none is absolutely accurate. Even the U.S. Department of Justice in its strategic plan for fiscal years 2003 to 2008 reports that "precise financial losses resulting from white collar crime for consumers, government, and business are unknown since no systematic data collection exists" (U.S. Department of the Treasury 2003). Sources include those collected at the federal, state, and city level. The FBI measures some incidents of white-collar offending with its Uniform Crime Reports (UCRs), which include offenses such as embezzlement, fraud, and forgery/counterfeiting. The problem is that the UCR program underestimates crime in general—and vastly underestimates corporate crime because their statistics do not measure all types of corporate offenses. Through these official statistics then, it appears as if arrest rates for corporate offending are lower than those for property offenses and for crime in general. Again, however, UCR statistics may be misleading due to the fact that not all offenses are included in their report. Other problems with using UCR data involve a lack of offender characteristics for each type of crime. No occupational or socioeconomic variables about the offender are available in the data

(Barnett 2006), and no characteristics of corporate structure are included either. As such, using these characteristics as definitions of corporate crime is meaningless.

The Bureau of Justice Statistics, a division of the U.S. Department of Justice, also collects information on corporate offending. Offenses in their database include tax law violations, food and drug offenses, bribery, antitrust cases, environmental violations, fraud, obstruction of justice, and perjury. The National White Collar Crime Center (NW3C) is another organization that gathers statistics on white-collar crime. The center is a federally funded nonprofit organization that provides support for agencies in prevention, investigation, and prosecution of economic and high-tech crimes. The NW3C conducted a survey in 2005 to measure public perceptions and past-year experiences with white-collar and corporate crime victimization. The 1,605 adult respondents reported their opinions about the seriousness of these offenses and their individual experiences with account fraud, credit card fraud, product pricing, unnecessary repairs to property, as well as any losses because of false stock information, national corporate scandals or fraudulent business ventures, and fraud involving the Internet (Kane and Wall 2005).

Results of the study revealed that 46.5 percent of households and 36 percent of the individuals surveyed reported at least one form of victimization within the 12-month period. This rose to 62.5 percent when respondents were asked about any victimizations in their lifetime. The most prevalent forms of victimization were the result of credit card fraud, unnecessary repairs, product pricing fraud, and national corporate scandals. The survey results also showed that the two most common factors for being victimized were use of the Internet and residing in an urban area. When asked about reporting behavior, 67 percent of respondents said they reported the victimization to at least one source, whether it was the credit card company, the business itself, or law enforcement; only 30.1 percent reported the victimization to a law enforcement or crime control agency (Kane and Wall 2005).

Regarding the public's perception of the seriousness of white-collar offenses, the results revealed that respondents consider them to be as serious as street crime; however, crimes that involve physical harm are seen as more serious than those with monetary losses. Furthermore, those offenses committed by organizations are seen as more harmful than individual offenders, and persons with high status are seen as more culpable than those with lower status in the organization (Kane and Wall 2005). The results of the survey by the NW3C are interesting in that they show that corporate offending is more prevalent than official statistics suggest. The public evidently views these offenses as serious and in need of increased control, yet there is apathy among individuals in reporting these offenses to the appropriate crime control agencies. A similar survey was done by Pricewater-houseCoopers (PwC) in 2005, in which they interviewed 3,634 senior executives in 34 companies around the world, soliciting information on corporate fraud. The results of this survey show an increase in the number of companies worldwide that have fallen victim to economic crime—an increase from 37 percent of companies in 2003 to 45 percent of companies in 2005 (Bussmann 2005). Results also show that the larger the company, the more likely it is to be victimized by fraud. Of the companies victimized, 40 percent report they have endured significant "collateral damage" because of fraud. It also appears from the survey that no industry is safe—it did not matter whether these were industries that were regulated or not—and 38 to 60 percent of the companies in various industries reported serious frauds (Bussmann 2005). Probably the most interesting and disturbing finding from this survey on global economic crime was that despite all the recent efforts by governments to crack down on these offenses with new legislation and detection efforts (the Sarbanes-Oxley Act, for example), companies typically report that the fraud came to their attention by chance, with someone tipping them off that they had been victimized.

At the federal level, data and statistics are also collected and compiled by the USSC. Again, however, these would only reflect statistics on those offenses that have been reported and are in various stages of prosecution, conviction, or sentencing. Federal-level data collection methods differ in their reported incidence rates for corporate crime. There is also some confusion in using the terms *corporate crime* and *white-collar crime.* Corporate crime usually involves organizations, and most crime control agencies that collect crime statistics only gather information on individual offenses because of the idea that violations of the law can only be committed by individuals, who can then be punished for these violations. Further definitional issues stem from conceptual problems with what encompasses corporate crimes; these were discussed extensively in chapter 1.

The U.S. attorney general is responsible for prosecuting federal corporate violations. Within the Department of Justice, there are several regional offices of the attorney general. Because cases of wrongdoing appear in the various districts upon referral from the FBI or other crime control agencies, Simpson, Harris, and Mattson (1995) report that federal court records only show cases that have been adjudicated. Cases that were dismissed, or cases that were closed citing actions other than adjudication, are only available through Freedom of Information Act requests. Some regulatory agencies may keep information about corporate offending for their records, but usually these data are only available after a corporation has had charges brought against it (Clinard and Yeager 1980). Probably the best source of information on corporate crime data—at least on those corporations that have been prosecuted—comes from the USSC. Again, these data only include information on those corporations that were convicted and sentenced in federal district court. Simpson, Harris, and Mattson (1995) state that even if a case is properly "brought into the system, there is no guarantee that formal adjudication will result" (119).

State and Municipal Sources

The office of the state attorney general collects data on state corporate crime. Similar to federal-level statistics, most states do not report separate statistics for corporate criminal offending, nor do they have specialized units to apprehend and detect these kinds of offenses. And, as with federal-level record keeping, definitions and measurement of corporate and white-collar crime at the state level are ambiguous (Wellford and Ingraham 1994). City and municipal law enforcement authorities, if they report corporate offenses, would do so as part of the information they regularly give to the FBI for the UCR. These are official police statistics and for offenses such as fraud, forgery, embezzlement, and bribery. The data suffer from many problems, the chief one being that they are compiled together with conventional crime statistics (Simpson, Harris, and Mattson 1995).

Overall, the sources of data on corporate offending have several limitations with regard to measurement and accuracy. First, they vastly underestimate the amount of offending occurring in the United States. Second, there are various methodological issues in the measurement of these data as well as biases in the recording and reporting of the statistics. Third, and related to the first two, is that availability and public access to these data are limited. These data reveal that criminal penalties against corporations are not imposed as often, or as severely, as needed to effectively deter them from future offending.

Detecting and Controlling Corporate Crime

The idea behind the deterrent value of the sentencing structure in the United States relies on two things: retribution and the severity of a penal sanction. In order for retribution and deterrence to work, offenders have to fear being caught in the first place, and then the sentence has to be proportionately severe. The risk of a corporation getting caught for engaging in illegal activity seems to be low (Simpson 2002). As stated earlier, corporate crimes are often complex acts that involve multiple offenders; the indirectness of intention, as well as the inability to single out a victim, makes detection difficult. Another problem surrounding detection has to do with actual policing of these behaviors. In some cases, oversight of these actors has been transferred to regulatory agencies and out of the realm of law enforcement. "Traditional policing techniques . . . are unsuited for or unable to penetrate the corporate setting. . . . Police are trained for conventional crime investigation and generally lack many of the investigatory skills necessary to follow the paper trail left by corporate criminals" (Simpson 2002, 46). Moreover, federal agencies responsible for enforcement of these activities have been reluctant to work together in uncovering these types of offenses.

Traditionally—even after detection, investigation, prosecution, and conviction of corporations and their employees for criminal wrongdoing—the sanctions meted out are rarely severe enough to act as deterrents. The truth is that these cases are usually dismissed, settled through plea negotiations, or result in what amounts to a "slap on the wrist" fine (Simpson 2002). Due to the unlikelihood of discovery, corporate offenders are not caught as often as their street-offending counterparts. And when they are caught, corporations know many powerful people who can help them through their ordeal. Unlike the average criminal defendant who will more than likely end up in prison, corporate criminals and their attorneys make certain that if they serve any time at all, it will be under relatively acceptable conditions.

The U.S. Department of Justice has a Corporate Fraud Task Force (CFTF) that was created by President George W. Bush on July 9, 2002. Its mandate is to oversee and coordinate all corporate fraud matters under investigation by the department, as well as to enhance inter-agency cooperation on any investigations. The CFTF is also authorized to "provide direction for the investigation and prosecutions of cases, . . . provide recommendations to the Attorney General for allocation and reallocation of resources, . . . and make recommendations to the president" (Corporate Fraud Task Force, 2003). In March 2002, four months before the task force was created, the president outlined his 10-point plan to improve corporate responsibility and protect America's shareholders. The points contained in this plan are as follows:

1. Each investor should have quarterly access to the information needed to judge a firm's financial performance, condition, and risks.
2. Each investor should have prompt access to critical information.
3. Chief Executive Officers (CEOs) should personally vouch for the veracity, timeliness, and fairness of their companies' public disclosures, including their financial statements.
4. CEOs or other officers should not be allowed to profit from erroneous financial statements.
5. CEOs or other officers who clearly abuse their power should lose their right to serve in any corporate leadership positions.
6. Corporate leaders should be required to tell the public promptly whenever they buy or sell company stock for personal gain.
7. Investors should have complete confidence in the independence and integrity of companies' auditors.
8. An independent regulatory board should ensure that the accounting profession is held to the highest ethical standards.
9. The authors of accounting standards must be responsive to the needs of investors.

10. Firms' accounting systems should be compared with best practices, not simply against minimum standards. (Corporate Fraud Task Force 2003)

The Securities and Exchange Commission (SEC) took action to implement these directives by adopting rules and policies in line with the president's 10 reforms. In its first yearly report to the president, the CFTF summarized their efforts: task force members had obtained over 250 corporate fraud convictions, and as of May 31, 2003, prosecutors and law enforcement agents were working on 320 investigations involving over 500 defendants. The report also revealed that from July 1, 2002, to March 31, 2003, prosecutors won over $2.5 billion in fines, forfeitures, and restitution; however, of that sum, they actually recovered only $85 million, or about 30 percent of the monies owed. Regarding sentences for convicted defendants, the reports list information in only 64 of the 250 cases: 75 percent of the defendants in those 64 cases received a sentence of imprisonment, with 25 percent being in excess of 5 years in length (Corporate Fraud Task Force 2003).

The second annual report of the CFTF showed improvements from the previous year in combating fraud, punishing corporate wrongdoing, and adding inter-agency cooperation in investigation of cases. From the task force's inception up to May 31, 2004, prosecutors netted over 500 corporate fraud convictions or guilty pleas and had charged over 900 defendants and 60 CEOs and presidents (Corporate Fraud Task Force 2004). In the Enron case alone, according to the report, the task force had seized over $161 million to compensate the victims in that case.

Indeed, efforts to detect, punish, and control corporate crime do seem to be improving; however, these efforts are more likely the result of increased public scrutiny of political officials than a legitimate concern that these cases are increasing, that they result in numerous losses to the victims, and that the offenders need to be punished severely for their wrongdoing. Exemplifying the public's desire to expose corporate wrongdoing is the fact that a new ranking, the globe's worst corporations, is as highly anticipated as *Forbes* magazine's annual list of best businesses. One "worst" list is compiled by Russell Mokhiber and Robert Weissman of the *Multinational Monitor;* to be named to their list of the ten worst corporations of the year requires a less-than-distinguished business record rife with corporate fraud, scandal, and even violence (Mokhiber and Weissman 2005).

If we look at the various reports by the U.S. government on detecting and controlling corporate crime, the consensus is that we are doing better. More cases are being forwarded to the appropriate crime control agencies, and more corporations and their employee offenders are being charged, prosecuted, and punished for their actions. These statistics are probably accurate. If the government creates a special task force to detect and prosecute these crimes and encourages agencies in charge of these offenses to cooperate and work together on these cases, we will undoubtedly see an increase in the number of successful prosecutions. But the question remains, is this increased effort, detection, apprehension, prosecution, and punishment acting as a deterrent to future criminal offending by corporations and their employees?

Kane and Wall (2005) and Bussmann (2005) analyzed the results of the National White Collar Crime Center Survey and the PricewaterhouseCoopers Global Economic Crime Survey, respectively, and found that corporate offending and other types of fraud are on the increase. Furthermore, these agencies and others like them report that a majority of the offenses are detected by accident by the firms themselves, giving little credence to the idea that the federal government and crime control agencies are having an effect on the incidence of these crimes. According to Geis (2007), the likelihood of a corporation being audited is very minimal. As of 2007, it took 38 months for the IRS to audit the tax return of a corporation. In 2003, corporations paid about $133 billion in taxes—the second lowest amount collected by the government since 1983. In 1970, 17 percent of the nation's budget came from corporate taxes; today, it makes up only 7 percent (Geis 2007).

What can be done to further detect, apprehend, and deter corporate criminal offending? If we look deeper into the government reports, we find that most of the money (70 percent) awarded in the form of fines, forfeitures, and restitution is never recovered (Corporate Fraud Task Force 2003). Additionally, those defendants who do get convicted and sentenced to prison do not serve the time that the average defendant in federal criminal court serves; only about 25 percent of defendants received five or more years in jail (Corporate Fraud Task Force 2003). This pales in comparison to sentences for narcotics offenders; in fact, the mandatory minimums for first-time drug offenders convicted in federal court of *possession* of certain amounts of narcotics can be five or ten years depending on the amounts of drugs involved.

Improving Current Methods

Some observers have suggested that an annual report on corporate offending should be compiled each year and made available to interested parties, or for public consumption, similar to the way in which information for the UCR database is collected and made public. Other critics have proposed more severe sanctions for convicted individuals and corporations as a way to deter and control corporate offending. Coleman (1998) believes that corporate crime is perpetuated by the sense of mystery that corporations maintain around their business practices. This has helped to insulate them from scrutiny because their actions and practices seem very complex to the average observer. Indeed, the inner workings of organizations and their business practices are complex and therefore not well understood. For an investigator, then, it becomes difficult to determine which actions were deliberately undertaken and which were simply bad business decisions.

The Center for Corporate Policy (2006) has offered some suggestions for deterring corporate crime:

Strengthen criminal liability standards for corporations, executives, and directors. As discussed in chapter 1, because corporations are legal fictions, they are unable to have intent imputed upon them. Guilt under criminal law requires both the *actus reus,* guilty act, and the *mens rea,* guilty mind. If we could recognize that corporations, not just the individuals within the corporations, are to blame for harm, it would be much easier to hold them criminally liable, to prosecute them, and to punish them with the hope of also deterring them from future criminal acts.

Strengthen sanctions for corporations. As we have seen from some of the federal statistics, although more cases against corporations and their executives are making their way into U.S. federal courtrooms, the punishments given to those convicted are still not in line with the seriousness of harm done, the culpability of the offender, or the typical outcomes of other cases in federal court. Most corporate offenders avoid criminal prosecution in the first place by signing an agreement with the government that they, as a corporation, will reform and will continue to monitor their corporate activities. Some sanctions for corporations have been included in the USSC's organizational sentencing guidelines, but rarely are harsh sentences meted out; in fact, sentences may actually be shortened, not elongated, in light of the Supreme Court decision in *U.S. v. Booker* that rendered the guidelines only advisory and not mandatory. Essentially, judges can now more easily reduce the sentences of convicted corporate executives. The Center for Corporate Policy suggests adding a requirement that companies must announce to the public their crimes, as well as their plans for reform, in an effort to shame them into compliance. They also recommend that the government put a corporate probation officer in place to ensure that the organization adopts and follows through with specific reforms.

The corporate death penalty. This method of deterrence could be used for corporations that continue to violate the law. Death in this instance means that corporate licenses would be revoked, forcing the affected corporations to go out of business. Most states have the power to revoke corporate charters but rarely threaten this form of sanction. Obviously, this option would punish more than just the executives of the corporation—law-abiding employees and shareholders would also suffer. The Center for Corporate Policy offers other options that would attempt to reincorporate the organization under public ownership or compensate innocent parties in the cases where corporate death was imposed.

Ban corporations that violate the law from receiving federal contracts. The federal government contracts with more organizations than any other entity. The contracts they enter into amount to roughly $350 billion a year. The government has a list of people with whom they will not do business. This list could be expanded to include those corporations convicted of criminal offenses.

Make corporate crime a law enforcement priority. U.S. attorneys do not have the time or the financial or labor resources necessary to enforce the full power of the law. Most divisions are underfunded, have high employee turnover, and therefore cannot keep up with their caseloads. Passing tougher laws does little in the way of deterrence if the funding is not in place to enforce those laws and punish violators. The Center for Corporate Policy proposes that the Department of Justice not only increase its budget for enforcement of these laws but further establish a corporate crime division that would be a permanent part of the agency.

Grabowsky (2001) suggests that a more expansive system of corporate crime control needs to be implemented in an attempt to deter and prevent corporate criminal offending. "It is a combination of complementary institutions and instruments which will provide the best solution" (Grabowsky 2001, 138). Among Grabowsky's suggestions for implementation are mandatory third-party vigilance and disclosure, voluntary public interest organizations becoming active, private regulatory enforcement, self-regulation programs, and inducements for compliance.

Third-party vigilance—what Grabowsky (2001) refers to as conscription—would involve third-party actors aiding and overseeing the corporation's compliance process. Banks, for instance, could be required to alert authorities of anything out of the ordinary or any monetary transactions above a certain dollar amount. This would make it harder for corporations and individuals within them to siphon funds or cover up taxable income. Banks are already legally obligated to make such reports on their individual account holders.

Public interest groups are ubiquitous in every domain of society. It is often from these groups—not from government authorities—that we first hear about corporate malfeasance. These groups are influential in getting the media involved in reporting high-profile cases that may not otherwise come to the public's attention. Sometimes, public interest groups are the only recorders of annual facts and statistics on corporations and their activities. From health, labor, and environmental organizations to Nader's Raiders, young activists inspired by the work of Ralph Nader, and now some of the corporate watchdogs, these groups have been very successful in helping to set agendas for policy (Grabowsky 2001).

Private regulatory enforcement can also help to enforce current legislation. Grabowsky (2001) believes this is especially feasible where criminal justice authorities have budget restraints. Regulatory agencies make the job of law enforcement officers easier by taking over the responsibility for enforcement of regulations guidelines; politicians can also escape making unpopular decisions by relegating decision-making duties to regulatory agencies (Coleman 1998). Private entities can be endowed with certain rights that give them the ability to enforce rules and regulations, or they can be given the power to enforce the rules on behalf of the state. For some environmental laws, private enforcement already exists. Also, the False Claims Act allows private interests to bring suit against those who violate the law (Grabowsky 2001). Once a suit is filed and the facts discovered, the government can decide to prosecute as well. If the civil action is successful, the private party who brought the suit is entitled to a portion of damages awarded.

Self-regulation by a corporation is another method that can be implemented in an attempt to curb corporate wrongdoing. Many companies have quality control operations in place and have hired management to instill an atmosphere and reputation of excellence without having another entity impose these controls on them (Grabowsky 2001). Many corporations have set up compliance divisions or have, at the least, a compliance officer whose role is to ensure that the actions of the organization and its employees are law-abiding (Coleman 1998). This type of corporate governance requires the board of directors to oversee business operations, to guarantee that the safeguarding of shareholder interests is of principal concern, and to ensure that the law is not being violated (Geis 2007). Warren Buffett, the CEO of Berkshire Hathaway and one of the world's most successful investors, has been outspoken on this issue, calling for corporations to pay more attention to business practices, to be quicker to fire corrupt employees, and to allow corporate boards of directors more independence, which includes holding meetings without corporate executives present. In this way, according to Buffett, members of the board will be less reserved in discussing operations and more likely to have the interests of the shareholders in mind when making important decisions.

The government, however, can also impose self-regulatory controls as part of conditions attached to probation for past violations. This should be a requirement in every case where evidence exists that a corporation has violated the law; the corporation should be made to implement a program of self-compliance, and they should have to foot the bill for it.

Finally, Grabowsky (2001) says that inducements to corporations by the government can elicit lawful behavior from them. Making regulatory compliance and quality control costs tax-deductible can be an incentive for corporations to implement them as part of their business practices. If simply having a compliance program in place makes a corporation less likely to be audited or investigated by the government, this can induce compliance.

These suggestions, along with others that attempt to remedy definitional issues and alleviate some of the current problems with measurement, would do much to help make corporate offending more easily detectable and therefore punishable, but they might also help deter corporations from engaging in any illegal or harmful activities.

Conclusion

Whether stemming from definitional or conceptual issues of what constitutes corporate and white-collar crime, or from issues with detection, apprehension, and subsequent punishment of corporate wrongdoing, myriad problems continue to plague researchers, scholars, law enforcement officials, and even corporate executives themselves.

The increased awareness of corporate offending due to recent debacles involving Enron, WorldCom, Tyco, and their accounting firms such as Arthur Andersen has spurred the public to pressure the government and crime control agencies toward increased enforcement and prosecution of those involved with corporate malfeasance. We know from very conservative estimates (numbers on absolute costs of harms and losses are not known) that corporate crime costs the United States more annually than all other crime taken together. Estimates range from $200 billion to $600 billion each year. We also know that there are further consequences beyond monetary loss that result from corporate crime: countless injuries, job-related illnesses, and deaths occur every year due to negligence, false advertising, unsafe working conditions, poor product safety, unsafe food, and medical malpractice, among others.

However, a downside exists to holding corporations criminally liable for their actions. If hefty fines are levied and enormous amounts of monetary restitution must be paid, innocent employees and shareholders will be unduly punished. Indeed, there are other philosophical and theoretical reasons for not holding corporations liable: Imputing liability onto a corporation, for instance, is counter to our doctrine of criminal law, which requires that intent be established. Furthermore, corporations cannot be imprisoned, which is also an important element in deterrence against criminal offending. The government has, however, responded somewhat to the public outcry for increased corporate punishment. There is legislation in place supporting prosecutorial efforts in charging and punishing corporations.

The president has outlined a plan to improve corporate responsibility, the SEC has taken steps to implement the president's directives, the Department of Justice has initiated a Corporate Fraud Task Force designed to oversee all matters of fraud as well as enhance inter-agency cooperation in investigations, and the USSC has included a section on the sentencing of organizations in its federal guidelines manual. All of these efforts have greatly enhanced the government's ability to prosecute and punish corporations and their executives. Indeed, the numbers of those prosecuted have increased substantially, according to the CFTF.

Other observers, however, are more skeptical and believe the government is still not doing enough. They say that more legislation and increased punishment is not what is needed: there are already enough laws in place. For these critics, adding more laws is merely seen as a symbolic gesture that politicians are doing something to curb corporate offending. People supporting this point of view believe that the government is too closely tied to corporate America and that governmental authorities should do a better job of enforcing the laws that are already in place. Exemplifying this symbolic perspective is the fact that authorities are entering into more nonprosecution and deferred prosecution agreements with corporations than ever before. Also cited is the fact that there have not been any major convictions of corporations using recently added legislation.

These issues become especially problematic because, according to survey research, corporate offending is on the rise, and the agencies in charge of detection, apprehension, and punishment are sorely understaffed and underfunded to the point of lagging behind in clearing their caseloads. Even when corporations are found guilty of malfeasance, sentences handed out in court are paltry when compared with other federal crime convictions. Reduction in the rate of corporate criminal offending can only be accomplished with deterrence. The philosophy of deterrence relies on two things; retribution, or punishment for wrongdoing, and severity of penal sanction. For deterrence to work, offenders have to fear being caught, and if caught, the sentence must be proportionately severe. At the current time, the likelihood of being caught for engaging in illegal corporate activity is very low, and even if caught, prosecuted, and convicted, the sanctions given as punishment are insufficient to act as a deterrent. It should also be noted that deterrence theory has its critics as well, who cite that often those accused of wrongdoing are not rational or do not know what they are doing is wrong. Deterrence would not work in these cases.

Although we, as a nation and as a crime control community, are making strides, there is still a long way to go—especially considering the exponential increase of the global marketplace, which is making it easier for organizations to offend and harder for those in charge to detect these offenses. Current methods of corporate crime control have been overwhelmingly scrutinized and suggestions for improvement abound. There is no shortage of legislation or lack of mandates in place to apprehend, prosecute, and punish corporate and white-collar offenders: rather, some believe the problem is that the federal government and the powers that be are in bed with corporate America. In a capitalist society, the almighty dollar has power over the ordinary citizen. Corporate crime will continue to plague the United States—and the rest of the world—as long as the harmful acts of the power elite are not defined as crimes, nonprosecution or deferred prosecution deals with corporations and their agents who have violated the law continue to be negotiated, and self-regulation and informal social control by other institutions are not encouraged. As you will see in chapter 3, in other parts of the world, corporate offending and corruption by political and government leaders occur more frequently and are less often detected and punished. In most developing countries, a majority of government contracts are procured through bribery of government officials. The consequences for ordinary people around the world can be devastating.

References

Bachman, Ronet, and Russell K. Schutt. 2007. *The Practice of Research in Criminology and Criminal Justice.* Thousand Oaks, CA: Sage.

Barnett, Cynthia. n.d. "The Measurement of White-Collar Crime Using Uniform Crime Reporting (UCR) Data." Washington, DC: U.S. Department of Justice, Federal Bureau of Investigation. www.fbi.gov/ucr/whitecollarforweb.pdf.

Borger, Julian. 2001. "All the President's Businessmen." *The Guardian,* April 27. www.guardian.co.uk/bush/story/0,,479212,00.html.

Bussmann, Kai-D. 2005. "PricewaterhouseCoopers: Global Economic Crime Survey 2005." www.pwc.com/gx/eng/cfr/gecs/PwC_2005_global_crimesurvey.pdf.

Center for Corporate Policy. 2006. "Corporate Crime and Abuse: Cracking Down on Corporate Crime." www.corporatepolicy.org/issues/crime.htm.

Christie, Christopher J., and Robert M. Hanna. 2006. "A Push Down the Road of Good Corporate Citizenship: The Deferred Prosecution Agreement between the U.S. Attorney for the District of New Jersey and Bristol-Myers Squibb Co." *The American Criminal Law Review* 43: 1043–61.

Clinard, Marshall B., and Peter Yeager. 1980. *Corporate Crime.* New York: Free Press.

Coleman, James. 1985. *The Criminal Elite.* New York: St. Martin's.

Coleman, James. 1998. *The Criminal Elite: Understanding White-Collar Crime.* New York: St. Martin's.

"Corporate America's Woes, Continued." 2002. *The Economist*, November 28.

Corporate Crime Reporter. 2005. "Crime without Conviction: The Rise of Deferred and Non-Prosecution Agreements." *Corporate Crime Reporter,* December 28. www.corporatecrimereporter.com/deferredreport.htm.

Corporate Fraud Task Force. 2003. "First Year Report to the President." Washington, DC: U.S. Department of Justice.

Corporate Fraud Task Force. 2004. "Second Year Report to the President." Washington, DC: U.S. Department of Justice.

Drutman, Lee. 2003. "What about Three-Strikes-and-You're-Out for Corporate Criminals?" *Common Dreams News Center.* www.commondreams.org/views03/0307-02.htm.

Federal Bureau of Investigation. 2007. "2006 Preliminary Annual Uniform Crime Report." Washington, DC: U.S. Department of Justice, Criminal Justice Information Services Division. www.fbi.gov/ucr/06prelim/index.html.

Geis, Gilbert. 2007. *White-Collar and Corporate Crime.* Upper Saddle River, NJ: Prentice Hall.

Geis, Gilbert, and Joseph DiMento. 1995. "Should We Prosecute Corporations and/or Individuals?" In *Corporate Crime: Contemporary Debates,* ed. Frank Pearce and Laureen Snider. Toronto: University of Toronto Press.

Grabowsky, Peter. 2001. "The System of Corporate Crime Control." In *Contemporary Issues in Criminal Justice: Essays in Honor of Gilbert Geis,* ed. Henry N. Pontell and David Shichor. Upper Saddle River, NJ: Prentice Hall.

Gray, Kenneth R., Larry A. Frieder, and George W. Clark. 2005. *Corporate Scandals: The Many Faces of Greed.* St. Paul, MN: Paragon House.

Holder, Eric. 1999. Memorandum from Eric Holder, Deputy Attorney General, Department of Justice, to Component Heads and United States Attorneys: Bringing Criminal Charges against Corporations. June 16. www.abanet.org/poladv/priorities/privilegewaiver/1999jun16_privw aiv_dojholder.pdf.

Kane, John, and April D. Wall. 2006. *The 2005 National Public Survey on White Collar Crime.* Fairmont, WV: National White Collar Crime Center.

Khanna, Vikramaditya S. 2004. "Politics and Corporate Crime Legislation." *Regulation* 27 (Spring): 30–35.

Mokhiber, Russell, and Robert Weissman. 2005. "The 10 Worst Corporations of 2005." *Multinational Monitor* 26 (November–December). multinationalmonitor.org/mm2005/112005/mokhiber.html.

Mosher, Clayton J., Terance D. Miethe, and Dretha M. Phillips. 2002. *The Mismeasure of Crime.* Thousand Oaks, CA: Sage.

Reiman, Jeffrey. 2007. *The Rich Get Richer and the Poor Get Prison: Ideology, Class, and Criminal Justice.* 8th ed. Boston: Allyn and Bacon.

Reiman, Jeffrey, and Paul Leighton. 2004. *A Tale of Two Criminals: We're Tougher on Corporate Criminals, but They Still Don't Get What They Deserve.* Boston: Allyn and Bacon.

Simon, David R. 1996. *Elite Deviance.* Boston: Allyn and Bacon.

Simon, David R. 2006. *Elite Deviance.* Boston: Pearson/Allyn and Bacon.

Simpson, Sally S. 2002. *Corporate Crime, Law, and Social Control.* New York: Cambridge University Press.

Simpson, Sally S., Anthony Harris, and Brian A. Mattson. 1995. "Measuring Corporate Crime." In *Understanding Corporate Criminality,* ed. Michael B. Blankenship. New York: Garland.

Thompson, Larry D. 2002. Remarks by Larry D. Thompson, Deputy Attorney General, Department of Justice, to the American Bar Association Criminal Justice Section, Washington, DC: Corporate Fraud. August 10. www.usdoj.gov/archive/dag/speeches/2002/081002abacriminal justice.htm.

United States Sentencing Guidelines Manual. 2005. Chapter 8. www.ussc.gov/

United States Sentencing Guidelines Manual. 2005. §8A1.1–§8A1.2. www.ussc.gov/

United States Sentencing Guidelines Manual. 2005. §8B1.1–§8B1.4. www.ussc.gov/

United States Sentencing Guidelines Manual. 2005. §8D1.1–§8D1.4. www.ussc.gov/

United States v. Booker, 543 U.S. 220 (2005).

U.S. Code. Title 15.

U.S. Code. Title 18.

U.S. Constitution. Commerce Clause, Article I, §8.

U.S. Department of the Treasury. 2003. *Strategic Plan for Fiscal Years 2003–2008.* Financial Management Service, September 30.

U.S. Sentencing Commission (USSC). 2005. *Sourcebook of Federal Sentencing Statistics.* Tables 51–53.

U.S. Sentencing Commission (USSC). 2006. *2005 Annual Report.* www.ussc.gov/ANNRPT/2005/ar05toc.htm.

Wellford, Charles F., and B.L. Ingraham. 1994. "Towards a National White Collar Crime Reporting System." In *Critical Issues in Crime and Justice,* ed. Albert R. Roberts. Thousand Oaks, CA: Sage.

3

Worldwide Perspective

Corporate Offending outside the United States

Corporate crime is not something unique to the United States. As noted in the history of corporations (see chapter 1), many of the first big businesses sprang up in European countries. Any country in the world that has industrialized production of labor, or that favors free-market economies, is likely to have numerous corporations and therefore many incidents of corporate offending. Wherever people are in positions of power and have authority over resources or other individuals, the opportunity and temptation for embezzlement and bribery will exist. Countries like Japan, Australia, and Canada all report corporate wrongdoing, and in Europe, scandal and offending occur on a scale similar to that in the United States. No country is secure against corporate malfeasance, just as no country in the world is completely free of other types of criminal offending; some countries just experience more corporate crime than others. The southern half of the Western Hemisphere, for instance, deals with numerous incidents of criminal practices daily in both business and government, and no sector of South American society is exempt; recent reports have revealed that South America is one of the most corrupt regions in the world (Hodess 2004). In some South American countries, for instance, half of state contracts are awarded because of bribery. These revelations were exemplified in 2000, when the world watched the Peruvian government fall in the wake of presidential scandal. Alberto Fujimori was caught in a web of political corruption after being accused of embezzling upwards of $600 million from the Peruvian people.

Similar cases regarding political leaders have occurred elsewhere; in fact, political corruption is widespread in many countries around the globe. Mohammed Suharto, the former president of Indonesia, purportedly embezzled nearly US$35 billion throughout his years in office (1968–1998), making him one of the world's most corrupt leaders. Reports of corruption among such leaders as Suharto and Fujimori have been the impetus behind the lowering of public confidence in the polity around the globe. Hodess (2004) reports that "trust in political parties is lower than in any other public institution" (3).

For-profit corporations around the world attempt to misuse dominant market positions, and attempts by individuals and organizations to defraud governments and evade taxes are ubiquitous. Clinard and Yeager (1980) report that in France, corporations find numerous ways to violate the law—one of which includes cooking their books to evade the large commercial and industrial taxes that are levied by the French government. Minoru Yokoyama (2007) notes that throughout Japan's history, serious environmental crimes have been committed by the nation's leading corporations. He states that most of these were related to pollution and occurred because of "overzealous pursuit of profits, with little actual oversight by the government" (339). The *Multinational Monitor*'s 2006 list of the world's worst corporations includes several multinational companies (Mokhiber and Weissman 2006). The British weapons manufacturer BAE Systems is one of the world's largest military contractors, and it has been accused on numerous occasions of bribing governmental officials in many countries in order to secure large weapons contracts. The British government recently dropped an investigation of BAE Systems' practices in a Saudi Arabian weapons deal, citing that relations with the Saudi government were more important. Also on the list is Abbott, a U.S. manufacturer of infant formula that is used around the world. Abbott made the list for overpricing its formula in poor and developing countries, leading to thousands of infant deaths worldwide. When the Philippine government tried to implement new rules banning the use of the formula for infants under two years old in an attempt to encourage breast-feeding of infants in the country, Abbott sued them and tried to block the new rules. The Philippine Supreme Court decided in favor of the Philippine government; however, it reversed its own ruling after the head of the United States Chamber of Commerce wrote a letter to the Philippine president threatening decreased U.S. investment in the country (Mokhiber and Weissman 2006). U.S. drugmaker Pfizer also makes the list for its ruthless defense of patents and monopolistic practices in the availability of much-needed medicine in poor and developing countries. Pfizer has pressured the World Trade Organization to adopt worldwide rules related to intellectual property similar to patent law in the United States. This move would secure mega profits for the drugmaker at the expense of patients in countries that cannot afford the drugs.

The *Multinational Monitor*'s list for the previous year included a French water company, a Swiss drugmaker, and a British oil company (Mokhiber and Weissman 2005). To earn a spot on Mokhiber and Weissman's "worst" list, companies typically engage in bribery, fraud, racketeering, corruption, or other corporate criminal offenses without repercussion. Because these companies are so big and influential and have so much money to throw around, they seem to be able to buy their way out of prosecution. The results are very destructive for people throughout the world. Corruption around the globe increases the burden of debt that poor countries have to carry. Most world projects are financed by loans from the World Bank or other institutions in Western countries (Chatterjee 2003). If these projects go bust, Third World countries are the biggest losers; these poor countries ultimately pay the price for development.

This chapter outlines some of the effects of globalization and the impact the new global economy will have on corporate crime in the future. It also offers a global view of reports from various governmental and public watch groups on corporate criminal activity and summarizes some of the different types of international corporate offending. Corruption in government and the corrupt practices of government officials around the world—whether in the form of bribery and kickbacks for contract procurement, or extortion and embezzlement of monies from government coffers—seem to be the most widespread forms of corporate malfeasance. This type of criminal activity by political and government leaders exists in conjunction with big multinational corporations and small local businesses alike, causing devastating consequences for the least privileged people and the poorest countries on the planet. The legislation that various governments have implemented in an attempt to curb corporate offending and corruption is also discussed. Finally, this chapter takes a look at detection, prosecution, and punishment of corporate wrongdoers in other parts of the world.

Globalization and Its Effects on Corporate Offending Worldwide

Since the 1990s, a new buzzword has been used to describe the changing world economy: *globalization*. What is globalization? Although globalization can mean many things and can be tied to many different aspects of societies, it generally refers to the process of increased unity of societies around the world. The convergence of social, cultural, and economic practices, as well as increases in trade, technology, and business cooperation, is globalization. A more simplified definition would describe globalization as the mechanism by which life experiences are becoming standardized around the globe. Globalization has been occurring since World War II, but Theodore Levitt (1983) popularized the term in an economic context in his article "The Globalization of Markets." It was through this publication in the *Harvard Business Review* that Levitt brought forth his idea of globalization and the idea that when entities interact, things change. In other words, this idea of a global economic marketplace is not something that businesses discovered; rather it is the interacting of businesses that formed the globalized marketplace (Levitt 1983).

Charles Andrews (2000) simplifies the idea by saying that globalization is what is taking place with regard to economies on a world scale. Since the fall of the Berlin Wall and the advent of the Internet, there has been a rapid expansion in globalization of economies and world markets. The result has been increased movement of money, commodities, information, and people on an international scale. Friedman (2005) has spurred an increased awareness of this phenomenon with his bestseller *The World Is Flat*. Friedman's tome recounts the ways in which technology has reshaped the world. The author maintains that the world is flat in terms of politics, culture, and economics because of the enormous amount of information that can now be shared between ordinary people around the world. This phenomenon has also produced new multinational companies that do business on a global scale and with less resistance from governmental rules and regulations. Friedman (2005) believes global connectedness is inevitable, and, in order to survive, countries, companies, and individuals are going to have to adopt approaches that conform with global reality. The problem is that those who are unable to enter the market get left behind, and therefore become very susceptible to being influenced and taken advantage of by huge multinational corporations.

Andrews (2000) paints the ugly side of globalization. Some countries in the world have developed economies, and other countries' economies are still developing. Globalization means that multinational corporations in the developed world will dominate developing countries' economies. These First World corporations are exploiting the workforce and labor in developing countries. With globalization, world economic activity is more interconnected, but the production of labor in developing countries is now controlled and operated by multinational corporations. These corporations demand low wages as well as restraint of organized unions and collective bargaining power. What results is a lessening of already low standards of living for a large number of people in the developing world (Andrews 2000).

The appropriation of monies by developed nations to help Third World countries advance can also lead to corrupt practices and corporate wrongdoing. Hawley (2005) believes that international public financial institutions have further aggravated corruption. For the year 2002, 39 percent of the budget of the World Bank and regional development banks—roughly $16 billion— was spent on infrastructure worldwide. The Foreign Relations Committee of the U.S. Senate has reported that of the US$525 billion that the World Bank has lent since 1946, anywhere from 5 to 25 percent (or US$26 billion to US$130 billion) has gone missing due to corruption or misuse (Lugar 2006). Also, according to the U.S. General Accounting Office (2000), the World Bank does not adequately audit the projects for which it gives money; specifically, in the years 1998 and 1999, of the 1,500 projects it funded, only 54 were reviewed.

Obviously, the World Bank disputes the claims that these reports make. Lugar (2006) reported that the World Bank and its former chairman, Paul Wolfowitz, helped to enhance the anticorruption policies of the World Bank and suspended loans in several countries because of concerns of corruption. In an ironic twist, however, under pressure from the G8 nations, who are the largest funders and shareholders of the World Bank, Wolfowitz was forced to resign his post at the World Bank after being accused in a corruption scandal of his own. Wolfowitz admitted that he personally helped a bank official with whom he was romantically involved get a promotion, a large increase in salary, and a contract that would give her extraordinary annual raises (Guha and Callan 2007). Wolfowitz resigned on June 30, 2007, because he violated several rules for promotion and salary increase at the bank (Wroughton 2007).

The Extent of Corporate Offending in Other Countries

No country in the world is free from corporate offending and corruption by corporate business organizations, public institutions, and governmental entities at the highest and even most local levels. Throughout the world, developed countries with capitalistic and free-market economies suffer from the same types of corporate offending as the United States. Countries that are less developed seem to be most susceptible to governmental and political corruption. As in the United States, money, business, and politics in other nations are also interconnected. Whether through bribery, kickbacks, extortion, or other forms of criminal offending, political leaders and corporations around the globe have been involved in corporate malfeasance. Governments are responsible for many of the actions that a society undertakes. For instance, the granting of government contracts, using land, assessing taxes, and using public funds are all prone to corruption (Simon 2006). Often, these activities are conducted in conjunction with businesses and corporations within the country or with foreign business subsidiaries. In essence, corrupt practices by governmental officials and political leaders is corporate criminal offending because businesses are involved. Taking advantage of a political position of power for personal gain is defined as a political crime, but political crimes can also be corporate crimes. For example, a corporation could bribe a public official in exchange for favorable concessions, or a government official could demand money in exchange for a favor, which would be extortion (Simon 2006). Regardless of the type of offense committed, or whether it was the government official or the corporate employee who committed the act, such deals fall under the categories of political corruption *and* corporate crime.

The Global Corruption Barometer, a survey conducted by Gallup International for Transparency International (2006), reports that political parties and governments are seen around the world as the most corrupt sector. The report states: "While there are differences between countries in the extent to which people experience corruption in their everyday lives, there is a widespread perception that the authority vested in the institutions that ought to represent public interest is, in fact, being abused for private gain" (2006, 15). This statement seems to solidify the idea that corporations around the world are so entangled that the separation of corporate crime from political corruption is impossible. In fact, the very entities that are supposed to protect the people from being victimized are themselves offenders. The 2006 Global Corruption Barometer reveals that bribes are most commonly paid to the police, followed by bribes to obtain public services, bribes to the legal system and the judiciary, and finally bribes for medical and educational services. Bribery of this type greatly affects people's quality of life. The report also reveals that the average cost of bribes varies by country. For instance, in African countries, average bribes are US$100 to the legal system and judiciary, US$70 to the police and educational system, and US$40 for other public services. In Latin America, however, average bribes are the highest for medical services at over US$600, followed by those to the legal system, judiciary, and tax revenue at over US$300, and finally bribes to the police at an average of around US$200.

Transparency International (TI) also conducts an annual *Global Corruption Report* (*GCR*) that includes important studies on corruption around the world. These yearly reports cover a wide range of activity and include findings from 30–45 countries. TI is a global organization consisting of more than 90 locally established national chapters whose mission is to fight corruption on a global scale and to work toward a world free of corrupt and criminal practices. TI defines corruption as "the misuse of entrusted power for private gain," a definition similar to the one for political crime listed earlier. If this corruption involves any type of business, and it usually does, it can also be considered corporate crime. Corporate offending can occur in many sectors of society, but the most prevalent areas seem to be in the political arena, public service contracting, development and reconstruction, and access to health care.

Political Corruption and Corporate Crime

Whether we know it or not, political corruption concerns everyone. Politicians in the United States are elected by the people, and we expect that they will govern in our best interest. Democratically elected government officials are given the power to make decisions that affect citizens' lives and are given control of the use of national resources. It is often because of this power that corruption and corporate offending occur; whether to furnish favors to those who contributed to their campaign, or simply out of personal greed, corporate criminal activity in politics is ever present. According to the definition used by Hodess (2004), political corruption occurs when political leaders abuse their entrusted positions for personal gain. There are many facets of political corruption; these vary from buying votes to abusing state resources. The problem with corporate offending by politicians is not only that political leaders line their pockets with corporate monies in return for policy influence, which is ethically wrong, but they misuse or embezzle public funds to the point that services to the public suffer. Corporate offending by politicians means compromised access to health care, housing, sanitation, clean drinking water, and lifesaving services. Lack of these services, for many areas of the world, means loss of life. But the link between corporate offending and politics is not just about money; it can be about favors as well.

Politicians are very influential, and trading favors and abusing their influence threatens the very democratic process that the public believes in. Hodess (2004) reports that corruption in politics covers a wide range of illegal behavior, and politicians can engage in these behaviors before, during, and even after vacating their positions. Offending by politicians and government officials is rarely prosecuted, much to the public's dismay. Leaders are often out of office before any of their wrongdoing is uncovered. When asked if they could eliminate offending from one institution, most of the general public stated that they would like to see a crackdown on political parties more than any other institution (Transparency International 2003). Business leaders also believe that these types of offenses have an impact on policy. According to the *Global Competitiveness Report 2002–2003* issued by the World Economic Forum (2003), in about 20 percent of countries surveyed, bribery is the usual method by which policy goals are achieved. Furthermore, 50 percent of participating countries reported that illegal political contributions occur regularly. Offending in the political arena goes against the very notions of equality and justice; it keeps human needs from being met.

The *Global Corruption Report* for 2004 outlines large-scale offending by political leaders and government officials. The report gives information on the dollar estimates alleged to have been embezzled by some of the most corrupt political leaders in the last 20 years. They include Mohamed Suharto, president of Indonesia from 1967 to 1998, who is estimated to have embezzled anywhere from $15 billion to $35 billion; Ferdinand Marcos, president of the Philippines from 1972 to 1986, believed to have stolen $5 billion to $10 billion; Mobutu Sese Seko, president of Zaire from 1965 to 1997, who reportedly stole $5 billion; Sani Abacha, president of Nigeria, said to have embezzled $2 billion to $5 billion; Yugoslavian president Slobodan Milosevic, who siphoned an estimated $1 billion from his government; Jean-Claude "Baby Doc" Duvalier, president of Haiti, accused of pillaging between $300 million to $800 million from his country; and Alberto Fujimori, president of Peru, is said by the Global Corruption Report to have looted over $600 million. And the list goes on. When compared to the gross domestic product of the victimized countries, these figures make it obvious that many people have suffered unnecessarily at the hands of their corrupt leaders. Some of these individuals have been tried for international criminal offenses and human rights violations, but not all have been brought to justice.

Hodess (2004) also states that the legal system overseeing the political behavior of national leaders is insufficient. Many countries have set rules governing public contributions to candidates, with regulations stipulating that the candidate release the names of campaign donors. But these rules are not in place everywhere. According to Hodess, one in four countries lacks disclosure requirements for political officials, and one in three has no system in place to govern the financial practices of the countries' political parties. Enforcement and oversight in this realm need to be conducted by autonomous agencies. Many governments, however, are reluctant to take the steps needed to make this happen. Efforts to bring corrupt leaders to justice have been hampered in the past. Laws giving them immunity from prosecution and holes in extradition treaties continue to allow these individuals to avoid punishment. Although some of these offenders have been forced to pay back millions to the countries from which they stole, many corrupt political leaders have their pilfered fortunes tucked away in Swiss bank accounts, making it virtually impossible to recover any of the monies stolen. The *GCR* for 2004 puts forth some key recommendations for curbing political offending. These include the following requirements:

- Governments must enhance legislation on political funding and disclosure. Public oversight bodies and independent courts must be endowed with adequate resources and skills and the power to review, investigate, and hold offenders accountable.
- Governments must implement adequate conflict of interest legislation, including laws that regulate the circumstances under which an elected official may hold a position in the private sector or a state-owned company.
- Candidates and parties should have fair access to the media. Standards for achieving balanced media coverage of elections must be established, applied, and maintained.
- Political parties, candidates, and politicians should disclose assets, income, and expenditures to an independent agency. Such information should be presented in a timely fashion, on an annual basis, as well as before and after elections.
- International financial institutions and bilateral donors must take political corruption into account when deciding to lend or grant money to governments. They should establish sensitive criteria to evaluate corruption levels.
- The United Nations (UN) Convention against Corruption must be swiftly ratified and enforced.
- The Organisation for Economic Cooperation and Development (OECD) Anti-Bribery Convention must be strengthened and properly monitored and enforced. Signatory governments should launch an educational campaign to ensure that businesses know the law and the penalties for breaching it. (2004, 5)

Corporate Offending in Services, Development, and Post-Conflict Construction

Directly related to corporate crime by political and government officials are offenses in the granting of government contracts in countries around the world. Especially vulnerable to this type of offending are those countries that need development or reconstruction. The United Nations has stated that "the negative impact of corruption on development is no longer questioned" (Pilapitiya 2004, 9). When development and reconstruction contracts are not awarded in a fair and legal manner, the developing countries are the ones that lose out. They become further burdened with debt and, to make matters worse, are left with shoddy infrastructure. According to Peter Eigen (2005), roughly US$4 trillion is spent annually around the globe on government projects. From the construction of schools and public buildings to providing clean water and waste disposal, provision of these services is prone to corruption. Corporate criminal offending in construction is especially devastating because second-rate work puts lives at risk. Lewis (2005) reports that since 1990, approximately 156,000 persons have died in earthquakes. Although earthquakes are not preventable, substandard building construction is. "Earthquakes don't kill people," notes Lewis; "collapsing buildings do" (23). Although it is hard to ascertain blame for loss of life in an earthquake situation, two such disasters in Turkey and Italy illustrate the consequences of criminal activity in the construction of public buildings. Inspectors often turn a blind eye to regulations and safety codes if given sufficient bribes by the company contracted to construct the building. Not having to build the infrastructure to specified minimum standards saves the construction company a great deal of money.

In Italy, a 1980 earthquake brought devastation to the town of Avellino, located east of Naples. Many buildings, including the maternity wing of a six-story hospital, collapsed, crushing all the occupants inside. An investigation of this collapse revealed that the materials used to build the structure were not up to standards, and that the necessary inspections and controls were not done in order to cut costs (Alexander 2005). It was alleged that the Italian mafia siphoned funds from these construction projects, and costs were cut by violating building regulations.

Turkey has also been ravaged by earthquakes. The people of Turkey experienced two earthquakes in 1999 alone that killed more than 15,000 people (Mitchell and Page 2005). Should the Turkish people assume that these deaths were not preventable and that earthquake deaths are something beyond a government's ability to prevent? To the contrary, Mitchell and Page (2005) believe that corporate criminal offending in the "construction industry and in the enforcement of building codes" is to blame, and the government should be held accountable (28).

The stories above are just two examples of what can occur when bribery leads to second-rate construction. Obviously, loss of life is the worst result of this type of corporate offending, but bribery in development and reconstruction can also have serious economic costs. In order to gauge the actual economic loss from these crimes, we need to understand the reasons why construction is so prone to bribery. Paul Collier and Anke Hoeffler (2005) point out two reasons: "First it is intensive in 'idiosyncratic' capital, meaning that its capital has to be designed specifically for installation. Second, it is a 'network' activity, requiring government regulation" (12–13). Since calculating the cost of a new building or structure is very complex, the builders and the suppliers know more about actual costs than the customers. This gives the builder the chance to cut actual costs by using cheaper materials or to drag out the project longer than needed, thereby charging more for construction time and ensuring extra funds to bribe those in charge of inspection. The corollary effects of shady business practices are that governments pay more in capital costs for infrastructure, leaving less money available for services needed by the people. These practices also allow government officials to allocate more monies in areas where pilfering can occur. Placing a larger percentage of budgets on infrastructure than on education or health care results in "more being spent but less being delivered" (Collier and Hoeffler 2005, 13). This, in turn, raises the costs of building and providing services in the future.

Attempts have been made to judge what the outcome of a corruption-free public sector would look like. Kaufmann, Leautier, and Mastruzzi (2004) studied 412 cities from 134 countries. Their study measured city level performance with regard to access to a number of services. The authors used various controls to gauge whether government wrongdoing influences access and delivery of services above and beyond other city level factors. Findings reveal that bribery has significant effects on all of the service-related variables. Furthermore, the level of globalization of a country has effects on city-level performance. The authors report that "city performance for network infrastructure (electricity grid, sewerage, telephone lines) is impacted by two aspects of governance (bribery in utility at the city level, control of corruption at the country level) and per capita income" (26). The bottom line is that controlling bribery at both the city and country level would help cities improve provision of access to services.

Antonio Estache and Eugene Kouassi (2002) conducted a study of water utility companies in Africa using a 16-point scale for measuring corruption and controlling for many variables. Their results reveal that corruption significantly affects operating efficiency; a one-level reduction in corruption led to an increase of 6.3 percent in operating efficiency. The authors also report that if this type of corporate offending among water utility companies in Africa was zero, operating efficiency would increase 64 percent. In other words, almost two-thirds of the cost of providing this service is attributable to offending by the company that provides it. Think of the reduced costs to the consumers of this service if this offending could be halted. Dal Bo and Rossi (2007) conducted a similar study of electrical utility companies in Latin America (Argentina, Bolivia, Brazil, Chile, Colombia, Costa Rica, Ecuador, Mexico, Panama, Paraguay, Peru, Uruguay, and Venezuela) using two measures of offending. Their research controlled for various effects on electrical efficiency and looked at two outcome measures: labor productivity, and operational and maintenance costs. The authors found offending at the country level to be negatively associated with labor productivity and efficiency; in other words, an increase in offending by these corporations decreases productivity and efficiency. They also found that "public firms are substantially less efficient in their use of labor than private firms" (959). Both anecdotal and empirical evidence show that criminal offending by corporations around the world significantly hurts infrastructure as well as access to, and efficiency of, public services. But the costs are far greater than wasted construction expenses and costs of providing services. Collier and Hoeffler (2005) report that this type of offending causes schedule delays, reduces expenditures, raises operating costs, and reduces growth; furthermore, "it amounts to lower current living standards, with the poorest hit hardest" (18). The United Nations Development Programme has declared that "large-scale corruption should be designated a crime against humanity, as for many around the world it falls into the same category as torture, genocide, and other crimes against humanity that rob humans of human dignity" (Pilapitiya 2004, 9).

Corporate Crime and Reconstruction in the Wake of Conflict

The cost of corporate offenses is especially detrimental to people in countries that are rebuilding infrastructure in the wake of conflict. According to Philippe Le Billion (2005), countries in the aftermath of conflict tend to be some of the most prone to these offenses. He states that often the malfeasance was occurring prior to conflict and may even be the reason the conflict escalated. Part of the problem lies in the breakdown of government that comes with conflict. Those seeking power in times of governmental weakness resort to wrongdoing to gain influence and control. Post-conflict, however, wrongdoing also flourishes as the road to peace, democracy, and a free-market economy facilitates many opportunities to engage in criminal activity and abuse new positions of power. Laws, legal authority, and the manpower to enforce and deter these kinds of violations are also very unstable in times of rebuilding. Post-conflict areas, because of new regimes or modes of political power, are often characterized by informal procedures. With inadequate numbers of troops or police forces, or ones that lack training, criminal activity is more likely to occur. Le Billion also notes that even foreign troops and the influx of outside aid can "inflate local prices and salaries, thereby contributing to an economic context favorable to corruption" (74).

Numerous reports have surfaced of the offenses that are tolerated in post-conflict countries. The long-standing view has been that as long as the governments in these countries remain allies to the developed world, a blind eye will be turned to corporate criminal and other criminal practices, and the continued flow of aid to these regions will be given under the guise of support for the displaced and disturbed populace. Alberto Alesina and Beatrice Weder (2002) report that the United States in particular has continued to give aid to the most criminal of administrations in the world. The U.S. government cites reasons such as backlash from local governments, political instability, and the potential undermining of a new administration's credibility as reasons for continuing aid in these regions.

Rebuilding Iraq

Reconstruction and democracy building in Iraq provide a recent and alarming example of how conflict presents an abundant opportunity for corporate offending and corruption by officials to thrive and undermine the stability and prosperity of a devastated region. Reinoud Leenders and Justin Alexander (2005) report that when the regime of Saddam Hussein was demolished in 2003, many Iraqis celebrated; many others, however, watched with horror as a new era of offending, conflict, and pilfering of state assets began. The political void that was created when Saddam was dethroned encouraged many politicians to take over state property, buildings, and areas of cities in attempts to seize power over the country. The Iraqi people, who were oppressed and not able to participate in any political processes under Hussein, felt largely left out again as many factions tried to usurp power. This seizing of power and pilfering of state assets is not conducive to building stability or attempting to thwart violence in the building of a new government. Indeed, numerous reports have cited corruption as one of the major problems in the reconstruction of Iraq.

Although reconstruction efforts in Iraq are getting better, the Special Inspector General for Iraq Reconstruction (SIGIR) in its *October 2007 Report* explains that information is still not being disseminated on the cost of projects and whether or not they are fully completed. SIGIR, in its reports, has made several recommendations to agencies with reconstruction contracts in Iraq "designed to achieve management improvements and corrective actions needed in reconstruction and relief activities" (153). The Government Accountability Office (GAO) (2007) also released testimony on the rebuilding of Iraq. Their report states that "U.S. efforts lack an overall strategy, no lead agency provides overall direction, and U.S. priorities have been subject to numerous changes" (9). The U.S. Congress is demanding better oversight and success in the reconstruction of Iraq, and on August 29, 2007, the army set up a committee to review all army contracts in Iraq in order to "achieve greater effectiveness, efficiency, and transparency in future operations" (12). Dominic

Nutt and John Davison (2003) exemplify concerns when they note that despite the influx of large sums of money, effective reconstruction in Iraq has not occurred: "Hospitals still lack medicines and basic equipment, clean drinking water is not available in many areas, and raw sewage can be seen on the streets of many towns" (3). Leenders and Alexander (2003), in interviews with Iraqi businessmen, report that almost all tell accounts of how criminal offending is influencing the government's ability to function. The authors say that although these businessmen may not be telling the whole truth, high-ranking government officers have admitted that criminal wrongdoing is a real problem. Saddam's regime left malfeasance at every level because of the control he had over the economy. Trying to undo and correct these practices in government will bring even more chances for corporate criminal offending to thrive.

The other issue in Iraq is its inability to keep track of where its oil revenue goes. Leenders and Alexander (2005) report that there has been no attempt to devise a more effective method to manage Iraq's oil revenues. Shortly after the takeover of Iraq by allied forces, its oil profits were put into a development fund for Iraq, authorized by the United Nations. In 2004, the management of this fund was handed over to the Iraqi ministry of finance and managed by the International Advisory and Monitoring Board (IAMB). IAMB (2006) cites in its reports numerous problems with fraud-related activity. Pre- and post-war oil sales and assets seized from Saddam Hussein were estimated at around US$5 billion, yet somehow, US$4 billion of these profits remain unaccounted for (Nutt and Davison 2003). Part of the Iraqi oil revenue fraud and embezzlement is the fault of the U.S. handling of contracts in Iraq. Estimates for the reconstruction of Iraq range anywhere from US$56 billion (UN and World Bank estimates), up to US$100 billion (U.S. Congressional Budget Office estimate). Criticisms are that most contracts thus far have gone to large companies that either donated huge sums of money to the Republican party or have had Republican party officials on their boards in the past (Leenders and Alexander 2005). The U.S. government under the Bush administration has allowed "Indefinite Delivery" and "Indefinite Quantity" contracts that permit companies to continue to receive contracts without opening them up for bidding (Leenders and Alexander 2005, 85). A lot of money has been wasted in cost-plus contracts and subcontracting, as well. (Some examples of this type of waste were provided in chapter 1 in the section on types of corporate crime.)

Since early reconstruction problems have surfaced, there have been some improvements in Iraq. The Coalition Provisional Authority (CPA) has set up an independent office of inspectors to oversee the Iraqi government's affairs. A new law has also been developed called the National Integrity Law that requires Iraqi officials and politicians to disclose their assets prior to taking office (Leenders and Alexander 2005). In addition, the CPA has ensured that contractors are providing training in ethics and management to subcontractors. These subcontractors, however, have complained that the CPA itself is untrustworthy because it fails to reveal why some companies are awarded contracts and others are not. In its first quarterly report to the U.S. Congress, the CPA (2004) noted that 1,500 contracts had been awarded at a value of $9.7 billion. The report revealed that 32 percent of the contracts were awarded on a noncompetitive basis, and 68 percent were awarded in a competitive process—but 48 percent of those used *limited* competition. Criminal wrongdoing in the reconstruction of Iraq is likely to continue considering that much of the process of rebuilding remains to be done. Tougher legislation needs to be passed and proper systems of accountability put in place if it is to be stopped. Some of this burden rightly falls on the Iraqi government, which must demand accountability for the rebuilding of its country; the rest must fall on the countries that are in charge of and involved in its reconstruction. Leenders and Alexander (2005) state that foreign governments should create corporate-offending legislation that covers the companies working in Iraq and make the management of oil revenues of utmost priority in order to safeguard against further fraudulent activity. Nutt and Davison (2003) add that members of the international community, taking the lead from the U.S. and British governments, need to use their authority to make certain that appropriated monies and oil revenues are applied to the development of Iraq and to the benefit of its citizens.

Access to Health Care Worldwide

Access to adequate health care is an issue for most persons around the globe. Even in the United States, 2005 data, which are the latest statistics available, estimate that roughly 47 million people do not have health insurance and, consequently, do not have access to adequate health care resources (DeNavas-Walt, Proctor, and Lee 2006). This statistic exists despite the fact that the United States spends more on health care per capita than any other industrialized nation (Anderson, Hussey, Frogner, and Walters 2005; Organisation for Economic Cooperation and Development 2007). But the large amount of money spent by the U.S. government does not necessarily mean that more or better services are delivered to the citizens who need them most (Bureau of Labor Education 2001). Obviously then, the amount of money spent by governments is not equated with the level of services. One reason for this is that health care systems are often susceptible to embezzlement, theft, bribes, kickbacks, and illegal billing. The problem is even worse for many countries that are less developed than the United States. As stated earlier, one of the biggest problems worldwide is access to *adequate* health resources. Limited access to needed medicine stems from pharmaceutical supply distribution.

Pharmaceutical companies make up one of the biggest profit-making businesses in the world. In recent years, while the profits of most other Fortune 500 companies have dropped, the top 10 U.S. drugmakers had increases in profits (Public Citizen's Congress Watch 2002). Pharmaceutical companies are also some of the biggest violators of human rights. Corporate offending in health care causes is responsible for loss of numerous lives each year. Nussbaum (2006) reports that the consequences of corruption in health care are serious and that often "corruption might mean the difference between life and death." According to the World Health Organization (WHO) in 2002, roughly 30 million children worldwide lack access to routine immunization. In their report on key trends in health, they cite that "more than two million children under five continue to die each year from diseases that can be prevented by currently available vaccines" (Schirnding and Mulholland 2002, 8). Malfeasance in one country's health care industry can have severe consequences for the rest of the world as well. Depravity of essential health care anywhere increases the spread of communicable diseases and allows drug-resistant strains of disease to become more prevalent.

Other factors unique to the health care industry make it especially difficult to detect and curb corporate offending: Health care systems worldwide are very diverse and involve numerous entities for payment and provision of services. Each system is administered in a distinct way; therefore, it is difficult to oversee management and detect instances of mismanagement. Resources in the health care sector are very valuable because the stakes are so high. Every year more than US$3 trillion is spent on health care worldwide; Europe spends $1 trillion, the United States spends about $1.6 trillion, and Latin America spends approximately $136 billion (Savedoff and Hussman 2006). This is an enormous sum of money, and because most of it consists of public finds, it is an easy target for misuse. Corporate crime in the health care sector is so upsetting because the monies embezzled or abused could have been used to purchase much-needed medicines, repair badly maintained hospitals, acquire lifesaving equipment, or hire and train desperately needed health care workers. According to the World Health Organization (2006), "It is now accepted that the dire shortage of health care workers in many places is among the most significant constraints to achieving the three health related Millennium Development Goals: to reduce child mortality, improve maternal health, and combat HIV/AIDS and other diseases" (19). Because of the amount of money involved in the administration of health care, both rich and poor countries alike are affected by corporate crime in this sector. Poor persons, however, are definitely worse off due to lack of access. Offending by corporations and government officials "affects the poor disproportionately, due to their powerlessness to change the status quo and inability to pay bribes, creating inequalities that violate their human rights" (Pilapitiya 2004, 5).

The cost of offending in the health care sector is difficult to estimate. Sales of counterfeit drugs alone have been estimated at $30 billion annually. Losses are said to be in the tens of billions of dollars. The following examples provide a small glimpse of the types of offending that plague health care on a global scale.

Corporate Crime and HIV/AIDS

Corporate criminal activity limits efforts to control many diseases around the world. One of the biggest disease epidemics facing the world today is HIV/AIDS. According to the international AIDS charity AVERT (2007), over 25 million people from around the world have lost their lives to AIDS; in 2006 alone, almost 3 million persons died and over 4 million new cases were diagnosed. Current estimates are that almost 40 million people across the globe are living with AIDS. The number of persons contracting and dying of AIDS continues to climb despite the number of prevention programs that have been put in place. Part of the reason is that corporate crime hinders the efforts of these prevention programs to control the spread of the disease (Tayler 2006). Africa and Asia are disproportionately affected by the AIDS epidemic: 85 percent of those infected are living on these two continents (AVERT 2007). Since AIDS was first identified in 1981, a great deal of time and money (billions of dollars) has been directed toward treatment of the disease. In the West, effective drug treatments have been created, and their use has resulted in a decline in death rates.

As of 2007, AIDS patients who received proper treatment could expect to live two to three times longer than those who did not receive treatment. Pharmaceutical companies have been blamed for keeping the costs of AIDS drugs too high to be accessible to those around the world who need them the most. The World Trade Organization (WTO), with pharmaceutical companies backing them, was also criticized for the adoption of an agreement called Trade-Related Aspects of Intellectual Property Rights (TRIPS). Under this agreement, member states had to adopt patents for pharmaceutical products for a minimum 20-year period (Velásquez and Boulet 1999). This meant that for at least two decades, any newly formulated drug effective in the treatment of AIDS could not be made generically and sold at a substantially reduced cost. In essence, pharmaceutical companies producing drugs for AIDS treatment were raking in billions of dollars at the expense of Third World governments and charitable organizations; meanwhile, millions of people were dying because the drugs were not affordable.

Although the WTO has since amended some portions of TRIPS to exclude countries facing national health crises (mostly under pressure from citizen advocacy groups), and more affordable, generic brands of effective AIDS drugs are reaching those in the developing countries who need them, demands for the drugs still exceed the supplies. Further problems exist in delivery of the drugs, mainly due to criminal activity. Because of shortages, administrators and doctors in charge of controlling the distribution of the drugs "have a valuable commodity that can be traded for financial, political or other inducements" (Tayler 2006, 2). The result has been the emergence of a black market in many countries, especially in Africa, Asia, and South America; some of the AIDS drugs are sold on the black market by health officials, some by patients themselves, but most are counterfeit. Liz Tayler notes that certain officials in charge of procurement of these drugs receive incentives for obtaining the drugs from suppliers who are less than trustworthy (2006). This leads to a reduced effectiveness in controlling the disease. Despite some progress, the HIV/AIDS epidemic continues to be a critical health problem for the world. Large amounts of money will continue to flow to countries whose health systems are burdened with control and prevention. Corporate crime will continue to flourish in these areas where demand for treatment is high, oversight is minimal, and the potential for profit—illegal and otherwise—is ripe.

Corporate Crime in Mexico's Public Health System

In 2002, the Mexican congress announced it was appropriating 600 million pesos (US$56.5 million) for promotion of women's health issues, 30 million (US$2.8 million) of which would go to a private health care company called Provida. Originally the money had been allocated for HIV/AIDS prevention. Hofbauer (2006) recounts the story of how several civil society organizations in Mexico investigated the change in the budget and uncovered large-scale corporate offending involving ministry of health officials and employees of Provida. The organizations were able to uncover the wrongdoing because of access to a public information law that was passed in Mexico in 2002. They discovered a 6,000-page file detailing how the re-appropriated money was spent. Eighty percent of the money went to hire a public relations firm for a campaign against emergency contraception; money was also spent on "importing overpriced medical equipment . . . the rent of a ballroom . . . luxury pens, clothing and groceries" (Hofbauer 2006, 44). A campaign was initiated in 2004 demanding the government explain how the 30 million pesos had been spent, why a private organization with health policies contradictory to the Mexican government was given money, and how the money would be returned to the budget. In 2005, the auditor general of Mexico, in a separate investigation, stated that 90 percent of the 30 million pesos given to Provida had been misused, and that three officials from the health ministry were fired as a result (Hofbauer 2006). This case offers a prime example of how legislation allowing citizen access to public information and the initiatives by civil society organizations can uncover corruption and maybe even help prevent it in the future.

Health Care Reform: Colombia versus Venezuela

Colombia and Venezuela are similar in many ways: they share a border in South America, and they have similar histories and cultures. Both countries have also been plagued by embezzlement and bribery in the delivery of public services, and their health care systems are fraught with corporate crime (Di Tella and Savedoff 2001). In the early 1990s, however, Colombia undertook major reforms in its health care system, making it more equitable by creating a national fund that subsidized lower income individuals with payments from higher income persons (Savedoff 2006). In surveys conducted by Di Tella and Savedoff (2001) 59 percent of Colombian health care workers reported that criminal offenses in the health system had declined since new reforms were in place. In the same study, "staff in Venezuelan hospitals reported that doctors were absent from work about 37 percent of the time while absenteeism in Colombia's public hospitals apparently accounted for less than 6 percent of doctors' time" (14). Although still not perfect—some of the new monies have become targets of abuse—it appears that countries making a concerted effort at sweeping reforms can effect change. Colombia is a good example of attempts to curb corporate crime in the health care sector. In fact, in *The World Health Report 2000,* Colombia ranked number one in affordability of health care (World Health Organization [WHO] 2000).

Recommendations for the Health Sector

World health is one of the greatest issues facing the world today. Health care systems worldwide are vast, varied, complex, and costly, and as such they are especially susceptible to corporate crime. Occurrences of offending in the health care sector are some of the most egregious because of what is at stake: human life. Typical examples of corporate crime in the health care sector include fraud and embezzlement as well as bribery in procurement, payment, and delivery of services. Many organizations have made recommendations to curb corporate offending in health care and thereby improve these services worldwide. Managing offending means that, first and foremost, the problem must be dealt with openly. A government that accepts that there is a crisis and then implements strategies to address and reduce incidence rates will have far greater success and also see tangible improvements over those that attempt to sweep the problems under the rug. Transparency International (2006) offers a number of recommendations in thwarting criminal practices in health care; some of these include that governments regularly publish information on their systems' budgets and performance, that codes of conduct be introduced with training for all workers, that public oversight be introduced so that there is more account-ability and transparency in delivery of services, that govern-ments monitor payment methods in order to reduce incentive, that rules for conflict of interest be adopted, that pharmaceutical and other biotech and equipment companies implement policies for counterbribery, and that those caught engaging in these of-fenses are rigorously prosecuted. The WHO (2000) states that "poorly structured, badly led, inefficiently organized and inade-quately funded health systems do more harm than good" (xiv).

The WHO (2000) also states that health care workers in many nations are paid poorly, lack training, lack equipment, and work in facilities that are archaic. Governments need to set their priorities, and "clinical protocols, registration, training, li-censing, and accreditation processes need to be brought up to date and used" (WHO 2000, xvi). Tayler (2006) states that the conditions and terms under which health care personnel work need to be improved worldwide; consequently, the motivation to accept bribes or embezzle monies will be lowered. She offers a couple of suggestions for improvement, especially regarding corporate crime in the treatment and prevention of disease: First, monitoring of pharmaceutical sales needs to be improved, so that drugs are not stolen and re-imported. Second, the WTO, WHO, and other international development organizations also need to end corporate crime by putting the health of the world before the profits of pharmaceutical companies. The poor of the world are disproportionately affected by not having access to health care. "In trying to buy health from their own pockets, sometimes they only succeed in lining the pockets of others" (WHO 2000, xiv). Recent adoptions of agreements restricting the import and export of generic drugs have hindered the treatment and prevention of disease and helped pharmaceutical compa-nies secure billions in profits for years to come. Some exposure of this wrongdoing has helped. "In response to allegations of smuggling, and to minimise the risk of drugs for developing countries being re-imported, GlaxoSmithKline are re-branding and changing the colour of all their anti retroviral [anti-HIV] drugs that are sold in developing countries" (Tayler 2006, 6).

Ultimately, the responsibility for health care systems worldwide falls to individual national governments. Every country must facilitate and maintain the best and fairest system possible. Simply dumping more money into a system can actually be the impetus for increased embezzlement and fraudulent activities. Effective monitoring and oversight of where each dollar goes are crucial to deterring health care crimes.

What in the World Can Be Done?

Some of the examples above show that globalization and global conflict increase the opportunities for criminal practices to go on and that the consequences are not only monies wasted but also inadequate health services, lack of access to reparations, and premature and preventable death. What can be done in today's globalized economy to safeguard funds for infrastructure and basic human services from corporate malfeasance? What can be done to ensure that the developing countries do not fall further behind because of government embezzlement and bribery in building contracts? Le Billion (2005) believes that for corporate offending to be minimized in post-conflict areas, three needs must be met. These include guaranteeing public support, providing adequate economic and regulatory rules to eliminate opportunities for offending, and finally, paying adequate salaries to overseers of political financing and reconstruction. He also states that governments need to begin "securing a legal framework for transparency and accountability" in order to set rules and regulations for, and punishment against, corporate criminal activity (77).

Laws and Legislation against Corporate Offending around the World

In many industrialized nations—Canada, Australia, England, and Japan to name a few—there are in place laws against corporate crime similar to those present in the United States. Industrialized nations are powerful entities in the global marketplace; as such, corporations in these countries have engaged in unlawful practices in the name of profit. In response, most industrialized nations' governments have enacted legislation in attempts to deter criminal wrongdoing. Japan has passed numerous laws, especially regarding the environment and practices that affect the health and well-being of its citizens (Clinard and Yeager 1980; Yokoyama 2007). Canada, Australia, and most countries in Europe all have enacted new laws with stiffer penalties for those involved in corporate offending, including laws for offenses where death occurs. Australia, for instance, adopted the Australian Capital Territory Crimes Amendment Act in 2004 that enacted a law against industrial manslaughter (Sarre 2007). Furthermore, these countries have created official sectors of government similar to the Corporate Fraud Task Force (CFTF) in the United States to deal with these offenses. In Germany, a corporate governance code that is legally binding has been established, and the European Union has adopted the stance that country leaders and private companies need to be held more accountable for their financial practices (Shirreff 2002).

As in the United States, many countries have citizens' rights groups and nonprofit oversight organizations that investigate and disseminate to the public reports of corporate wrongdoing. Groups like Australians against Corruption, the Council of Europe's Anti-Corruption Monitoring Group, and Canada's Global Organization of Parliamentarians against Corruption were all established to help the fight against corporate criminal activities at home as well as abroad. Indeed, the message is out that corporate crime is something that affects everyone, and it should not, and will not, be tolerated. Corporate crime as an international endeavor has garnered more attention as well. Both national and international efforts have been strengthened by added legislation and resources; however, efforts are hampered by their ineffective use. In many nations, people still do not trust their governments to act in the best interest of its citizens. They believe that the polity in their country is involved in much of the corporate offending that lingers. Reports from the media and various public organizations reveal a degree of skepticism about the doggedness of current cleanup efforts:

> The very existence of anti-corruption campaigns and institutions in so many countries is an encouraging sign that the battle against corruption has become entrenched. If these anti-corruption initiatives are poorly

implemented, however, their existence is of little benefit. In continuing the fight against corruption, it is important therefore to continue assessing progress, not
just to identify needs for new anti-corruption laws and
institutions but to evaluate whether those already in
place are being effectively employed to curb corruption.
(Hodess 2007, 295)

The United Nations Office on Drugs and Crime (UNODC)
has urged the leadership of many countries to take what they call
"practical action," querying governments as to whether they are
freezing assets of individuals involved in corporate crime and
enforcing codes of conduct for public officials; the UNODC
maintains that the public has a right to hold the leadership of nations accountable for the enforcement of laws against corporate
offending (2006). The executive director of the UNODC since
2002, Antonio Costa, speaking at the first session of the Conference of the States' Parties to the United Nations Convention
against Corruption, stated that it is the responsibility of the individual countries to do more. Over 150 countries have signed the
UN Convention against Corruption, and 80 of those have ratified
it. The remaining 70 have cited a need to overhaul poor domestic
legislation against this type of offending before ratification can
take place. In his speech, Costa declared that the people of the
world have done their part by bringing corporate criminal offending to the fore, and now it is up to the world law enforcement community and the governments of individual countries to
do their part. He stated:

As recently as ten, fifteen years ago, the "C" word was
only whispered—almost as if it were bad to talk about
it. Dishonest people were often considered clever for
beating the system. Few corruption cases were brought
to trial, even fewer the convictions. For multi-national
companies, bribery was part of the cost of doing business—even tax deductible, in some cases. Many countries were ruled by strong men who looted the entire
state treasury, hiding billions of dollars in financial
sanctuaries where the stolen assets were protected by
banking secrecy. Entire financial communities pros-
pered from dirty money while the victims of corruption
were left to drink dirty water, without electricity,
schools or hospitals. . . . Ladies and Gentlemen, at one

point in the future I would like to give you a report on the state of corruption in the world, and the advances we are making thanks to the Convention. After all, I do such a thing once a year in relation to drug cultivation, trafficking and abuse, through the evidence submitted at the Commission of Narcotic Drugs (CND) and with the *World Drug Report.* Unfortunately, at the United Nations, the "C" word is still not fully appreciated: we simply do not have any way to unveil its shape, form and movements. . . . The UN Convention against Corruption was negotiated, signed and ratified by governments. But it belongs to all people. With corruption, everybody pays. Therefore we have to fight it together. (Costa 2006)

Indeed, many international laws against corporate crime have been enacted. These initiatives continue to be strengthened by many organizations around the world that are devoted to developing international laws, disseminating international recommendations for best practices, and encouraging cooperation and information sharing among world nations. Some of the organizations involved in this international effort include the United Nations, the Council of Europe, the Organization of the American States, the Global Organization of Parliamentarians against Corruption, the World Customs Organization, the Organisation for Economic Cooperation and Development, the Latin American Centre for Development Administration, the Organization for Security and Co-operation in Europe, the Inter-American Development Bank, ANCORAGE-NET, and the Asia-Pacific Economic Cooperation.

Recommendations from some of these organizations have been made available to the public, to corporations, and to governments regarding deterrence of corruption.

Inter-American Convention against Corruption

This document, which is over 10 years old, contains 28 articles. A multilateral treaty by the Office of American States set forth by its member states, it recognizes that "corruption undermines the legitimacy of public institutions and strikes at society, moral order and justice, as well as at the comprehensive development of peoples" (Office of American States 1996). Article II lays out the convention's purposes:

1. To promote and strengthen the development by each of the States Parties of the mechanisms needed to prevent, detect, punish and eradicate corruption; and
2. To promote, facilitate and regulate cooperation among the States Parties to ensure the effectiveness of measures and actions to prevent, detect, punish and eradicate corruption in the performance of public functions and acts of corruption specifically related to such performance. (Office of American States 1996)

Some of the preventive measures of this convention include the creation, maintenance, and support of standards of conduct for public function; mechanisms to enforce these standards of conduct; instruction to government personnel for understanding of responsibility; mechanisms for recording income, assets, and liabilities of those in public positions; laws that disallow special tax treatment for those violating anti-corruption laws of the convention; methods for the protection of those who report corruptive practices; boards to oversee execution of systems to prevent, discover, and punish corrupt acts; and systems to promote citizen and nongovernmental bodies in endeavors in prevention of corruption (Office of American States 1996). This convention does not stop the member states from using their own domestic laws against acts of corruption. The signatory countries of this convention include Argentina, Antigua and Barbuda, the Bahamas, Barbados, Belize, Bolivia, Brazil, Canada, Chile, Colombia, Costa Rica, Dominica, the Dominican Republic, Ecuador, El Salvador, Grenada, Guatemala, Guyana, Haiti, Honduras, Jamaica, Mexico, Nicaragua, Panama, Paraguay, Peru, St. Kitts and Nevis, St. Lucia, St. Vincent and the Grenadines, Suriname, Trinidad and Tobago, the United States, Uruguay, and Venezuela.

The convention encompasses the following acts of corporate offending:

The solicitation or acceptance, directly or indirectly, by a government official or a person who performs public functions, of any article of monetary value, or other benefit, such as a gift, favor, promise or advantage for himself or for another person or entity, in exchange for any act or omission in the performance of his public functions;

The offering or granting, directly or indirectly, to a government official or a person who performs public functions, of any article of monetary value, or other benefit, such as a gift, favor, promise or advantage for himself or for another person or entity, in exchange for any act or omission in the performance of his public functions;

Any act or omission in the discharge of his duties by a government official or a person who performs public functions for the purpose of illicitly obtaining benefits for himself or for a third party;

The fraudulent use or concealment of property derived from any of the acts referred to in this article; and

Participation as a principal, coprincipal, instigator, accomplice or accessory after the fact, or in any other manner, in the commission or attempted commission of, or in any collaboration or conspiracy to commit, any of the acts referred to in this article.

This Convention shall also be applicable by mutual agreement between or among two or more States Parties with respect to any other act of corruption not described herein. (Office of American States 1996)

The Global Organization of Parliamentarians against Corruption (GOPC)

This organization is an international group of parliamentarians devoted to fighting corporate crime and supporting superior governance throughout the world. The group has over 400 members worldwide and was established in 2002 at a conference hosted by the Canadian House of Commons and Senate (Parliamentary Centre 2005). The GOPC, a nonprofit organization under Canadian law, has several regional chapters and provides a number of resources for combating and controlling corporate offending and wrongdoing by public officials. According to its Web site, the organization has compiled a downloadable handbook with information on detection and control of criminal acts, as well as a training package on budget and finance oversight for governments, a code of conduct for governments to abide by, and a database on performance indicators for governmental administration. The GOPC encourages implementation of the United Nations Convention against Corruption (GOPC 2007).

United Nations Convention against Corruption

In 2000, the General Assembly of the United Nations recognized the need for an international legal instrument that was independent of the existing United Nations Convention against Transnational Organized Crime. In October 2003, the General Assembly adopted the United Nations Convention against Corruption. This convention is a 71-article instrument that contains numerous measures against corrupt and criminal activities and aims to increase international cooperation of criminal prevention and enforcement (UNODC 2003). Article I of the convention lists its three statements of purpose: "To promote and strengthen measures to prevent and combat corruption more efficiently and effectively; to promote, facilitate and support international cooperation and technical assistance in the prevention of and fight against corruption, including in asset recovery; [and] to promote integrity, accountability and proper management of public affairs and public property" (UNODC 2003, Article I). Those advocating for this convention wanted it to be an instrument that would be "binding, effective, efficient and universal, and . . . a flexible and balanced instrument taking into account the legal, social, cultural, economic and political differences between countries, as well as their different levels of development" (Rooke 2004).

Significant issues addressed by the UNODC relating to corporate crime include prevention, criminalization, international cooperation, asset recovery, and implementation mechanisms (UNODC 2005). The Convention against Corruption believes that wrongdoing by officials and corporations can be stemmed with adequate prevention; indeed, offending can be prosecuted after the fact, but the convention devotes a lot of attention to deterrence measures for both the private and public sector. The convention mandates that states criminalize acts of corporate and government wrongdoing if, under domestic laws, they are not already considered criminal. It also requires cooperation in efforts against offending, especially regarding legal assistance, gathering of evidence, extradition, and seizing of assets (UNODC 2005). Indeed, asset recovery is one of the greatest tools in the fight against corporate and political crime, particularly in developing countries where vast amounts of embezzled national resources need to be returned to the country for the sake of the public. The Convention against Corruption established a Conference of the States Parties to the Convention that will meet regularly to review and discuss the implementation of the mechanisms mandated by the convention.

United Nations Global Compact

The UN Global Compact is an international initiative that seeks to bring together corporations, UN agencies, and civil and labor associations to work on universal social and environmental principles. The goal of the collective is to "promote responsible corporate citizenship so that business can be part of the solution to the challenges of globalization" (United Nations Global Compact Office [UNGCO] 2000). This compact is voluntary and has two key objectives: to conventionalize the ten principles for business activities around the world, and to bring about actions that are supportive of UN goals (UNGCO 2000). This compact involves six UN agencies: the Office of the High Commissioner for Human Rights, the United Nations Environment Programme, the International Labour Organization, the United Nations Development Programme, the United Nations Industrial Development Organization, and the United Nations Office on Drugs and Crime.

The Global Compact is designed to cultivate favorable relationships between business and society. It gives attention to the world's poorest people and looks to involve them in the global economy by promoting sustainable and inclusive global markets.

The Global Compact asks companies to embrace, support, and enact, within their sphere of influence, the following principles:

Human Rights

Principle 1: Businesses should support and respect the protection of internationally proclaimed human rights; and

Principle 2: make sure that they are not complicit in human rights abuses.

Labour

Principle 3: Businesses should uphold the freedom of association and the effective recognition of the right to collective bargaining;

Principle 4: the elimination of all forms of forced and compulsory labour;

Principle 5: the effective abolition of child labour; and

Principle 6: the elimination of discrimination in respect of employment and occupation.

Environment

Principle 7: Businesses should support a precautionary approach to environmental challenges;

Principle 8: undertake initiatives to promote greater environmental responsibility;

Principle 9: encourage the development and diffusion of environmentally friendly technologies.

Anti-Corruption

Principle 10: Businesses should work against all forms of corruption, including extortion and bribery. (UNGCO 2005)

Many of those voluntarily undertaking the Global Compact have modified their business practices and codes of conduct, and looked for methods to put into action the principles set forth by the compact. Through an impact assessment, the UN reports that 50 percent of companies taking part in the compact made changes to business policies as they related to the compact's principles.

Other Resources in the Global Fight against Corruption

The United Nations Office on Drugs and Crime has a multitude of resources available on its Web site for prosecutors, government officials, and researchers alike. Some of these include *The United Nations Handbook on Practical Anti-Corruption Measures for Prosecutors and Investigators,* which provides information on the development and implementation of anti-corruption approaches for countries interested in fighting against corporate and political crime; *The United Nations Manual on Anti-Corruption Policies,* which is geared toward politicians and policy makers and outlines the nature and scope of offending and the critical components to policy making; and *The United Nations Anti-Corruption Toolkit,* which includes the tools necessary for officials to develop and implement an agenda for fighting corporate and political offending. In addition, the United Nations publishes a *Compendium of International Legal Instruments on Corruption,* listing all key international and regional treaties, agreements, and resolutions.

Detecting and Controlling Corporate Crime Worldwide

The aforementioned organizations involved in the global fight against corporate crime—and others like the World Trade Organization (WTO), the International Monetary Fund (IMF), and the World Bank—have a tough job. The business world is so multifaceted and vast that detection and prosecution of international corporate violations are easier said than done. Couple this with the fact that many nations do not have legislation in place that encourages transparency and accountability, and control becomes almost impossible. These organizations set forth many treaties, agreements, and tools in the fight against corporate crime. They have proffered many recommendations for those involved in this fight; however, it is up to individual governments to implement the necessary tools and make them a priority, and for multinational corporations to take charge in self-regulation of business activities. Andrews (2000) states that the financial cops of the world—the WTO, the IMF, and the World Bank—as well as national governments have given in to big business and accepted the idea that the global economy and opportunity for profit must not be impeded. Governments and organizations are making progress, but much is left to be done. Technological advances like the Internet have helped organizations to disseminate information and make the bidding process for contracts available in the public arena, thereby creating a fair process that is less subject to bribes and poor construction. This effort needs to be maintained.

The UNODC (2004) set forth some minimum requirements for the world to make an impact in the fight against corporate criminal offending at the signatory meetings of the Convention against Corruption in Merida, Mexico:

1. Civil society has to play a central role in oversight of business and government but also act as a vehicle for reform.
2. The media must continue to uncover and report on abuse, misuse, and corruption in the public and business sector, thereby holding those responsible accountable.
3. Countries need to establish a helpful system of checks and balances and adopt specific codes of conduct. This is needed for an increased effort at prevention, not just prosecuting and punishing wrongdoing after the fact, but seeking out the sources of corruption as targets of reform.
4. Governments need to create a framework to facilitate the implementations of legislation, including the establishment of independent anti-corruption agencies with extensive mandates to recognize, investigate, prosecute, and prevent corruption. This has proved to work in many jurisdictions thus far.
5. The financial system of a nation also needs to be on board. There needs to be a system for governing and supervising financial institutions within the institution itself as well as by outside agencies. Such a system would make it possible to track transactions and record suspicious activity.
6. Professional associations and working professionals also need to be involved. Legal systems and lawyers and accounting associations and accountants have to play a role in oversight and monitoring and upholding compliance standards.
7. States must participate in quick and helpful international cooperation to address issues of corruption by providing legal assistance, information sharing, and extradition treaties.

Prosecution of Corporations in Other Countries

In order to make an attempt at controlling corporate crime, the necessary laws must be enacted and law enforcement agencies must be created. As of the writing of this book, while some nations are still struggling to pass effective measures, most countries have these laws in place. Since the late 1990s, the international community has fought hard for the implementation of stricter and more effective controls. In the next decade, the challenge will be to ensure that these laws are actually put to use in the global fight against corporate crime, both domestically and on an international level. Houssain states that the biggest challenge for deterring corporate crime is to make certain that "laws are enforced and that legal redress for injustice can be secured through a functioning judicial system. The failure of judges and the broader judiciary to meet these legitimate expectations provides a fertile breeding ground" (2007, xix). He further notes that for countries with legal systems and judiciaries that are themselves offenders, even the best laws are useless.

Eigen (2003) reports that international cooperation has increased, the European Union has adopted new directives, and there have been many stories of success, especially in the case of money laundering and the returning of pilfered funds to the countries from which they were stolen. Nigerians saw US$1.2 billion returned from the accounts of their deceased dictator Sani Abacha; however, this occurred only after charges were dropped against his son. The Peruvian government has also taken steps by freezing assets of some of the associates of ex-president Albert Fujimori. Furthermore, after accusations of criminal offending, a vice president in South Africa was removed from office; Ecuadorian and Bolivian presidents were forced to resign; trials have begun in Venezuela, Nepal, and France; and investigations commenced against past politicians in Israel and Costa Rica (de Swardt 2007). Still, inconsistencies in extradition laws and reluctance by governments to prosecute make it difficult to bring criminal leaders to justice or to recoup lost funds. For instance, it took almost seven years for the Peruvian government to extradite Fujimori to answer for his crimes because Chilean court officials made several rulings against extradition until September 2007, when Chile's supreme court finally ruled that he be extradited back to Peru (McCarthy 2007). After being arrested on a return trip to Chile, Fujimori took up residence in an upscale apartment in Santiago, Chile, close to the Japanese embassy (Witte 2007). He continued to live freely in this apartment until his extradition. Progress is also slow in getting the Swiss banking system to release funds that were embezzled and deposited in Swiss accounts. For instance, international prosecutors spent five years trying to get back some of the millions that Benazir Bhutto stole from Pakistan, eventually recovering only US$250,000 (Transparency International 2004).

Punishment of Corporations Worldwide

Mennen, Frye, and Messick (2007) believe that the success of deterring corporate criminal activity relies on prosecution of these acts. They report that "courts must expeditiously, but fairly, adjudicate the resulting cases, and the penalties imposed on those convicted must be sufficient to dissuade others from similar acts" (310). Enforcement data by governments also need to be collected and maintained. This means that governments need to create agencies whose sole purpose is combating corporate crime. The United Nations and the Council of Europe recommend that countries employ agencies as an important part of the fight against corporate criminal activity. The European Union has also stipulated that these types of agencies be present in a nation's statutes as a prerequisite for EU membership (de Sousa and Triães 2007). Many countries have created these agencies, and data are now slowly being collected on their activities and progress. An online research network of anti-corruption agencies called ANCORAGE-NET was founded in 2006. The goal of this network is to supply practitioners and researchers with extensive and accessible information on the control of corporate crime (de Sousa and Triães 2007). Although still in its infancy, this network hopes to increase the ability of agencies to make progress in the punishment and deterrence of corporate criminal offending.

Criminal law, however, is not the only avenue for punishment. Governments also need to employ noncriminal actions; the loss of positions and pension funds can be equally effective in deterring individuals from engaging in criminal behaviors (Mennen, Frye, and Messick 2007). Citizen rights groups and the media also play an important role. In Kuwait, Morocco, and Uganda, the media has been integral in exposing corporate and governmental scandals, and South Korea has adopted strategies to combat offending that involve civil groups, the private sector, and the government (de Swardt 2007).

At the individual country level many reforms have been implemented:

- Cameroon, Finland, France, Guatemala, Malaysia, South Korea, and the United States have increased transparency in public procurement.
- Croatia and Slovakia have reduced political corruption.
- Slovakia, Switzerland, and Panama have all increased public access to all types of information.
- Brazil, Georgia, Greece, Poland, and Romania are ensuring that the independence and transparency of the judiciary remains in place.
- Croatia, New Zealand, and Panama have enhanced integrity in the public sector by establishing codes of conduct and conflict of interest rules.
- Japan, Papua New Guinea, and Romania have all enacted reforms aimed at protecting whistleblowers.
- Ireland, Malaysia, and South Africa are improving transparency in financial services (de Swardt 2007, 120).

The United Nations Convention against Corruption is partially responsible for the increase in reforms at individual country levels. Other international organizations such as the Organisation for Economic Cooperation and Development and the Latin American Centre for Development Administration have been integral in pressuring countries around the globe to effect reform as well. Enforcement, however, is still lacking in some countries and at the international level. The business sector in some nations has little information on or knowledge of many of the prevention strategies already in place at home (de Swardt 2007).

When prosecuted, punishments tend not to be severe enough to have a deterrent effect. In July 2007, however, the Chinese government took extreme measures and executed Zheng Xiaoyu, the head of its State Food and Drug Administration (SFDA), for accepting bribe money in exchange for approving untested medicines. Under Zheng, the SFDA approved six bogus medicines from 1998 to 2005 (NPR 2007). One of those drugs, an antibiotic, was the cause of at least 10 deaths. Zheng was found guilty of accepting bribes totaling over $800,000 in the form of gifts and money during his time as head of the agency (Associated Press 2007). Even though China executes more persons annually than all of the other nations in the world combined, this execution was an especially harsh punishment for a bribery conviction. Zheng's death sentence came in the wake of a scandal involving the import of numerous unsafe Chinese products. His execution was most likely a message from the Chinese government that offenses such as these will not be tolerated because the reputation of the Chinese food and drug industry is at stake. The U.S. Food and Drug Administration refused 253 shipments of Chinese seafood alone in 2006 due to drug residue or diseases such as salmonella (Associated Press 2007). Chinese officials have already admitted this year that they were responsible for distributing cough syrup that contained deadly chemicals and tainted pet food that caused the deaths of many cats and dogs in the United States. U.S. officials have also found deadly chemicals used in antifreeze in some toothpaste that was shipped from China, as well as toys containing lead paint (Webley 2007).

In October 2007, oil giant British Petroleum, which is Europe's second largest company, agreed to pay fines totaling $373 million related to a refinery explosion in Texas where 15 workers were killed and 170 others were injured (PBS 2007). Part of the fine is related to criminal penalties, part of it is for environmental violations, and some is for artificially manipulating propane gas prices.

Conclusion

Corporate crime around the globe is ever present; the industrialized production of labor, free-market economies, and the globalization of the world marketplace have all contributed to an increase in incidents of corporate offending. The message is clear: no country is fully protected against corporate crime. In some countries, however, the outlook is bleaker than in others. Latin America, Africa, and some parts of Asia are especially susceptible to corporate offending in both business and government. The poor around the world pay an especially high price for corporate offenses, whether in development, access to basic services like sanitation and clean water, or necessary and affordable health care; those less fortunate are always the most severely affected. In the globalized, shrinking world of the early 21st century, the effects can also be widespread. Corporate criminal activity anywhere costs the whole world. Depriving persons of essential health care can facilitate the spread of disease and create drug-resistant strains of diseases. Criminal behavior by corporations around the globe causes daily loss of human life.

Some see globalization as progress; others say the faster and the more reckless we proceed with the idea of a global economy without taking precautionary steps to ensure the health and well being of all, the more widespread and deadly corporate offending will become. Developed countries have the responsibility to ensure that multinational corporations are not dominating developing nations' economies in the name of profit. Giving monies to help those in the Third World can lead to more offending—and, consequently, more human suffering— if not monitored properly. Corporate crime plagues every sector of society: business, politics, services, development, construction and reconstruction, health care, disease prevention, and the military, to name a few.

Many laws, treaties, compacts, and recommendations for combating corporate offending are in place, both domestically and in the international arena. It is now time for all involved to work hard to see that these laws are enforced. The United Nations is calling for governments and other entities to take "practical action" to ensure that no criminal act goes unnoticed, uncharged, unprosecuted, and unpunished. Numerous countries have made many strides in uncovering, prosecuting, and punishing those involved in corporate crime. Governments and other agencies have been involved in freezing, confiscating, and returning assets and monies stolen, but obstacles remain. Some governments are still reluctant to prosecute corporate criminals; some countries' judicial systems are still susceptible to bribery; Swiss and other offshore banking institutions are still surrounded by secrecy. Research suggests that international public financial institutions in charge of development may, in some cases, be further aggravating corporate crime. The World Bank, the IMF, the WTO, and other international organizations need to be effectual, too. The World Bank alone has awarded nearly 40,000 contracts for development and reconstruction in recent years; obviously, oversight and monitoring by these agencies is imperative in the global fight against corporate crime. The public and private sectors, the business community, governments, citizen rights organizations, the media, and various other agencies all have the responsibility to undertake this cause as well. The global fight against corporate crime will no doubt require a global effort.

References

Alesina, Alberto, and Beatrice Weder. 2002. "Do Corrupt Governments Receive Less Foreign Aid?" *American Economic Review* 92 (September): 1126–37.

Alexander, David. 2005. "The Italian Mafia's Legacy of High-Rise Death Traps." *Global Corruption Report 2005.* Transparency International Web site. www.transparency.org/publications/gcr/download_gcr/download_gcr_2005.

Anderson, Gerard F., Peter S. Hussey, Bianca K. Frogner, and Hugh R. Walters. 2005. "Health Spending in the United States and the Rest of the Industrialized World." *Health Affairs* 24 (July–August): 903.

Andrews, Charles. 2000. "Globalization: What Is This Monster, and What Do We Do About It?" www. mail-archive.com/pen-l@galaxy.scu.chico.edu/msg48969.html.

Associated Press. 2007. "China Executes Former Watchdog Chief." *USA Today.* www.usatoday.com/news/world/2007-07-10-china-tainted-goods_N.htm.

AVERT. 2007. "Aids around the World." www.avert.org/around world.htm.

Bureau of Labor Education. 2001. "The U.S. Healthcare System: Best in the World, or Just the Most Expensive?" Orono: University of Maine. Summer.

Chatterjee, Pratap. 2003. "Megacrime Scenes." *New Internationalist,* July.

Clinard, Marshall B., and Peter Yeager. 1980. *Corporate Crime.* New York: Free Press.

Coalition Provisional Authority (CPA). 2004. "First Quarterly Report to Congress." www.sigir.mil/reports/quarterlyreports/Mar04/cpaig_march_30_report.pdf.

Collier, Paul, and Anke Hoeffler. 2005. "The Economic Costs of Corruption in Infrastructure." *Global Corruption Report 2005.* Transparency International Web site. www.transparency.org/publications/gcr/download_gcr/download_gcr_2005.

Costa, Antonio Maria. 2006. "Let's Make History at the Dead Sea: Implementing the UN Convention against Corruption." Speech of the Executive Director of the United Nations Office on Crime and Drugs at the First Session of the Conference of the States Parties to the United Nations Convention against Corruption. www.unodc.org/unodc/speech_2006_12_10.html.

Dal Bo, Ernesto, and Martin A. Rossi. 2007. "Corruption and Efficiency: Theory and Evidence from Electric Utilities." *Journal of Public Economics* 91: 939–962.

DeNavas-Walt, Carmen, Bernadette Proctor, and Cheryl Hill Lee. 2006. "Income, Poverty and Health Insurance Coverage in the United States: United States Census Bureau." Washington, DC: United States Government Printing Office.

de Sousa, Luís, and João Triães. 2007. "ANCORAGE-NET: Sharing Knowledge-Based Solutions to Corruption Control." *Global Corruption Report 2007*. Transparency International Web site. www.transparency.org/publications/gcr/download_gcr.

de Swardt, Cobus. 2006. "Lessons Learned from Anti-Corruption Campaigns around the World." *Global Corruption Report 2006*. Transparency International Web site. www.transparency.org/publications/gcr/download_gcr/download_gcr_2006.

Di Tella, Rafael, and William D. Savedoff, eds. 2001. *Diagnosis Corruption: Fraud in Latin America's Public Hospitals*. Washington, DC: Inter-American Development Bank.

Eigen, Peter. 2003. "Introducing the Global Corruption Report 2003." *Global Corruption Report 2003*. Transparency International Web site. www.transparency.org/publications/gcr/download_gcr/download_gcr_2003.

Eigen, Peter. 2005. "Introduction." *Global Corruption Report 2005*. Transparency International Web site. www.transparency.org/publications/gcr/download_gcr/download_gcr_2005.

Estache, Antonio, and Eugene Kouassi. 2002. "Sector Organization, Governance, and the Inefficiency of African Water Utilities." World Bank Policy Research Working Paper 2890. ssrn.com/abstract=636253.

Friedman, Thomas L. *The World Is Flat: A Brief History of the Twenty-first Century*. New York: Farrar, Straus, and Giroux.

Global Organization of Parliamentarians against Corruption. 2007. www.parlcent.ca/gopac/index_e.php.

Government Accountability Office. 2007. *Stabilizing and Rebuilding Iraq: Serious Challenges Confront U.S. Efforts to Build the Capacity of Iraqi Ministries*. Testimony of David M. Walker before the Committee on Oversight and Government Reform, House of Representatives. Washington, DC: GAO.

Guha, Krishna, and Eoin Callan. 2007. "Pressure Grows on Wolfowitz to Resign." *Financial Times*, April 12.

Hawley, Susan. 2005. "Financing Corruption? The Role of Multilateral Development Banks and Export Creedit Agencies." *Global Corruption Report 2005.* Transparency International Web site. www.transparency .org/publications/gcr/download_gcr/download_gcr_2005.

Hodess, Robin. 2004. "Introduction." *Global Corruption Report 2004.* Transparency International Web site. www.transparency.org/publications/gcr/download_gcr/download_gcr_2004.

Hofbauer, Helena. 2006. "Citizens' Audit in Mexico Reveals Paper Trail of Corruption." *Global Corruption Report 2006.* Transparency International Web site. www.transparency.org/publications/gcr/download_gcr/download_gcr_2006.

Houssain, Kamal. 2007. "Foreword." *Global Corruption Report 2007.* Transparency International Web site. www.transparency.org/publications/gcr/download_gcr.

International Advisory and Monitoring Board. 2006. Development Fund for Iraq (DFI) Audit Reports. www.iamb.info/dfiaudit.htm.

Kaufmann, D., F. Leautier, and M. Mastruzzi. 2004. "Governance and the City: An Empirical Investigation into the Global Determinants of Urban Performance." Washington, DC: World Bank.

Le Billion, Philippe. 2005. "Overcoming Corruption in the Wake of Conflict." *Global Corruption Report 2005.* Transparency International Web site. www.transparency.org/publications/gcr/download_gcr/download_gcr_2005.

Leenders, Reinoud, and Justin Alexander. "Case Study: Corrupting the New Iraq." *Global Corruption Report 2005.* Transparency International Web site. www.transparency.org/publications/gcr/download_gcr/download_gcr_2005.

Levitt, Theodore. 1983. "The Globalization of Markets." *Harvard Business Review* 61: 92–102.

Lewis, James. 2005. "Earthquake Destruction: Corruption on the Fault Line." *Global Corruption Report 2005.* Transparency International Web site. www.transparency.org/publications/gcr/download_gcr/download_gcr_2005.

Lugar, Richard. 2006. Senate Committee on Foreign Relations Chairman Richard G. Lugar's Opening Statement for Hearing on "Multilateral Development Banks: Promoting Effectiveness and Fighting Corruption." Washington, DC: United States Senate. March 28. www.senate.gov/~foreign/testimony/2006/LugarStatement060328.pdf.

McCarthy, Julie. 2007. "Former Peru President Fujimori Faces Extradition." Washington, DC: National Public Radio. September 22. www.npr.org/templates/story/story.php?storyId=14620504.

Mennen, Tiernan, Eric Frye, and Richard E. Messick. 2007. "Enforcement of Anti-Corruption Laws: The Need for Performance Monitoring." *Global Corruption Report 2007*. Transparency International Web site. www.transparency.org/publications/gcr/download_gcr.

Mitchell, William A., and Justin Page. 2005. "Turkish Homeowners Demand an End to Earthquake Devastation." *Global Corruption Report 2005*. Transparency International Web site. www.transparency.org/publications/gcr/download_gcr/download_gcr_2005.

Mokhiber, Russell, and Robert Weissman. 2006. "J'Accuse: The Ten Worst Corporations of 2006." *Multinational Monitor* 27 (November–December). www.multinationalmonitor.org/mm2006/112006/mokhiber.html.

Mokhiber, Russell, and Robert Weissman. 2005. "The 10 Worst Corporations of 2005." *Multinational Monitor* 26 (November–December). multinationalmonitor.org/mm2005/112005/mokhiber.html.

National Public Radio (NPR). 2007. "China Executes Ex-Food and Drug Chief." July 10. www.npr.org/.

Nussbaum, David. 2006. "Preface." *Global Corruption Report 2006*. Transparency International Web site. www.transparency.org/publications/gcr/download_gcr/download_gcr_2006.

Nutt, Dominic, and John Davison. 2003. "Iraq: The Missing Billions; Transition and Transparency in Post-War Iraq." Briefing Paper for the Madrid Donors' Conference on Iraq. October 23–24.

Office of American States. 1996. "Inter-American Convention against Corruption." www.oas.org/.

Organisation for Economic Cooperation and Development. 2007. *OECD in Figures: 2006–2007 Edition*. Paris: OECD Observer.

Parliamentary Centre. 2005. *Thirty-seventh Annual Report of the Parliamentary Centre*. Ottawa, ON: Parliamentary Centre.

Pilapitiya, Thusitha. 2004. *The Impact of Corruption on the Human Rights Based Approach to Development*. Oslo: United Nations Development Programme, Oslo Governance Centre. September.

Public Broadcasting System (PBS). 2007. "Oil and Gas Giant BP to Pay Fines Totaling $373M." October 25. www.pbs.org/.

Public Citizen's Congress Watch. 2002. "Pharmaceuticals Rank as Most Profitable Industry, Again." April 16. www.citizen.org/.

Rooke, Peter. 2004. "The UN Convention against Corruption." *Global Corruption Report 2004*. Transparency International Web site. www.transparency.org/publications/gcr/download_gcr/download_gcr_2004.

Sarre, Rick. 2007. "White-Collar Crime and Prosecution for 'Industrial Manslaughter' as a Means to Reduce Workplace Deaths." In *Interna-*

tional Handbook of White-Collar and Corporate Crime, ed. Henry N. Pontell and Gilbert Geis. New York: Springer.

Savedoff, William D. 2006. "A Tale of Two Health Systems." *Global Corruption Report 2006*. Transparency International Web site. www.transparency.org/publications/gcr/download_gcr/download_gcr_2006.

Savedoff, William D., and Karen Hussmann. 2006. "Why Are Health Systems Prone to Corruption?" *Global Corruption Report 2006*. Transparency International Web site. www.transparency.org/publications/gcr/download_gcr/download_gcr_2006.

Schirnding, Y., and C. Mulholland. 2002. "Health and Sustainable Development: Key Health Trends." Geneva: World Health Organization.

Shirreff, David. 2002. "After the Chaos." *Economist*, September 14.

Simon, David R. 2006. *Elite Deviance*. Boston: Pearson/Allyn and Bacon.

Special Inspector General for Iraq Reconstruction. 2007. *October 2007 Quarterly Report to Congress*. Special Inspector General for Iraq Reconstruction Web site.

Tayler, Liz. 2006. "Corruption and AIDS—An Overview of the Issues." London: HLSP Institute. February.

Transparency International. 2004. Executive Summary. *Global Corruption Report 2004*. Transparency International Web site. www.transparency.org/publications/gcr/download_gcr/download_gcr_2004.

Transparency International. "Frequently Asked Questions About Corruption." www.transparency.org/news_room/faq/corruption_faq#faqcorr1.

Transparency International. 2006. "Report on the TI Global Corruption Barometer 2006." Berlin: Transparency International Policy and Research Department. December 7.

Transparency International. 2003. "The TI Global Corruption Barometer: A 2002 Pilot Survey of International Attitudes, Expectations and Priorities on Corruption." London: TI Centre for Innovation and Research. July 3.

United Nations Global Compact Office. 2000. "About the Global Compact." New York: UNGCO. www.unglobalcompact.org/AboutTheGC/index.html.

United Nations Global Compact Office. 2005. "The United Nations Global Compact: Advancing Corporate Citizenship." New York: UNGCO www.unglobalcompact.org/docs/about_the_gc/2.0.2.pdf.

United Nations Office on Drugs and Crime. 2005. *Compendium of International Legal Instruments on Corruption*. 2nd ed. New York: UNODC.

United Nations Office on Drugs and Crime. 2004. "Global Action against Corruption." Vienna: UNODC.

United Nations Office on Drugs and Crime. 2003. "United Nations Convention against Corruption." Vienna: UNODC.

United Nations Office on Drugs and Crime. 2006. "UNODC Chief Says Tangible Progress Needed in Fighting Global Corruption to Overcome Public Skepticism." Vienna: UNODC. December 10.

United States General Accounting Office. 2000. "World Bank: Management Controls Stronger, But Challenges in Fighting Corruption Remain." Washington, DC: GAO. April. www.gao.gov/new.items/ns00073.pdf.

Velásquez, Germán, and Pascale Boulet. 1999. "Globalization and Access to Drugs: Implications of the WTO/TRIPS Agreement." Geneva: World Health Organization.

Webley, Kayla. 2007. "List of Problem Chinese Imports Grows." Washington, DC: National Public Radio. July 10. www.npr.org/templates/story/story.php?storyId=11656278.

Witte, Benjamin. 2007. "Prosecutor Backs Fujimori's Extradition to Peru." *The Santiago Times.* June 10. www.worldpress.org/Americas/2821.cfm.

World Economic Forum. 2003. *Global Competitiveness Report: 2002–2003.* New York: Oxford University Press.

World Health Organization. 2006. *Working Together for Health: The World Health Report 2006.* Geneva: WHO Press.

World Health Organization. 2000. *The World Health Report 2000: Health Systems: Improving Performance.* Geneva: WHO Press.

Wroughton, Lesley. 2007. "Wolfowitz to Resign June 30 as World Bank President." Reuters. www.reuters.com/article/topNews/idUSN2444199220070517?feedType=RSS.

Yokoyama, Minoru. 2007. "Environmental Pollution by Corporations in Japan." In *International Handbook of White-Collar and Corporate Crime,* ed. Henry N. Pontell and Gilbert Geis. New York: Springer.

4

Chronology

This chapter provides a timeline of corporations from their inception through 2007. Included are some of the important legislation and court cases that have given corporations more rights, but that have also made it easier for the government and law enforcement officials to hold them liable for their actions. Major prosecutions against corporate offenders are also listed. As a whole, this chronology attempts to outline important events, crucial court cases, significant pieces of legislation, organizations formed to control corporate wrongdoing, as well as other historical events that have shaped and reshaped corporations into the conglomerates they are today.

1443   Inventors Bylaws is passed, which grants patents for inventions and is the oldest patent law in the world.

1553   The English Joint Stock Company is formed to pay for a journey to the East by Sir Hugh Willoughby and Richard Chancellor. Willoughby would lose his life on the journey, but Chancellor would make it back to England.

1600   The East India Company is established, which is said to be the first multinational corporation to issue stocks. The East India Company was founded by the Royal Charter of Queen Elizabeth I. This charter bestowed upon the company a monopoly on trade in the East Indies. The company's power reached across all continents and had influence over half the world's

1600 (cont.)	trade. It internationalized the systems of weights and measures, built entire industries, and created its own currency.
1624	The Monopoly Act is passed in England, which protects patents.
1661	The London Board of Trade is founded.
1661	The Corporation Act is passed, which expressly forbids members of the Church of England from holding municipal office; it is enacted to restrain the power of the church.
1711	The South Sea Company in London is incorporated.
1720	The French Mississippi Company collapses when its head, John Law, decides its shares are too high and begins devaluing them. Intense protest and subsequent selling pressure cause the stock to drop tenfold; fortunes are lost by many investors, and the collapse causes an economic depression in France and parts of Europe. In the same year, the English South Sea Company experiences a similar fate.
1776	Adam Smith pens *The Wealth of Nations*, which is a seminal work for contemporary economics. In it, he maligns companies and corporations, stating that they are useless and, if anything, have harmed trade.
1790	In the case of *The Rev John Bracken v. the Visitors of William and Mary College*, the Court of Appeals of Virginia decides that William and Mary College can change its curriculum and its faculty, and that this will not violate its original charter. Corporations can now make decisions about themselves and changes to their structure without reorganizing their charters. Patent law develops in Colonial America based on the constitutional provisions set forth in Article I, Section 8. The act federalizes patent power; states can no longer grant patents.

1819   In the case of *Dartmouth College v. Woodward*, the United States Supreme Court rules that states cannot interfere with the operations of a corporation and do not have the right to amend or repeal a corporation's charter.

1827   The Mechanics' Union of Trade Associations forms in Philadelphia, Pennsylvania, and the American trade union movement begins.

1830   In the case of *Society for the Propagation of the Gospel in Foreign Parts v. Town of Pawlet,* the U.S. Supreme Court expands the rights of corporations to be similar to those of natural persons.

1833   The Factory Act in Britain is promulgated to establish a normal working day. It states that the working day is to begin at 5:30 a.m. and will end by 8:30 p.m. Also, those ranging in age from 13 to 18 cannot work longer than 12 hours in a day, and children ranging in age from 9 to 13 cannot work longer than 9 hours in a day. Thus, children and young adults can no longer be put to work at night.

1842   Massachusetts is the first state in the United States to enact child labor laws.

1844   The UK Joint Stock Companies Act is passed by the British parliament, expanding the access of a company to incorporate. Prior to this act, incorporation was only granted by Royal Charter. The act also establishes that joint stock companies need to be registered.

1855   The UK Limited Liability Act is passed to make investors less liable for company losses. Shareholders in a company are now not personally responsible for the company's debts if it goes bankrupt; they are liable only up to the amount of their shares in the company.

1858   The East India Company is dissolved. India is now ruled by the British Crown.

1870   The Standard Oil Company is incorporated in Ohio by John D. Rockefeller.

1886   The U.S. Supreme Court grants corporate personhood in the case of *Santa Clara County v. Southern Pac. R. Co.* (118 U.S. 394 [1886]). Corporations now have many of the same rights and responsibilities as individuals, such as the right to own property, sign contracts, and pay taxes.

1890   The United States passes the Sherman Antitrust Act, the first legislation against monopolistic practices. It makes monopolizing any trade or commerce a felony.

1892   England passes the Shop Hours Act, which limits the number of hours that those under 18 can work in a week to 74 hours.

1909   The U.S. Supreme Court holds in the case of *New York Central & Hudson River Railroad Co. v. United States* that corporations can be held liable and receive punishment for the actions of their agents.

1911   The U.S. Supreme Court orders that the Standard Oil Company be broken up. Chief Justice Edward Douglass White writes that conglomerations of capital in the hands of a few are analogous to slavery.

1913   The Trade Union Act in Britain establishes a union's right to use its fund for political purposes.

1914   Congress amends the Sherman Antitrust Act with the Clayton Antitrust Act, which bolsters and clarifies the previous act. The Clayton Act legalizes striking, picketing, and boycotting by employees. It states that human labor is not a commodity and acts as the foundation for many lawsuits against corporations.

        The Federal Trade Commission (FTC) Act is passed by the U.S. Congress in order to protect consumers from unfair competition or deceptive actions and to prevent restraints on competition. The act, which is enforced by the FTC, guards against business practices that cause harm and protects the market of free enterprise from large mergers and conspiracies to fix prices. A business, under this act, could be liable for any of the above actions committed by its employees, agents, or representatives. The FTC has five commissioners and the power to examine both interstate and foreign commerce.

1929   Wall Street stock market crashes. From 1921 to 1929, the Dow Jones rose from 60 to 400 points. Many millionaires are made and stock trading seems like a sure thing. Fraudulent companies spring up, aiming to bilk investors out of money. This overinflated bubble cannot hold, and the Federal Reserve raises interest rates. The resultant panic forces large-scale selling, which leads the market to crash.

1934   The Securities Exchange Act creates the Securities and Exchange Commission (SEC) in an attempt to restore confidence in the stock market. The SEC has broad power over the securities industry, including the registration and regulation of brokerage firms and the authority to punish violators of the act's terms. In addition, the Securities Exchange Act requires companies with publicly traded securities to report reliable information to investors.

1939   Edwin H. Sutherland coins the term "white-collar crime" in his presidential address to the American Sociological Society in Philadelphia, Pennsylvania.

1945   The United Nations is established. Its charter is ratified by the five permanent members of the Security Council: China, France, the Soviet Union, the United Kingdom, and the United States.

1946   The Hobbs Act is enacted. It criminalizes any attempt at robbery or extortion and in doing so it affects both commerce interstate or foreign. The Hobbs Act was enacted for the main purpose of combating racketeering and labor disputes, but it has been used on

1946
(cont.)
several occasions against extortion and public corruption. It stipulates fines and imprisonment not more than 20 years, or both.

1947
The International Monetary Fund (IMF) begins its operations at its headquarters in Washington, DC. According to the IMF Web site, the organization consists of "185 countries, working to foster global monetary cooperation, secure financial stability, facilitate international trade, promote high employment and sustainable economic growth, and reduce poverty."

1948
The Organization of American States (OAS) is founded in Bogota, Colombia, consisting of 21 nations who together confirm their commitment to common goals and regard for each nation's sovereignty.

1949
Sutherland publishes his seminal book *White Collar Crime,* which details criminal offending by many U.S. corporations.

1956
The Federal Water Pollution Control Act is passed, creating new standards for water quality in the country.

1959
The Inter-American Development Bank (IDB) is established as an international finance institution for the development of Latin American countries. It will help finance sustainable economic and social development, and support projects to decrease poverty and increase trade, investment, and modernization.

1961
The Organisation for Economic Cooperation and Development is formed in Paris, bringing together the governments of countries committed to the ideals of democracy and the market economy.

1962
The ruling in the case of *Standard Oil Company of Texas v. United States* establishes limits on corporate criminal liability: it states that liability cannot be imputed on a corporation if an employee's behaviors were counter to the benefit of that corporation.

1966   The National Traffic and Motor Vehicle Safety Act is passed, which establishes the National Highway Traffic Safety Administration. Subsequently, auto accidents decline.

1970   Environmental groups Greenpeace and Friends of the Earth begin campaigning against toxic waste and pollution by corporate America.

The Occupational Safety and Health Act (OSHA) is passed by the U.S. Congress in an attempt to ensure workplace safety for American workers.

The Bank Secrecy Act, passed by U.S. Congress, is the first law enacted to battle money laundering in the United States. The act requires banks to report cash transactions over $10,000; keep records and file reports that may be used in tax and regulatory matters; file Suspicious Activity Reports (SARs) when they identify any violations of federal law or suspicious activity related to monetary transactions; establish programs to ensure compliance with the act; maintain internal controls and independent compliance testing; and delegate an officer to coordinate the program.

Congress passes the Racketeer Influenced and Corrupt Organizations Act (RICO) as part of the Organized Crime Control Act of 1970, which is designed to punish organized criminal activity. RICO prohibits criminal activity committed through the use of *enterprise* (any individual, partnership, corporation, association, or other legal entity, and any union or group of individuals associated in fact although not a legal entity). Racketeering includes such offenses as gambling, extortion, bribery, mail or securities fraud, prostitution, and narcotics trafficking. The punishments under the act are harsh, with penalties of up to 20 years in prison for each violation.

1972   The Consumer Product Safety Act is promulgated. It creates the Consumer Product Safety Commission (CPSC) to make sure that laws are in place to protect consumers from unsafe products.

A governmental report entitled the *President's Report on Occupational Safety and Health* cites the number of deaths from industrial disease at 100,000 annually.

The Latin American Centre for Development Administration is founded to provide international cooperation for development in Latin America and the Caribbean.

1977   The Foreign Corrupt Practices Act is enacted, prohibiting individuals and corporations in the United States from bribing or paying foreign officials with the intention of obtaining business contracts. It also mandates that publicly held companies maintain records showing company assets and ensure internal accounting controls, including that financial transactions have been authorized, recorded, and reviewed.

1984   The world's largest corporation, AT&T, is broken up because it is monopolizing telecommunications in the United States.

1988   Ronald Reagan signs the Major Fraud Act, which increases penalties for those who defraud the government.

1991   Exxon Corporation and Exxon Shipping Company agree to pay a record $1 billion to settle all federal and state civil claims stemming from the *Exxon Valdez* oil spill in 1989.

1992   Tom Harkin, the senator from Iowa, introduces the Child Labor Deterrence Act, which would prohibit the importation of products that were produced with child labor and sets penalties, both civil and criminal, for violators. This bill has yet to be passed into legislation.

The European Union (EU) is formed.

1994   A jury in Anchorage, Alaska, awards $5 billion in punitive damages against Exxon for the 1989 *Valdez* oil spill.

1995   The World Trade Organization (WTO) is born and becomes an organization for liberalizing trade. It is a forum for negotiation of trade agreements between governments as well as a place for the settlement of trade disputes. It also sets forth a system of rules of trade.

1996   The Office of American States adopts the Inter-American Convention against Corruption, which is one of the first international legal instruments adopted in the fight on corruption. The convention identifies acts of corruption and sets forth obligations for member states under international law. It lists specific actions that need to be criminalized, and gives information on extradition, asset forfeiture, legal assistance, and technical assistance. This convention was adopted to acknowledge the importance of an international instrument in the fight against corruption as well as the need to foster and assist in multination cooperation to combat it. The convention set forth two goals: To promote and toughen each of the member states' development methods to prevent, detect, punish, and eliminate corruption, and to promote and assist cooperation among the member states.

The False Statements Accountability Act is passed, making it a crime to knowingly and willfully make false statements, or to cover up any facts or make fraudulent statements or representations, or to make or use fraudulent documents in any matter involving the three branches of government. If found guilty under this act, the offender is subject to fines or imprisonment of not more than five years, or both.

1997   The Organisation for Economic Cooperation and Development (OECD) adopts the Convention on Combating Bribery of Foreign Public Officials in International Business Transactions, recognizing that bribery is a universal phenomenon in international business practices and has severe consequences. This convention seeks to foster good governance and economic development and aid countries in the fight against bribery. It maintains that all countries have a duty to combat bribery in international business transactions.

     The European Union (EU) adopts the Convention on the Fight against Corruption. The purpose of the convention is to strengthen judicial cooperation between the EU member states in an attempt to combat corruption among European officials.

     Archer Daniels Midland Company, a leader in agribusiness, is fined $100 million by the U.S. Department of Justice for price fixing commodities used in common processed foods.

1998   Exxon and Mobil merge to form the largest oil company in the world; these two companies were offshoots of the original Standard Oil Company breakup in 1911.

     President Bill Clinton signs the International Anti-Bribery and Fair Competition Act, which implements the OECD's previous Convention on Combating Bribery of Foreign Public Officials in International Business Transactions and amends the Foreign Corrupt Practices Act. It gives the Department of Justice the power to subpoena documents and witnesses in the investigation of certain civil cases.

1999   The Council of Europe adopts the Criminal Law Convention on Corruption, designed to strengthen the bonds that unite its members and promote cooperation among them. Members will work together to formulate a general criminal policy—including the adoption of legislation and preventive measures—aimed at protecting society against corruption. In conjunction with this convention, the council creates the Group of States against Corruption (GRECO) to monitor compliance with the convention's anti-corruption strategies. At the same time, the Council of Europe, also recognizing the undesirable consequences of corruption financially, adopts the Civil Law Convention on Corruption to aid civil law in the fight against corruption and to compensate for damages those who have been victimized.

The World Trade Organization (WTO) summit in Seattle sees tens of thousands of protesters and rioters who believe that the organization encourages corporate dominance around the globe.

Hoffman-La Roche, a Swiss vitamin company, is hit with a $500 million fine by the Antitrust Division of the U.S. Department of Justice for price fixing violations. This is the largest fine ever imposed in a criminal prosecution.

Deputy Attorney General Eric Holder sends memorandums to United States Attorneys outlining methods for the prosecution of corporations.

2000   Hospital Corporation of America (HCA) pleads guilty to criminal charges and agrees to pay $840 million in fines, civil penalties, and damages from false claims.

The Peruvian government falls in the wake of Alberto Fujimori's presidential scandal of political corruption, which accuses him of stealing more than $180 million.

The United Nations Convention against Transnational Organized Crime is opened for signature in Palermo, Italy, in December 2000, and enters into force in September 2003. This convention has three supplemental protocols, which are aimed at specific acts of organized crime: trafficking in persons,

2000
(cont.)
especially women and children; smuggling of migrants; and illicit manufacturing and trafficking in firearms. It becomes a key tool in fighting transnational organized crime. States that ratify this convention must take action against organized crime by creating domestic criminal laws, adopting extradition treaties, collaborating with legal and law enforcement cooperation assistance, and promoting training and technical assistance for national authorities. For the first time, official definitions of *trafficking in persons* and *smuggling of migrants* are developed and agreed upon. The protocol against illicit firearm manufacturing and trafficking enters into force in July 2005, making it the first instrument on small arms at the global level that is legally binding.

Congress passes the International Anticorruption and Good Governance Act, which mandates the State Department to disseminate annual reports on all anticorruption practices. The act's purpose is to ensure the promotion of good governance at all levels of government and the private sector. The act also specifies that the secretary of state, the secretary of commerce, and the administrator of the Agency for International Development provide reports to Congress that outline the U.S. government's anticorruption efforts.

Arthur Andersen LLP bills Enron $25 million in auditing fees and $27 million in consultation service fees.

2001
A Republican administration (the administration of George W. Bush) wins the presidency in the United States, with more than 70 percent of presidential campaign contributions coming from corporations.

In the case of *In re Hellenic,* the Fifth Circuit Court of Appeals rules that corporate criminal liability may be charged on a corporation without regard to the offending employee's hierarchical position. Liability can be imputed based on the responsibilities of the agent, not his/her rank. This is a significant shift from the traditional belief that, to be guilty of a corporate offense, the acting agent must be in a high-ranking position in the company.

The world witnesses the collapse of Enron, Global Crossing, WorldCom, and Tyco, revealing widespread fraud and deception among major corporations.

2002   Twelve major countries in Europe begin using the Euro as their national form of currency. The UK opts out and the Euro begins trading at 0.625 British pounds.

The Global Organization of Parliamentarians against Corruption is founded at a conference hosted by the Canadian House of Commons and Senate. The group is made up of over 400 members dedicated to good governance and combating corruption around the world.

A U.S. District Court in the case of *United States v. Bainbridge Management* rules that in order to impute liability to a corporation for the actions of an individual, the government must show that the individual did indeed have a relationship to the corporation.

The Sarbanes-Oxley Act is passed in response to the fallout from Enron, WorldCom, and others. It is legislation aimed at punishing fraud and corruption while protecting shareholders and investor interests. The act focuses on improving financial reporting and auditing of publicly held companies. It also creates the Public Accounting Oversight Board to oversee the accuracy of corporate disclosure of financial and accounting practices. George W. Bush creates the Corporate Fraud Task Force, whose chief mandate is to oversee and coordinate all corporate fraud matters for the Department of Justice.

George W. Bush outlines his 10-point plan to improve corporate responsibility and protect the shareholders of America.

2002 *(cont.)*	Wal-Mart is hit with a record 43 lawsuits charging unfair labor practices.

A 9th U.S. Circuit Court of Appeals orders a judge in Anchorage to reduce the punitive damages against Exxon from $5 million to $4 million in the *Valdez* oil spill case.

WorldCom files for bankruptcy protection, cataloging $107 billion in assets and $41 billion in debt, the largest bankruptcy protection filing in U.S. history.

2003　　　AOL Time Warner reports losses for the fiscal year 2002 at $98.7 billion, which is one of the largest corporate collapses in history.

Hospital Corporation of America (HCA) again pays fines for civil penalties and damages related to false claims, this time in the amount of $631 million.

The Corporate Fraud Task Force files a report to the president on its first-year efforts. The report details over 250 corporate fraud convictions and 320 ongoing investigations involving roughly 500 defendants. Also, in its first year, prosecutors secure over $2.5 billion in fines but recover only about 30 percent of the monies.

2004　　　Former chairman and CEO of Enron Kenneth Lay is charged with 11 counts of bank fraud, share trading fraud, and making false statements. If convicted, he faces up to 175 years in prison and almost $6 million in fines. The SEC also charges Lay with securities fraud and insider trading, seeking $90 million in damages.

George W. Bush signs the Antitrust Criminal Penalty Enhancement and Reform Act, which raises the upper-limit penalties in cases where corporations are found guilty of antitrust violations to fines of $1 million and 10 years in prison for individuals, and fines of $100 million for corporations.

Dukes v. Wal-Mart becomes the largest class action lawsuit in U.S. history, representing over 1.6 million current and past female employees of Wal-Mart and seeking $11 billion in damages.

Sam Waksal is sentenced to seven years in prison and made to pay $4 million for insider trading and securities fraud. Martha Stewart is convicted of lying to investigators during the investigation and spends a few months in federal prison.

Adelphia founder John Rigas and his son are convicted of conspiracy and bank and securities fraud.

The Corporate Fraud Task Force's second-year report to the president details over 500 corporate fraud convictions, charges against over 900 defendants and 60 CEOs and presidents of corporations, and a seizure of $161 million from Enron.

2005   The U.S. Supreme Court overturns a 2002 conviction against Arthur Andersen, the auditor for Enron's books, citing that vague jury instructions allowed conviction without proof of criminal intent. Prosecutors decide not to retry the firm, as it has now been reduced from 28,000 employees to 200 employees who primarily handle pending lawsuits.

Serono, a company that manufactures a human growth hormone to combat AIDS, pays a $704 million settlement in a fraud case involving kickbacks to doctors and pharmacies who prescribed and recommended their drug.

John Rigas, founder of Adelphia Communications, is sentenced to 15 years in prison for fraud and conspiracy. His son gets 20 years.

The National White Collar Crime Center conducts a survey of public perceptions related to white-collar and corporate victimization. Results reveal that

2005
(cont.)

46.5 percent of households and 36 percent of individuals surveyed report at least one victimization within the last year.

A survey by PricewaterhouseCoopers of 3,634 executive in 34 companies around the world reveals that 45 percent of companies report being victimized by economic crimes. Of these, 40 percent report significant collateral damage, and most claim they discovered the fraud by accident.

Tyco CEO Dennis Kozlowski and CFO Mark Swartz are convicted. Later in the year they are each sentenced to 8 to 25 years in prison.

2006

Enron founder Kenneth Lay and former Enron CEO Jeffrey Skilling are convicted of conspiracy to commit securities and wire fraud. Skilling is sentenced to 24 years in federal prison. Lay dies of an apparent heart attack before his sentencing hearing.

Tenet Healthcare agrees to pay back to the federal government and those who filed lawsuits $900 million for violations of Medicare billing. They allegedly stole $1.9 billion.

A 9th Circuit Appellate Court reduces the punitive damages against Exxon to $2.5 billion for the *Valdez* oil spill.

The International Advisory and Monitoring Board, the manager of Iraq's oil proceeds, reports numerous fraud-related problems with the rebuilding and development of Iraq.

2007

The 9th Circuit Court of Appeals denies Exxon Mobil's request for another hearing, upholding the award of $2.5 billion in punitive damages. Exxon says it will appeal to the U.S. Supreme Court.

World Bank president Paul Wolfowitz is forced to resign over a corruption scandal at the bank that involves his securing a promotion and a pay increase for himself and large annual raises for his girlfriend.

Former Peruvian president Alberto Fujimori is extradited to Peru from Chile to face charges of embezzlement and human rights abuses.

British Petroleum agrees to pay fines totaling $373 million for violations related to a Texas refinery explosion as well as for price fixing propane gas.

Drugmaker Merck agrees to pay $4.85 billion to settle thousands of lawsuits stemming from its pain-relieving drug Vioxx. This will be the largest ever settlement by a drug company.

5

Biographical Sketches

Henry Clayton (1857–1929)

Henry Clayton was a Democrat in the U.S. House of Representatives from 1879 to 1914. He later served as an Alabama federal judge. Clayton was born in Alabama in 1857. He obtained a literary arts degree in 1877 and a law degree in 1878, both from the University of Alabama. He served as the Democratic National Convention chairman in 1908. He is the namesake behind the Clayton Antitrust Act of 1914, which was promulgated in an attempt to overcome some of the deficiencies of the earlier Sherman Antitrust Act of 1890. The Clayton Antitrust Act provided continued support of laws against monopolies. The act has been widely used in many publicized lawsuits against large corporations. Henry Clayton died in 1929 in Montgomery, Alabama.

Marshall B. Clinard (b. 1911)

Marshall B. Clinard is professor emeritus of sociology at the University of Wisconsin–Madison. He received his BA and MA from Stanford University and his PhD from the University of Chicago. An accomplished criminology scholar, Clinard has authored or co-authored more than 10 books, 40 articles, and 25 book chapters. He is best known for his work on the sociology of deviant behavior and corporate crime, and he is considered one of the top researchers on deviance and deviant behavior. Some of his books include *Cities with Little Crime: The Case of Switzerland; Corporate Crime* (with Peter C. Yeager); and *The Sociology of Deviant Behavior* (with Robert F. Meier).

Bernard Ebbers (b. 1941)

Canadian businessman Bernard Ebbers was born in Edmonton, Alberta, in 1941. He made headlines in an accounting scandal as CEO of the telecommunications giant WorldCom. It is estimated that the accounting fraud at WorldCom cost investors $180 billion.

Ebbers attended Mississippi College on a basketball scholarship and graduated in 1967 with a degree in physical education. He later received honorary doctoral degrees from Mississippi College and Tougaloo College. Having started in the telephone business in 1983 at Long Distance Discount Services (LDDS) in Jackson, Mississippi, he became CEO of the company after only two years, then began buying up other telephone companies in an attempt to develop LDDS. By 1995, Ebbers had changed the name of the company to WorldCom. The next year, he secured one of the largest corporate buyouts in U.S. history, acquiring the company MFS Communications for roughly $12 billion. In 1998, WorldCom took over MCI, then the second-largest long distance telephone service provider, for about $40 billion. Ebbers also tried to take over Sprint Communications in 1999 for a reported $100 billion; however, the deal was quashed by antitrust regulators.

The price of WorldCom's stock fell because of the failed deal with Sprint, and Ebbers's image as a savvy businessman also began to decline. His troubles stemmed mostly from the fact that his deals and acquisitions had all been bought with loans held up by his shares in WorldCom stock. The board of directors of WorldCom continued to give loan guarantees to creditors despite the decline in WorldCom's stock prices. By 2002, the Securities and Exchange Commission (SEC) requested that WorldCom hand over accounting information relating to the company's business transactions as well as to loans to its executive officers. The Department of Justice also began an investigation of its own and requested that Ebbers give testimony before the House Financial Services Committee. In his testimony, Ebbers claimed that there was no wrongdoing on the part of his company, WorldCom. The SEC levied civil charges against WorldCom and ordered that the company not destroy any of its accounting and financial documents. In July 2002, however, WorldCom filed for Chapter 11 bankruptcy. Its financial reports revealed $11 billion in fraud, and shares in WorldCom stock were selling for 9 cents. Ebbers was ultimately charged criminally, tried, and convicted of nine counts of conspiracy and securities fraud. He was sentenced to 25 years in prison and is currently serving out his sentence at a federal facility in Louisiana. His earliest parole date is 2028.

Andrew Fastow (b. 1961)

Andrew Fastow was born in 1961 in Washington, D.C. He was a business executive with Enron when the company collapsed in the wake of accounting and fraud scandals. Fastow is well known because he garnered a deal with the government, pleading guilty to charges of tax fraud in exchange for his testimony against other Enron executives. Fastow earned a BA in economics from Tufts University as well as an MBA from Northwestern University. He first started working in Chicago for Continental Illinois National Bank and Trust. His career at Enron began in 1990, and by 1998, he was Enron's chief financial officer. Fastow has been singled out as the mastermind behind Enron's fraudulent activities, including the debt that was not listed anywhere in accounting documents.

He was forced to resign in 2001 and later gained notoriety for testifying against other key Enron officials, implicating them in the accounting fraud as well. His testimony confirmed that both Kenneth Lay and other members of the board of directors had knowledge of—and approved of—each of Enron's financial decisions and that the accounting fraud was deliberate. Indictments against Fastow included 78 counts of fraud, conspiracy, and money laundering, and in 2004, he came to an agreement with the federal government to plead guilty to 2 counts of fraud. He was given a 10-year prison sentence. Fastow's wife, Lea, was also implicated in the scandal because she was an assistant to the treasurer of Enron. Lea also pleaded guilty, was charged with tax fraud, and was given one year in prison to be followed by one year of probation. A judge recently reduced Andrew Fastow's sentence to six years in prison to be followed by two years' probation. He is currently being held at the Federal Detention Center in Oakdale, Louisiana. His projected release date is 2011.

Alberto Fujimori (b. 1938)

The birthplace of Alberto Fujimori is uncertain. Some have argued that he was born in Japan and emigrated with his parents to Peru. Fujimori himself claims to have been born in Peru in 1938. His true birthplace matters because if he were born in Japan, he would have been ineligible to become the president of Peru. Nevertheless, Fujimori was the first person of Japanese origin to become the head of a foreign country. He became the president of Peru in 1990. To most observers, Fujimori was seen as an outstanding leader who put the Peruvian economy back on its feet. Fujimori was an ardent fighter of terrorism, forged a peacemaking process with the Ecuadorian people, and aided in the destruction of the coca crops used for the production of cocaine. But, as it turns out, Fujimori was not the unselfish leader that some thought he was. His leadership style was very authoritarian, and his presidency was not without controversy.

In 2000, on a visit to Japan, Fujimori resigned as president via the Peruvian embassy in Tokyo. The pressure against Fujimori began mounting after footage of his second-in-command bribing a congressman was released to the public. Subsequent investigations revealed that upwards of $800 million in assets had been pilfered from the Peruvian government. The government refused to accept Fujimori's resignation and instead removed him from office, levied criminal charges against him, and banned him from government. Fujimori decided in 2006 to ignore the ban and attempt another run at the Peruvian presidency. He traveled to Chile to start his campaign but was subsequently arrested by Chilean officials. Fujimori was released on bail but ordered to remain in Chile. The government of Peru has since issued new charges against Fujimori, some of which include human rights violations and embezzlement. Fujimori remained in Chile, living in a very wealthy Santiago neighborhood near the Japanese Embassy. Finally, in September 2007, after several years of appellate review in Chilean courts, the

Chilean Supreme Court granted Peru's request to have Fujimori extradited back to Peru to face embezzlement and human rights abuse charges.

Gilbert Geis (unknown)

Gilbert Geis is currently professor emeritus at the University of California at Irvine. Geis obtained a bachelor's degree from Colgate University and a doctorate from the University of Wisconsin at Madison. Prior to joining the Department of Criminology, Law, and Society at UC–Irvine in 1972, he served as a professor at the University of Oklahoma and California State University. His foremost research interest has been the study of white-collar crime. Geis has published over 350 articles relating to crime and criminal justice, held the post of president of the American Society of Criminology (ASC), and won the Edwin H. Sutherland Award from the ASC for outstanding research. Some of his publications include "Scrutiny on the Bounty: Business Rewards for Crime Tips," *Prescription for Profit: How Doctors Defraud Medicaid* (with Paul Jesilow and Henry N. Pontell), "The Evolution of the Study of Corporate Crime," *International Handbook of White-Collar and Corporate Crime* (with Henry N. Pontell), and *White-Collar and Corporate Crime.*

L. Dennis Kozlowski (b. 1946)

L. Dennis Kozlowski was born in 1946 in Newark, New Jersey. Kozlowski graduated from Seton Hall University in 1968, has given generously to his alma mater, and was even named to its board of regents. He began working at the Tyco Corporation in 1976 as an accountant. Kozlowski eventually became CEO of the company and turned it from a $40 million company to a $40 billion corporation. While at Tyco, Kozlowski was one of the highest paid CEOs in the United States, reportedly earning over $100 million a year. With his jumbo salary, Kozlowski purchased million-dollar yachts, mansions, and priceless art. Ultimately, it was his art purchases that led to his demise. The New York district attorney in Manhattan conducted an investigation of several art galleries that were helping their customers evade New York taxes on high-end art purchases and stumbled upon Kozlowski's name. He owed about $1 million in taxes on art he had purchased for Tyco. Kozlowski resigned as CEO because of the charges against him. However, when the Tyco board took up their own investigation, they uncovered numerous excesses Kozlowski was enjoying at the expense of the shareholders. Some of the luxuries shareholders funded included a $19 million apartment in New York, with $11 million in furnishings, a $2 million birthday party for his wife, and a now-infamous $6,000 shower curtain. Kozlowski was accused of falsifying the company's financial documents and charged with theft of $170 million and the illegal selling of $430 million in Tyco stock. His first trial ended in a mistrial, reportedly due to threats the jury had received and fear on the part of jurors to convict. In the second trial, however, Kozlowski was convicted of 22 counts of grand larceny, conspiracy, and falsifying business records. He was sentenced to eight and one-third to twenty-five years and ordered to pay $200 million in restitution. Kozlowski is serving his sentence at Mid-State Correctional Facility in upstate New York. His earliest release date is 2014.

Kenneth Lay (1952–2006)

Kenneth Lay was born in Missouri in 1952 and died in Colorado in 2006. He is remembered for his role as CEO of Enron and its widely publicized corruption scandal. The collapse of Enron caused thousands of employees and investors to lose their retirement savings plans.

Lay received his BA and MA in economics from the University of Missouri in 1964 and 1965, respectively. He went on to obtain a PhD in economics from the University of Houston in 1970. He began working for Humble Oil as an economist in 1965. Lay also worked for the U.S. Navy and the Federal Power Commission and served as the deputy secretary of energy for the U.S. Department of the Interior. In 1974, Lay joined Florida Gas Company and served as vice president of corporate development. He left that company in 1981 and joined Transco Energy in Houston. Three years later, Lay left Transco to become chairman of Houston Natural Gas Company, which later became Enron. His annual salary and benefits package from Enron is believed to have been $40 million.

Lay claimed that he knew nothing of the impending collapse of Enron, but records show that he was selling large amounts of stock while encouraging other employees at Enron to continue to buy more. When Enron went bankrupt in December 2001, roughly 20,000 employees lost their jobs and their retirement funds. The company had been committing accounting fraud with the help of its accountant firm, Arthur Andersen. Enron's financial reports were cooked to overstate sales and revenue that would help to inflate its stock prices. Arthur Andersen also collapsed in the wake of the Enron scandal, having been charged with obstructing justice by shredding important financial documents. Lay stepped down as CEO of Enron after the company filed for bankruptcy. Investigations in 2004 led to the indictment of Lay by a grand jury. They charged him with several counts of securities fraud and wire fraud. Lay was found guilty on six counts of fraud and conspiracy. Before his sentencing date, however, he died of a heart attack at his Aspen, Colorado, vacation home. His conviction was vacated in October 2006, but civil suits are still pending against his estate from the thousands of former employees of Enron who lost their jobs and their retirement funds.

Patrick Leahy (b. 1940)

Patrick Leahy is a Democratic senator from Vermont and chairman of the Senate Judiciary Committee. Leahy was born March 31, 1940, in Montpelier, Vermont, graduated from Saint Michael's College in 1961, and obtained a J.D. from Georgetown University in 1964. He then practiced law until 1974, when he was elected to the U.S. Senate. Leahy has been re-elected for all five terms since 1974. He served as chairman of the Senate Committee on Agriculture, Nutrition and Forestry from 1987 to 1995. He chaired the Senate Judiciary Committee from 2001 to 2003 and became chairman of the Judiciary again in 2007. He is the third-highest-ranking Democrat on the Senate Appropriations Committee. Leahy authored the criminal provisions of the Sarbanes-Oxley Act of 2002, which enhanced criminal penalties for corporate crime. He has repeatedly supported stronger criminal penalties and accountability for war profiteering and contractor fraud. Leahy has been critical of the Bush administration's alleged use of the National Security Agency to spy on U.S. citizens without first obtaining a warrant. In 2004, Leahy and Orrin Hatch introduced the Pirate Act, backed by the Recording Industry Association of America (RIAA), as part of an ongoing crusade against Internet file sharing, as well as the INDUCE Act, which focuses on combating copyright infringement.

Ferdinand Marcos (1917–1989)

Ferdinand Marcos was the president of the Philippines from 1965 to 1986. He is remembered for his corruptive practices, embezzlement, and luxurious lifestyle—vividly illustrated by the thousands of pairs of shoes owned by his wife, Imelda—despite the fact that many Filipinos barely had enough to eat. Marcos studied law at the University of Philippines; however, his studies were interrupted by accusations that he murdered one of his father's political opponents. Despite being detained, he finished law school in prison. Marcos was found guilty of the murder, but the conviction was overturned on appeal. After getting out of prison, he served as a trial attorney in the city of Manila. He also served in the Philippine army during World War II. In 1947, Marcos became the assistant to the president of the Philippines and was eventually elected a representative in parliament. Marcos married Imelda in 1954, and they had four children.

Ferdinand Marcos was affiliated with the Liberal Party of the Philippines and was elected president in 1965. He promised great things for the Filipino people, including an enhanced economy, new infrastructure, and trade with the free world. In the late 1960s, the vision of a better Philippines was crushed: crime was on the rise and the quality of life for the Filipinos began to decline. Marcos suspended habeas corpus in 1971 and declared martial law in 1972. Doing so nullified the Philippine constitution and essentially turned the presidency into a dictatorship. During this time, however, Marcos remained friendly with the United States. The U.S. government did nothing about his actions because he was a strong critic of communism.

Eventually the world came to know about the corruption of the Marcos administration. Marcos fled to Hawaii in 1986. Customs officials in Hawaii reported suitcases full of gold bricks, jewelry, and gold certificates worth billions. The Marcos family was estimated to have stolen somewhere between $3 billion and $35 billion from the Philippines. Most of the money was supposedly held in Swiss bank accounts. When Marcos fled, the Philippines had a debt load of around $28 billion, most of which was incurred under the Marcos regime; as of 2007, it was about 54 billion. Marcos was eventually indicted by a New York grand jury for obstruction of justice and mail fraud. He died in 1989 before a trial could begin. Five years after his death, a Hawaiian district court found Marcos guilty of the torture and execution of thousands of Filipino people and awarded damages of $2 billion to the surviving victims. The Philippine government stopped the payment, citing that they are owed roughly $700 million from the Marcos family. As of the writing of this book, there is still a battle between the Philippine government and the Marcos family over the Marcos fortune.

Stephanie A. Martz (b. ca. 1970)

Stephanie A. Martz is the current director of the White Collar Crime Project for the National Association of Criminal Defense Lawyers. As director, her main goal is to defend the rights of people charged with corporate malfeasance. Specifically, the director's duties include monitoring legislative and judicial policies that may infringe upon justice and due process for white-collar defendants. Before becoming director of the White Collar Crime Project, Martz wrote for *The New York Times* and *The Charleston Gazette*. She graduated from Stanford Law School in 1997 and served as law clerk for the Hon. James Robertson of the United States District Court in Washington, D.C., and the Hon. Patricia Wald of the United States Court of Appeals for the D.C. Circuit. Martz also worked as staff counsel of the National Litigation Center of the Chamber of Commerce of the United States and was an associate at the law firms of Mayer, Brown, Rowe & Maw and Miller, Cassidy, Larroca & Lewin.

Paul J. McNulty (b. 1958)

Paul J. McNulty was sworn in as deputy attorney general of the United States on March 17, 2006, and resigned in the summer of 2007. He was the most senior official from the Justice Department to resign over the scandal involving the firing of nine U.S.

attorneys. McNulty obtained a bachelor's degree from Grove City College in Grove City, Pennsylvania, and a juris doctor from Capital University School of Law in Columbus, Ohio. He has two decades of experience in federal and state government. He has served as the United States Attorney for the Eastern District of Virginia, where he made prosecuting terrorism, drug trafficking, gun violence, and corporate fraud his main concerns. McNulty has also served under President George W. Bush as principal associate deputy attorney general and as the Justice Department's director of policy. During his years in Congress, McNulty served as chief counsel and director of Legislative Operations for the majority leader of the U.S. House of Representatives and as chief counsel to the House Subcommittee on Crime. In Virginia, he played an important role in the state's criminal justice policy, serving on the board of the Department of Criminal Justice Services and the advisory committee of the Office of Juvenile Justice and Delinquency Prevention.

Robert F. Meier (b. 1944)

Robert F. Meier is a professor and past chair of the School of Criminology and Criminal Justice at the University of Nebraska at Omaha. He has also held professorships at Iowa State University, Washington State University, and the University of California at Irvine. Meier has written 15 books and over 50 articles for sociological and criminological journals. His research interests center on deviance and social control. Specifically, Meier has conducted research on crime etiology, victimization, white-collar crime, deterrence, and legal processes. Some of his publications include *The Process and Structure of Crime: Criminal Events and Crime Analysis* (edited with Leslie Kennedy and Vincent Sacco), *White-Collar Crime: Classic and Contemporary Views* (edited with Gil Geis and Lawrence Salinger), and *Sociology of Deviant Behavior* (with Marshall B. Clinard).

Michael Milken (b. 1946)

Michael Milken was a financier who earned the title of "junk bond king" for his heavy investments in high-risk bonds. He invested a great deal of money in the stock market in the 1970s and

1980s and was indicted in the late 1980s on almost 100 counts of racketeering and fraud. Milken's investments in industry facilitated growth and also created an abundance of wealth for U.S. investors. Milken graduated from the University of California at Berkeley and obtained an MBA from the University of Pennsylvania's Wharton School of Business. He was initially employed by Drexel Harriman Ripley, an investment bank, and through mergers, he became head of the investment bond department. During his tenure at Drexel, the company went from $1.2 million in profit to $4 billion. These successes earned Milken huge salaries and bonuses. He is said to have earned $500 million in 1987. Two years later, however, a federal grand jury indicted him on 98 counts of fraud and racketeering. Milken pleaded guilty to charges of securities fraud in exchange for dropping of the racketeering charges. Milken was given a ten-year-long prison sentence that was later reduced to just two years, followed by three years of probation. He actually spent only 22 months in prison before being released. Upon his release, he was still worth an alleged $1 billion. As part of his punishment, Milken was barred from future trading in securities. He found himself in trouble again, however, after violating his parole by working as a business consultant. Subsequently, he was ordered to pay back to the government the $42 million that he earned as a consultant. Milken has remained clean since his probation violation and has recently given extensively to charities and to medical research. As of 2007, his estimated net worth was almost $2 billion.

Slobodan Milosevic (1941–2006)

Slobodan Milosevic was born in Yugoslavia (now Serbia) in 1941. He died in his prison cell at The Hague in the Netherlands in 2006. Milosevic obtained a law degree from the University of Belgrade in 1964. After his graduation, he was employed as an economic advisor to the mayor of Belgrade. A great deal of Milosevic's life was spent in the economic and banking sector. He eventually worked his way up to president of the biggest bank in the former Yugoslavia. This position helped him gain political prominence and the posts of leader of the Belgrade Communist Party and the League of Communists of Serbia. Milosevic became president of Serbia in 1989. Considerable tension arose between Serbia and the countries around it during his tenure.

Many countries in the region became fearful of Milosevic, believing he would attempt to overtake smaller countries in the region to form a more powerful Serbian empire. In 1991, Croatia and Slovenia declared independence from Serbia. Milosevic sent in troops and tanks to regain the areas. In the aftermath, Slovenia agreed to a deal with Milosevic: the Slovenes promised to help take over Croatia in exchange for their independence. The war against Croatia that followed resulted in the deaths of 20,000 people and the recapturing of about a third of Croatian territory.

A year later, Bosnia-Herzegovina attempted to gain independence from Serbia. In response, Milosevic's Serbian forces seized most of the Bosnian land and then crossed over into Croatia. The human suffering and loss of life that resulted eventually evoked a response in 1995 from the North Atlantic Treaty Organization (NATO), which attempted to force a cease-fire and the withdrawal of the Serbian army. These attempts failed, prompting NATO to launch air strikes against Serbian forces. Later that year, Milosevic signed a peace accord with the Bosnian and Croatian presidents. During the war, though, problems arose back in Serbia. Many of Milosevic's opponents won local elections, and he was eventually barred from the Serbian presidency. This did not stop him, however; he became the president of Yugoslavia, where his troubles continued. Albanians living in Kosovo attempted to gain independence from Yugoslavia, and again Milosevic quelled the succession attempt with military force. The outcome of the fighting was catastrophic; over 10,000 people were dead and 700,000 more were forced to flee the region. In 2001, the United Nations sent peacekeepers to the region, and the Serbian government arrested Milosevic. He was charged with corruption, embezzlement, and war crimes, including genocide, and was extradited to The Hague to be tried at the International Court. His trial started in 2002 and ended 467 days later when he was found dead in his prison cell.

Ralph Nader (b. 1934)

Ralph Nader is well known as a consumer advocate, lawyer, and presidential candidate in three different elections, but he first gained national attention in 1965, when he authored a book on car safety titled *Unsafe at Any Speed,* which criticized the automobile industry. Nader earned a bachelor's degree from Princeton

University in 1955 and went on to study law at Harvard, graduating with distinction in 1958. Through his publications and other endeavors, Nader has established himself as a renowned activist, a fierce consumer-interest watchdog, and an outspoken critic of corporate America. Through this political and corporate activism, he has attracted many followers. These fans and followers have been labeled "Nader's Raiders." Nader's political aspirations began when he ran for president in 1996 as the Green Party's candidate. (He ran a second time in 2000 as a Green Party candidate and again in 2004 as an independent.) However, his political campaigns failed to generate the success of his role as consumer advocate. Nader is the founder of such organizations as the Center for Auto Safety, Clean Water Action Project, and Public Interest Research Groups (PIRGs). In recent years, he has criticized American foreign policy decisions.

Michael Oxley (b. 1944)

Michael Oxley was a Republican representative from the Fourth Congressional District of Ohio from 1980 to 2007. He was born in Ohio in 1944, graduated from Miami University of Ohio, and obtained his law degree from Ohio State University. An FBI agent from 1969 to 1972, Oxley was then elected to the Ohio House of Representatives, where he served until 1981. He cosponsored the Sarbanes-Oxley Act, which was promulgated in 2002 to provide protection to shareholders and investors in the wake of accounting scandals at Enron and WorldCom. The act set forth new rules for the recording and reporting of corporate financial information. It also enhanced the penalties for noncompliance. Oxley announced his retirement from the U.S. House of Representatives at the end of the 2007 term.

Henry N. Pontell (b. 1950)

Henry N. Pontell is a professor of criminology, law and society, and sociology at the University of California, Irvine. Pontell received his BA, MA, and PhD, all in sociology, from the State University of New York at Stony Brook. An award-winning researcher and lecturer, he has written about criminology, criminal justice, and sociology. Pontell received the Donald R. Cressey

Award for major lifetime contributions to research on white-collar crime from the Association of Certified Fraud Examiners in 2001 and the Albert J. Reiss, Jr. Distinguished Scholarship Award from the American Sociological Association that same year. He has served as vice president of the American Society of Criminology and president of the Western Society of Criminology. His research and teaching interests include white-collar and corporate crime, deviance and social control, punishment and criminal justice system capacity issues, identity theft, financial crime, and cybercrime. Some of his publications include *Social Deviance, Prescription for Profit: How Doctors Defraud Medicaid, Profit without Honor: White Collar Crime and the Looting of America, Big Money Crime: Fraud and Politics in the Savings and Loan Crisis,* and *Contemporary Issues in Crime and Criminal Justice.*

John Rigas (b. 1924)

John Rigas was born in Wellsville, New York, in 1924. He founded Adelphia Communications Corporation, which would become one of the largest cable organizations in the United States. Rigas enlisted in the U.S. Army right after high school and saw combat in France during WWII. After the war, Rigas enrolled in Rensselaer Polytechnic Institute in Troy, New York, where he received a degree in management engineering. His business career started in 1952, when he purchased a cable television franchise in Pennsylvania. He then built up Adelphia by buying out other franchises. Rigas made Adelphia into one of the biggest providers of cable services in the United States, with more than 5 million customers prior to its demise in 2002. Until then, the Rigas family led a very lavish lifestyle, highlighted by the purchase of an NHL hockey team, 17 company cars, and $1 million per month in fun money. However, like many other CEOs of the post-Enron era, Rigas was forced to resign from Adelphia after being indicted for conspiracy, bank fraud, and securities fraud. Rigas, his sons, Timothy and Michael, and two of his sons-in-law were accused of embezzling nearly $100 million and of hiding $2 billion in liabilities from investors. Rigas and Timothy were both convicted on numerous charges and required to pay restitution. Both John and Timothy were out on bail pending appeals of their convictions of 20 and 15 years, respectively.

That appeal was rejected in May 2007 and they are currently serving their sentences at a federal facility in North Carolina. The Rigases plan to appeal their case to the U.S. Supreme Court.

Paul Sarbanes (b. 1933)

Paul Sarbanes was a member of the Democratic Party and served as a senator from Maryland from 1977 until his retirement in 2007. Sarbanes, along with Congressman Michael Oxley, cosponsored the Sarbanes-Oxley Act of 2002. This act was passed in the aftermath of the Enron and WorldCom accounting scandals with a goal of raising corporate ethics. A former Rhodes Scholar known for his sharp mind and simple ways, Sarbanes obtained degrees from Princeton University, the University of Oxford, and Harvard Law School. Prior to his years in the U.S. Senate, Sarbanes served in the House of Representatives. He was a ranking member of the Banking, Housing, and Urban Affairs Committee and a senior member of the Foreign Relations and Budget committees. Sarbanes did not seek reelection in 2006.

Sally S. Simpson (b. 1954)

Sally S. Simpson is professor and chair of criminology and criminal justice at the University of Maryland, College Park. She received her PhD in sociology from the University of Massachusetts, her MA from Washington State University, and her BS from Oregon State University. A recipient of the Herbert Bloch Award from the American Society of Criminology, Simpson is past president of the White-Collar Crime Research Consortium and past chair of the Crime, Law, and Deviance Section of the American Sociological Association. Her research interests include corporate crime, criminological theory, and the connections between gender, race, class, and crime. Her writings include *Corporate Crime* (edited with Carole Gibbs); *Corporate Crime, Law, and Social Control; Of Crime & Criminality: The Use of Theory in Everyday Life* (editor); and "Integrating the Desire for Control and Rational Choice: Examining the Causality of Corporate Crime" (with Nicole Leeper Piquero and M. Lyn Exum).

Jeffrey K. Skilling (b. 1953)

Jeffrey Skilling was CEO of Enron when it collapsed following a corruption scandal. He was convicted in 2006 on numerous federal charges related to Enron's collapse. As of 2007, Skilling was serving a 24-year prison sentence at a Federal Correctional Institution in Waseca, Minnesota.

Skilling obtained a BS from Southern Methodist University in 1975 and an MBA from Harvard University in 1979, after which he became an energy consultant at McKinsey & Company. Perceived as harsh and arrogant by the press, he is remembered for a particularly foul reply to a Wall Street analyst who asked him why Enron was the only company that did not disseminate a balance sheet with its earning statements. Skilling also made jokes about the California energy crisis, remarking that the difference between California and the *Titanic* was that "at least when the *Titanic* went down, the lights were on." Skilling resigned from Enron in 2001, citing personal reasons, then began selling large amounts of his shares in Enron—almost $60 million worth. Kenneth Lay took over for Skilling as CEO until Enron declared bankruptcy later the same year. In testimony before Congress, Skilling denied any knowledge of the wrongdoing and practices that led to Enron's fall. He was eventually indicted on over 30 counts of fraud, conspiracy, and insider trading. Skilling pleaded not guilty and surrendered to the FBI in 2004. His trial began in 2006 in Houston, despite change of venue requests from his attorneys. Skilling was found guilty on 28 of the counts, sentenced to 24 years and four months in prison, and ordered to pay $45 million in fines. His release date is set for February 2028.

Adam Smith (1723–1790)

Adam Smith was born in Scotland in 1723, in a town north of Edinburgh. He became known as one of the greatest political economists and philosophers in the world. Smith attended the University of Glasgow and Oxford University; after graduation, he served as chair of logic and moral philosophy at Glasgow. In 1762, he received an honorary doctorate and shortly thereafter left university life to tutor a young duke. During this time, Smith met many influential intellectuals who would have a great impact on his life. After tutoring, he retired to Scotland, where he was elected a fellow of the Royal Society of London. He devoted much of his retired life to the writing of his famous multivolume work *An Inquiry into the Nature and Causes of the Wealth of Nations* (1776). *The Wealth of Nations* initiated the idea of free enterprise. In the book, Smith uses the idea of the "invisible hand" to explain that most business is guided by self-interest, but that competition is beneficial for society as a whole. Smith also advanced the notion that market forces are far more powerful than efforts by individuals or the state to effect change. *The Wealth of Nations* has been called the most influential economics book ever written. Smith died in 1790.

Arlen J. Specter (b. 1930)

Arlen Specter, a Republican senator from Pennsylvania, was first elected to office in 1980. He is the longest-serving senator in Pennsylvania's history, having been elected to five terms. In 1951, Specter graduated from the University of Pennsylvania with a major in international relations. He served in the U.S. Air Force from 1951 to 1953 and three years later graduated with a law degree from Yale Law School. As a lawyer in Philadelphia, Specter was very active in politics. He worked on the investigation of the John F. Kennedy assassination for the Warren Commission. Specter was a democrat at this time, but he changed parties and won the 1965 race for district attorney in Philadelphia by running on an anti-corruption platform. Specter has been referred to as a RINO (Republican in Name Only) by more conservative senators. A past chairman of the Senate Select Committee on Intelligence and the Committee on Veteran Affairs, he has been ranking member of the Senate Judiciary Committee and a senior member of the Appropriations and Veterans Affairs committees. Specter announced that he will seek a sixth term in the U.S. Senate in 2010. The senator has worked to reauthorize key provisions of the USA PATRIOT Act and has proposed legislation to better protect consumers and the privacy of their personal information. He authored the Armed Career Criminal Act of 1984, which mandates long prison terms for repeat offenders, and the Terrorist Tracking, Identification, and Prosecution Act of 2006, which permits prosecution in U.S. courts for assaults and murders of U.S. citizens anywhere in the world. Specter has been critical of the Bush administration's wiretapping of persons without warrants, and he is a resolute proponent of bettering the national security of the United States. He also drafted the legislation that would establish the Department of Homeland Security. In December 2006, Specter introduced a bill that would prohibit federal prosecutors from seeking attorney-client privilege waivers in cases against corporations. However, this legislation was not expected to pass.

Eliot Spitzer (b. 1959)

Eliot Spitzer was sworn in as New York's 54th governor on January 1, 2007. He campaigned on the idea that his administration would promote ethical government while rebuilding New York's economy. Spitzer graduated from Princeton University in 1981 with a BA and received a law degree in 1984 from Harvard Law School, where he edited the *Harvard Law Review*. After serving as a law clerk for Robert W. Sweet and working as an assistant district attorney in Manhattan, he became attorney general of New York, a position he held from 1999 until he became governor in 2007. Spitzer has been a steadfast investigator and prosecutor of white-collar and corporate offending. In the 1990s, his work brought down the Gambino Crime Family and gave him national recognition as he continued to prosecute landmark cases protecting consumers, the environment, investors, and low wage workers. Aside from organized crime bosses, Spitzer has successfully prosecuted Merrill Lynch, the mutual-fund industry, and insurance brokers, forcing many companies to get rid of their CEOs and pay millions of dollars in restitution. As of 2007, he was investigating companies—including 50 power plants—suspected of polluting the environment.

Nadine Strossen (b. 1950)

Nadine Strossen is professor of law at New York Law School and the first female president of the American Civil Liberties Union (ACLU). Strossen earned her juris doctor from Harvard Law School in 1975 and practiced law in Minneapolis and New York City before becoming a law professor. In addition to receiving six honorary doctoral degrees, she was twice named one of the 100 most influential lawyers in America by the *National Law Journal*. As president of ACLU, Strossen annually makes over 200 public presentations to college campuses. Strossen's publications include *Defending Pornography: Free Speech, Sex, and the Fight for Women's Rights* and *Speaking of Race, Speaking of Sex: Hate Speech, Civil Rights, and Civil Liberties*.

Mohammed Suharto (b. 1921)

Mohamed Suharto was the president of Indonesia from 1967 to 1998. His rise to political power stemmed from his advancement in Indonesia's military. Suharto was a sergeant during the Japanese invasion of Indonesia in World War II. After the Japanese surrendered, Indonesia gained its independence. Suharto was also successful in leading a fight against an attempt by the Dutch to take over Indonesia. As a veteran of war, he eventually earned the rank of chief of staff of the army. After a 1965 coup attempt, he convinced the then-president of Indonesia to give him executive authority. Suharto was finally appointed president in 1967 by the Indonesian parliament. During his six terms as president, Indonesia achieved economic and political stability. Indonesia rekindled relationships with many Western nations.

Suharto, however, was an authoritative ruler. He punished dissidents severely and used his position of power to make his family and friends wealthy. He was also accused of crimes against humanity including genocide in the Indonesian occupation of East Timor. Finally, in 1998 he was forced to resign under mounting pressure of corruption. Authorities later arrested Suharto on charges of corruption; the charges were ultimately dropped because of his ill health. Despite never being convicted, Suharto has been dubbed one of the most corrupt world leaders of the past 20 years. Investigations revealed that he and his family stole anywhere from $15 billion to $35 billion during his presidency. He regularly handed out government contracts to family and friends in exchange for large kickbacks. Indonesian companies and businesses were also forced to give some of their profits to the Suharto family. Anyone wanting to do business with Indonesia had to go through one of Suharto's companies. His family has denied all charges of corruption; as of 2007, Suharto was living in virtual isolation.

Edwin H. Sutherland (1883–1950)

Edwin H. Sutherland was one of the most prominent criminologists in the world. Sutherland was born in Nebraska in 1883 and earned a doctorate in sociology from the University of Chicago. He was an adherent of the Chicago School of crime etiology, which emphasizes that people's social and physical environments exert great influences on their behavior. Sutherland's writings include *The Professional Thief* (1937) and *White Collar Crime* (1949).

Sutherland is most widely known as the architect of the differential association theory, which states that crime is a behavior that is learned through interactions with others. Sutherland also coined the term "white collar crime." He first referred to crime by members of the upper class as "white collar crime" in his presidential address to the American Sociological Society in Philadelphia in 1939. In his address, he postulated that white-collar and corporate offending should be thought of as distinct from street crime, and he urged researchers to focus their efforts on the causes of white-collar crime. Prior to this time, researchers concentrated on criminal behavior in lower socio-economic classes. It is thought by some that Sutherland used this presidential address to show that both types of criminality (white-collar and street crime) could be explained by his differential association theory. Sutherland believed that the only difference between white-collar and lower-class criminals was in the application of the law. Sutherland's concept of white-collar crime referred to crimes committed "on the job" by a respected person of high social status.

Larry D. Thompson (b. 1946)

Larry D. Thompson served as deputy attorney general of the United States from 2001 until August 2003. He obtained a bachelor's degree from Culver-Stockton College, a master's degree from Michigan State University, and a law degree from the University of Michigan. Prior to becoming deputy attorney general, he was the director of Providian Financial Corporation. In this position, he came under fire because he sold $4.7 million of stock just before the company was charged with consumer and securities fraud—allegations for which they paid over $400 million to settle. Thompson also served as district attorney for the Northern District of Georgia from 1982 to 1986.

John Ashcroft (who was then attorney general) put Deputy Attorney General Thompson in charge of the National Security Coordination Council, and President George W. Bush named him the head of the Corporate Fraud Task Force. Thompson led counterterrorism efforts and efforts to punish white-collar crime. He also headed up the prosecutions against officials at Enron, as well as other corporate fraud investigations, and issued a memorandum to U.S. attorneys outlining methods and procedures in prosecution of corporations. Thompson left the deputy attorney general's office to assume the role of senior vice president and general counsel for the PepsiCo Corporation. He also serves as a visiting professor of law at the University of Georgia and a senior fellow at the Brookings Institution.

Gary Winnick (b. 1948)

Telecommunications billionaire Gary Winnick grew up on Long Island, New York. In 1997, he invested $15 million of his own money to create a company called Global Crossing, so named because it laid fiber optic cable under the Atlantic Ocean. Winnick was the chairman of Global Crossing from 1997 until 2002. When Global Crossing went public, it started making billions of dollars, and like many other executives, Winnick spared no expense on corporate headquarter purchases, which included a Picasso painting worth $15 million and five corporate jets. Winnick spent to excess, and his financial waste incurred criticism from other employees of the company. Global Crossing ultimately collapsed, its stock dropping from a high of $61 to mere pennies, costing investors roughly $49 billion. Winnick sold over $700 million of his own Global Crossing stock—a portion of it just weeks prior to the company's collapse. After the company filed for bankruptcy in 2002, two Asian firms purchased a majority stake and Winnick stepped down as CEO. It was later revealed that Winnick was aware of Global Crossing's precarious financial situation back in mid-2000. The Securities and Exchange Commission investigated

Global Crossing's accounting and business practices and issued fines to some executives, but its investigation found no wrongdoing by Winnick. Winnick has since set up a fund of $25 million to compensate former employees who lost retirement money in the bankruptcy.

Peter C. Yeager (unknown)

Peter C. Yeager is an associate professor of sociology at Boston University. He received his Ph.D. from the University of Wisconsin at Madison in 1981. Yeager has served on the advisory committee of the Office of Research Integrity since 1999, has reviewed grants for the National Institutes of Health, and has acted as a consultant to the Institute of Medicine of the National Academies. Yeager's research interests include the limitations of legal requirements to control wrongdoing in powerful organizations, the social construction of ethical and legal requirements among professionals and management of organizations, and theories of organizational morality and rule-breaking. Some of his publications include *Corporate Crime* (with M.B. Clinard), *The Limits of Law: The Public Regulation of Private Pollution*, and "Understanding Corporate Lawbreaking: Progress and Prospects" (a chapter in *International Handbook of White-Collar Crime*).

6

Data and Documents

Facts and Statistics on Corporate Crime

Facts and statistics on white-collar and corporate offending are not as widely available as those on traditional offending and not systematically kept by any one organization. One of the reasons for this lack of record keeping is the debate that exists about what constitutes white-collar and corporate criminal offenses. The controversy over precise definitions of white-collar and corporate offending hinges on whether classification should be based on the type of offense, the type of offender, or the type of organization involved. The Federal Bureau of Investigation (FBI) and the information it collects on crime through the Uniform Crime Reports (UCRs) categorizes these crimes by the type of offense committed. There are no measures of occupation, socio-economic status, or an organization's structure listed in the UCR data, as such statistics can only be looked at in terms of offense (Barnett 2002). The UCR, therefore, is an imperfect measure of white-collar and corporate offending; fraud, forgery, counterfeiting, and embezzlement are the only offenses that the UCR collects information on. Furthermore, statistics in the UCR often include offenses that many critics would not group as white-collar or corporate offenses, but are nonetheless mixed in with the aggregate. Table 6.1 lists arrests for forgery and counterfeiting, fraud, and embezzlement according to the UCR in 2005.

These statistics include petty offenses, those committed by corporations or business executives, as well as local, city, and

TABLE 6.1
Number of Arrests for UCR White-collar Offenses in 2005

Offense	Arrests
Forgery and Counterfeiting	118,455
Fraud	321,521
Embezzlement	18,970

Source: Compiled by the author from 2005 UCR data.

state violations. As such, it is impossible to disaggregate which ones are true white-collar or corporate offenses; therefore, the true picture of the extent of white-collar and corporate crime remains blurry.

The National Incident-Based Reporting System (NIBRS) is also collected by the FBI and part of the UCR. NIBRS gives us a better idea of what proportion of these statistics constitutes white-collar and corporate offending; however, even these statistics leave much to be desired. A complete list of white-collar offenses included in the NIBRS database can be obtained from the FBI's Web site under UCR statistics at www.fbi.gov/hq/cjisd/ucr.htm. But Barnett (2002) notes that a number of white-collar offenses are recorded in NIBRS data under the category "all other offenses." This makes it difficult to get accurate measures of white-collar offenses because they cannot be differentiated from other types of offenses in this category. Furthermore, the NIBRS data are from state and local agencies, whereas most white-collar and corporate offenses fall under the jurisdiction of the federal government; federal offenses do not show up in these data. Therefore, the NIBRS data, although better than that of the UCR, are also of limited use in the measurement of white-collar and corporate offending.

Table 6.2 reveals that a majority of white-collar offenses fall under the categories of counterfeiting and false pretenses. False pretenses are offenses involving swindling and confidence games. Embezzlement accounts for almost 20,000 cases, and welfare fraud, wire fraud, bribery, and extortion make up only a little over two percent of cases. The total number of so-called white-collar cases in the NIBRS data is roughly 230,000. When we compare this to the overall absolute number of offenses measured with NIBRS data, these cases make up a very small

TABLE 6.2
Frequency and Percentage of White-collar Offenses

Crime	Frequency	Percent
False Pretenses	98,816	43
Welfare Fraud	682	0.3
Wire Fraud	3,032	1.3
Bribery	163	0.1
Extortion	906	0.4
Counterfeiting	106,945	46.5
Embezzlement	19,281	8.4
Total	**229,825**	**100**

Source: Compiled by the author from 2005 NIBRS data. Downloaded from the Inter-university Consortium for Political and Social Research, Study No. 4720.

percentage. The NIBRS data set includes information on over 5 million cases for 2005 alone, making white-collar offenses just under 5 percent of the cases for that year. Obviously, the NIBRS data set underestimates the amount of white-collar offending that actually occurs. We can, however, get some demographic information from these data that the UCR figures do not provide. Table 6.3 displays the type of offense by sex, and Table 6.4 displays the type of offense by race. For most of the offense types, males are represented at almost three times the rate of females. Female offenders make up 34,694 of the cases, whereas males make up 98,211 cases. Notice that in just over 30,000 of the cases, the sex of the offender is not known. It is not known whether this is because of a recording error or due to the fact that police have not cleared these cases by an arrest yet. Consequently, conclusions about this table must be considered with caution, as we do not know the sex of the offender in over 30,000 of the cases. Other data sets, however, do confirm that males are represented in white-collar crime statistics at higher rates than females.

Table 6.4 reveals that Caucasians make up the largest category of offenders in overall statistics on white-collar offenses; however, there are a few offenses, namely welfare fraud and wire fraud, where the number of African Americans arrested exceeded the number of Caucasians. Asians, Pacific Islanders, and Native Americans make up a small proportion of offenders. As

TABLE 6.3
White-collar Offenses by Gender

	Sex of Offender		
Offender	**Female**	**Male**	**Unknown**
False Pretenses	16,041	43,552	13,153
Welfare Fraud	107	283	57
Wire Fraud	540	1,200	320
Bribery	24	88	32
Extortion	149	423	195
Counterfeiting	15,598	45,499	14,159
Embezzlement	2,235	7,166	2,126
Total	**34,694**	**98,211**	**30,042**

Source: Constructed by the author from 2005 NIBRS data. Downloaded from the Inter-university Consortium for Political and Social Research, Study No. 4720.

TABLE 6.4
White-collar Offenses by Race

	Race of Offender				
Offense	**Asian/Pacific Islander**	**African American**	**Native American**	**Caucasian**	**Unknown**
False Pretenses	98	21,386	53	37,047	14,162
Welfare Fraud	0	248	0	138	61
Wire Fraud	2	875	0	844	339
Bribery	0	21	0	88	35
Extortion	3	198	1	344	221
Counterfeiting	719	14,656	213	43,872	15,796
Total	**956**	**38,460**	**296**	**90,030**	**33,205**

Source: Constructed by the author from 2005 NIBRS data. Downloaded from the Inter-university Consortium for Political and Social Research, Study No. 4720.

in the data on gender, there are around 33,000 cases where the offender's race is unknown. Again, whether this is because the offender has not been arrested is not known. Figure 6.1 displays the mean age of offenders by offense type. The mean age for all offenders—regardless of the type—is under 25 years old; for

FIGURE 6.1
Mean Ages of Offenders by Offense Type

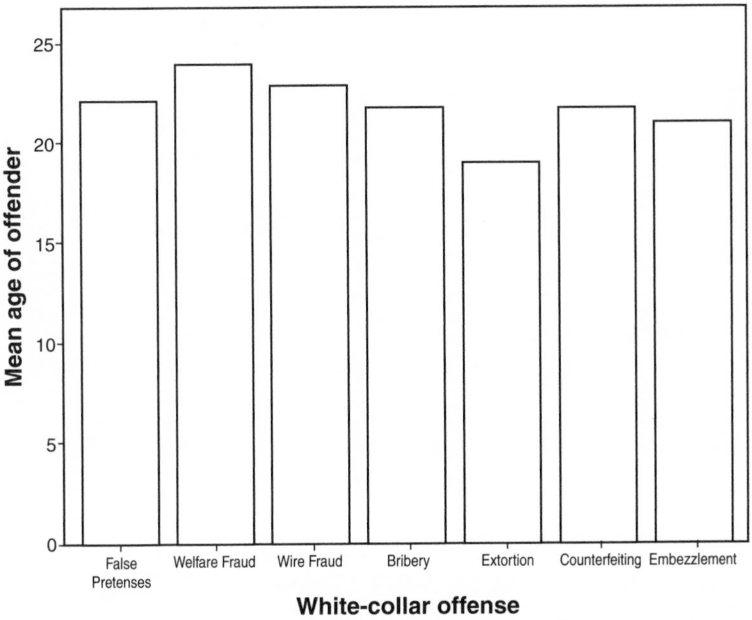

Mean age of offender — White-collar offense

Source: Constructed by the author from 2005 NIBRS data. Downloaded from the Inter-university Consortium for Political and Social Research, Study No. 4720.

embezzlement the mean age appears a little lower, and for extortion, the mean age is under 20. These ages seem low compared to stereotypical images of white-collar offenders. Most people probably think of someone older and higher up in a corporation as the main offenders. Keep in mind these data *do not* reflect federal white-collar cases. Most CEOs, presidents, and vice presidents of corporations who have violated the law are prosecuted in federal court.

Figure 6.2 shows the percentage of offenders above the age of 50 for each type of offense. This chart reveals that very low percentages (less than 5 percent) of white-collar offenders at the state and local level are above the age of 50.

As part of the NIBRS data, information is also collected on the amount of property taken in each case (see Figure 6.3). These data, however, are not as revealing as they may seem at first glance. Some property is considered to have no value—for

FIGURE 6.2
Percentage of Offenders above Age 50

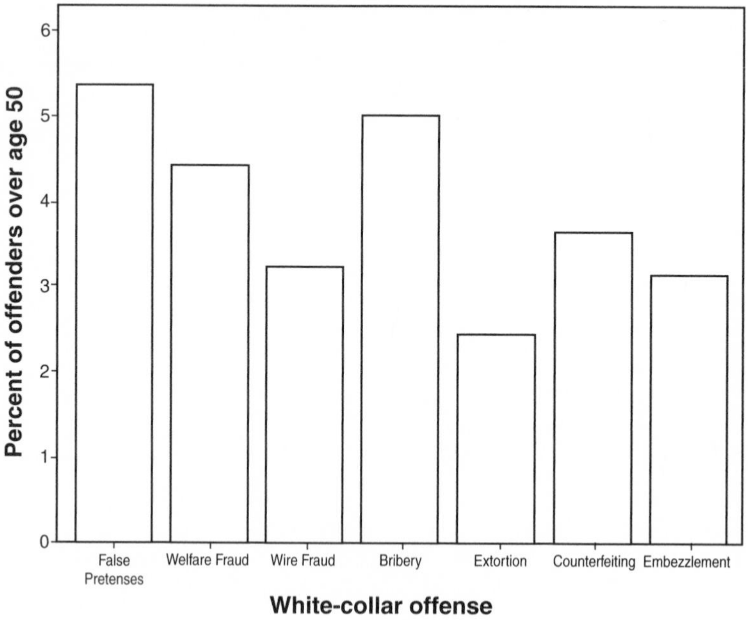

Source: Constructed by the author from 2005 NIBRS data. Downloaded from the Inter-university Consortium for Political and Social Research, Study No. 4720.

example, stolen credit cards. Therefore, regardless of whether the stolen card was used or not, it is considered to have no value. Furthermore, if the value of the property or amount of loss is unknown in the case, the value is set at $1. These statistics clearly underestimate the loss to victims in some cases.

For most offense types, the mean amount of loss is not great. The highest mean loss is for extortion, at around $1,400, and the lowest mean loss is for bribery, at about $700. The mean loss for all other offenses is somewhere in between $1,000 and $1,200. Again, we have to keep in mind that cases with an undetermined amount of loss are represented in these statistics with a value of $1. Indeed, there were just over 23,000 cases where the mean loss was $1. Even with these cases omitted from the data set, the average mean loss only increases by about $500 for each offense. All told, in less than 3 percent of cases for all offense types is the loss more than $10,000.

FIGURE 6.3
Mean Property Value Loss for White-collar Offenses, NIBRS

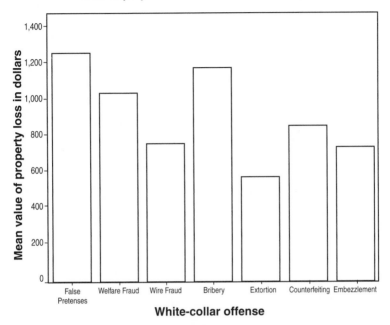

Source: Constructed by the author from 2005 NIBRS data. Downloaded from the Inter-university Consortium for Political and Social Research, Study No. 4720.

Consulting another source yields yet another snapshot of white-collar and corporate offending. The *Sourcebook of Criminal Justice Statistics 2003* (Pastore and Maguire 2003) lists information on a wider variety of offenses, but it only includes arrests for federal violations. Table 6.5 shows the number of persons arrested for federal white-collar offenses, according to the *Sourcebook.*

These numbers reflect individuals arrested on federal charges. There are fewer cases in federal court than in state courts. These may reflect more serious cases where larger amounts of money are involved and where federal statutes have been violated. The largest proportion of federal arrests fall into the offense category of fraud. The next highest arrest rate is for counterfeiting. Arrests for all other offenses number only in the hundreds. In 2003, there were only 6 arrests on antitrust violations. The numbers for white-collar arrests in the UCR and NIBRS data sets are much higher. Overall, however, arrest rates

TABLE 6.5
Persons Arrested for Federal White-collar Offenses

Offense	Number of Arrests
Property Offenses	
Embezzlement	845
Fraud	11,225
Forgery	358
Counterfeiting	1,304
Public-order Offenses	
Antitrust	6
Food and Drug	120
Civil Rights	72
Other Regulatory	22
Tax Law Violations	868
Bribery	175
Perjury/Contempt	284
National Defense	12
Racketeering and Extortion	582
Obstruction of Justice	485
Conspiracy	105
Environmental	126

Source: Compiled by the author from the *Sourcebook of Criminal Justice Statistics 2003.*

for white-collar offenses are much lower than they are for conventional crimes. For example, for the year 2005, the UCR reported 449,297 aggravated assaults and 1,146,696 thefts. Federal arrest statistics from the *Sourcebook* (2003) also show higher numbers of arrests for drug and immigration offenses at 33,066 and 27,347, respectively.

As can be seen from the data above, corporate criminal offense records are not kept with any consistency, and researching the true numbers of offenses, arrests, and prosecutions is very difficult. Another source that compiles records on white-collar offenses is the Transactional Records Access Clearinghouse (TRAC) at New York's Syracuse University. The purpose of this clearinghouse is to give information to the American people about the federal government's law enforcement activities. TRAC's most recent reports at the time this book was being written were for March 2007. According to these records, the federal government reported 663 prosecutions of white-collar criminals. What TRAC also reported, however, is that this figure represents a slight decrease in the number of prosecutions from 2006 and a decrease of roughly 10 percent from the same month five years ago (TRAC 2007c). TRAC (2007b) noted that in March 2007, the government secured 674 convictions for white-collar crime (there are more convictions than prosecutions because these are monthly data, and the convictions represent cases that are carried over from month to month). According to Alexandra Marks (2006), recent decreases in convictions for white-collar and corporate offending reflect the government's move to shift resources away from the fight against corporate crime and toward homeland security. In other words, the drop in convictions is not a reflection of a decrease in corporate offending, but rather a change in the priorities of the federal government. In fact, the number of federal investigators who focused solely on white-collar crimes decreased by 500 persons from 2000 to 2004. Figure 6.4 shows the number of federal criminal prosecutions from 2000 to 2005. As the figure illustrates, the focus of federal prosecutions from 2002 to 2005 has been on cases involving immigration offenses. Both drug prosecutions and white-collar prosecutions have decreased during the same time period, while prosecutions for weapons increased slightly. Drug and immigration cases, however, make up the majority of federal prosecutions.

TRAC data also reveal which agencies charged what percentage of cases. These data report that 30 percent of cases originate with the FBI, 19 percent with the IRS, 15 percent with the Secret Service, 9 percent with the Postal Service, 5 percent with Health and Human Services, and 23 percent with other agencies (TRAC 2007c). For convictions, 42 percent are secured by the FBI, 15 percent by the Secret Service, 10 percent by the IRS, 8 percent by the Postal Service, 5 percent by the Department of Homeland Security, and 20 percent by other agencies (TRAC 2007b).

Table 6.6 is a list of the number of counts and the top statutes under which white-collar and corruption charges were prosecuted in March 2007. Table 6.7 is a list of the number of counts and the top statutes under which white-collar and corruption charges were convicted for March 2007. Note that this is not an exhaustive list.

FIGURE 6.4
Federal Criminal Prosecutions, 2000–2005

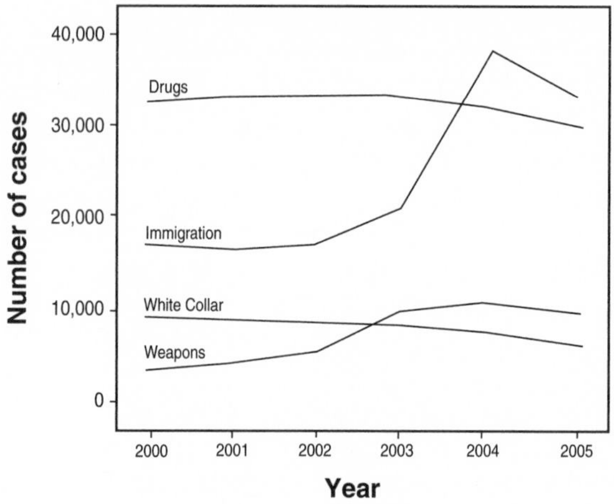

Source: Constructed by the author from information obtained from the Transactional Records Access Clearinghouse, Syracuse University (2007a).

Former Attorney General Alberto Gonzales spoke to the Corporate Fraud Task Force (CFTF) on its fifth anniversary, July 17, 2007. In his speech, he outlined the accomplishments of the task force in its first five years. Since its inception, the CFTF has obtained 1, 236 convictions for corporate fraud alone. Those convicted of this offense include over 200 CEOs and presidents of corporations, 53 CFOs, 23 corporate attorneys, and 129 vice presidents of corporations. Assets seized by the task force in its first five years amount to more than $1 billion, much of which has been given back to the victims in those cases (Gonzales 2007).

The U.S. Sentencing Commission also keeps records of individuals prosecuted in federal court for white-collar and corporate offenses, as well as organizations that are convicted and sentenced under the Federal Sentencing Guidelines set forth in the *United States Sentencing Guidelines Manual* (2005, chap. 8).

Table 6.8 is a list of offenses for which individuals were convicted in federal court in 2005 (October 1, 2004, to September 30, 2005), as well as the percentage of all federal cases those represent. There were 72,462 convictions in all federal districts in 2005. The cases in Table 6.8 make up approximately 15 percent

TABLE 6.6
Statutes and Number of Counts of White-collar Prosecutions

Charge	Counts
18 USC 1344: Bank Fraud	65
18 USC 1341: Mail Fraud	60
18 USC 371: Conspiracy to Commit Offense or Defraud the United States	44
18 USC 1343: Wire Fraud	35
26 USC 7206: Fraud and False Statements	29
18 USC 287: False or Fraudulent Claims	24
18 USC 641: Public Money, Property, or Records	22
18 USC 1001 and 7206: Fraud and False Statements or Entries	21
18 USC 513: Securities of the States and Private Entities	16

Source: List compiled by the author from TRAC (2007c).

TABLE 6.7
Statutes and Number of Counts of White-collar Convictions

Conviction	Counts
18 USC 1344: Bank Fraud	100
18 USC 1341: Mail Fraud	92
18 USC 1028 and 1029: Fraud and Related Activity	79
18 USC 1343: Wire Fraud	48
18 USC 371: Conspiracy to Defraud the Government	34
18 USC 1001: Fraud and False Statements	26
18 USC 641: Public Money, Property, or Records	24
18 USC 1347: Health Care Fraud	23
26 USC 7201: Attempt to Evade Tax	21

Source: List compiled by the author from TRAC (2007b).

of that number. The most frequent violations were fraud, followed by forgery and money laundering.

Table 6.9 reflects information on the percentage of persons incarcerated by offense type, as well as the range, mean, and median of their sentence length in months. The offenses with the

TABLE 6.8
Convictions in Federal District Court for 2005* by Offense Type

Offense	Frequency	Percent of all Federal Cases
Fraud	6,809	9.4
Embezzlement	577	0.8
Forgery	1,083	1.5
Bribery	199	0.3
Tax Violation	604	0.8
Money Laundering	934	0.3
Racketeering/Extortion	715	1.0
Antitrust Violations	18	Less than 0.1
Food and Drug Violations	78	0.1

* 2005 = October 1, 2004, to September 30, 2005

Source: Compiled by the author from 2005 U.S. Sentencing Commission data. Downloaded from the Inter-university Consortium for Political and Social Research, Study No. 4630.

highest incarceration rates were racketeering, antitrust violations, and money laundering. Those least likely to be incarcerated were individuals who committed food and drug violations and embezzlement. In looking at the *range* of sentences, the longest sentence was given for racketeering/extortion at 720 months, or 60 years, followed by money laundering at 564 months, or 47 years. For fraud, the longest sentence was 480 months, or 40 years, and the longest sentence for forgery was 10 years. The minimum sentence length given for a majority of offenses was just one month.

Table 6.9 also reveals that the *average* sentence lengths were highest for individuals convicted of racketeering/extortion at 80.5 months, followed by money laundering and fraud at 47 and 26 months, respectively. The lowest mean sentences were given for those convicted of antitrust violations and embezzlement. Keep in mind that these statistics refer to outcomes for individuals convicted of white-collar offenses; organizations themselves, however, can also wind up in federal district court.

Table 6.10 gives information for organizations that are convicted in federal district court. These data reflect information on organizations only, not individuals within the organization.

TABLE 6.9
Incarceration Rates and Sentences in Months by Offense, 2005*

Offense	Percent Incarcerated	Sentence Range in Months	Mean Sentence Length	Median Sentence
Fraud	57	1 to 480	26	18
Embezzlement	37	1 to 120	15.8	12
Forgery	61	1 to 240	21	17
Bribery	55	1 to 112	22	15
Tax Violation	55	1 to 156	19.5	14
Money Laundering	70	1 to 564	47	33
Racketeering/Extortion	84	4 to 720	80.5	60
Antitrust Violations	72	4 to 30	8.7	6
Food and Drug Violations	24	1 to 71	25	16

* 2005 = October 1, 2004, to September 30, 2005

Source: Compiled by the author from 2005 U.S. Sentencing Commission data. Downloaded from the Inter-university Consortium for Political and Social Research, Study No. 4630.

According to the U.S. Sentencing Commission (2005), an organization is "a person other than an individual" (18 U.S.C. §18). Corporations, associations, partnerships, unions, joint-stock companies, pension funds, unincorporated organizations, trusts, governments, and nonprofit organizations all qualify under this definition. In 2005, there were 187 organizations sentenced under chapter 8 of the Federal Sentencing Guidelines. According to this data set, sentenced organizations had an average of 3.6 conviction counts and received an average of 26 months of probation as punishment. Organizations cannot be incarcerated, so punishments mainly include probation and fines.

As shown in Table 6.10, organizations can be involved in non-white-collar offenses. In fact, 52 of the 187 organizations convicted were charged with gambling offenses. Others include firearms violations, immigration offenses, pornography and prostitution, as well as obstruction of justice. Fifty-three organizations were also convicted on environmental offenses, including air, water, wildlife, and hazardous material violations. These 187 cases represent a very small percentage of cases in federal district courts for the year 2005. Table 6.11 gives information on how the organizational cases were disposed of. More than 90

TABLE 6.10
Primary Offense Type, Organizations

Offense	Frequency	Percent
Antitrust	15	8.0
Bribery	5	2.7
Environmental Waste–Water	6	3.2
Environmental Waste–Air	30	16.5
Environmental Waste–Hazardous Materials	4	2.1
Environmental–Wildlife	13	7.0
Equity	5	2.7
Firearm	14	7.5
Food and Drug Violation	8	4.3
Gambling	52	28.3
Immigration	3	1.6
Embezzlement	4	2.1
Trafficking Automobile Parts	3	1.6
Obstruction of Justice	12	6.4
Pornography/Prostitution	4	2.1
Tax	1	0.7
Other	6	3.2
Total	**187**	**100**

Source: Compiled by the author from U.S. Sentencing Commission data, 2005.

percent of the time, a plea of guilt was given. Roughly 6 percent were convicted by jury trial, and only two organizations decided to have their case decided by a judge.

Other information about the organizations convicted in federal court in 2005 reveals that 51 percent of them had a prior history of misconduct that was known to federal officials. Likewise, roughly 52 percent also had civil cases either pending or in progress. Only 35 organizations had some type of compliance program implemented, and only 13 had community service ordered as part of their conviction and sentence. Almost 75 percent, however, had some type of fine ordered as part of their sentence. Table 6.12 gives information on the dollar amount of

TABLE 6.11
Disposition of Case, Organizations

Type of Case	Frequency	Percent
Guilty Plea	173	92.5
Trial by Jury	12	6.4
Trial by Judge	2	1.1
Total	187	100

Source: Compiled by the author from U.S. Sentencing Commission data, 2005.

the fines ordered in these organizational cases. Approximately 15 percent of organizations had fines over $500,000, another 15 percent had fines less than $10,000. Roughly 20 percent of the fines were in the $100,000 to $499,000 range. In two cases, however, fines were ordered against the organization in excess of $100 million. It should be noted, however, that almost 25 percent of the organizations that had fines imposed were unable to pay any of the fine imposed against them, and another 3 percent were unable to pay a portion of the fine imposed. Most cases (90 percent) did not have any assets forfeited and were not required to perform community service or implement a compliance program—all this despite the fact that over 50 percent had a prior history of misconduct. Fines, then, are the most frequent punishments for organizations that violate federal law.

A legal print newsletter called the *Corporate Crime Reporter* monitors and highlights corporate crime and corruption. This publication disseminates information on corporations and their offending, as well as government officials and legislation fighting to prevent corporate violations. Table 6.13 is a list of the top 10 white-collar criminal defense attorneys, according to a survey conducted by the *Corporate Crime Reporter* in 2003. Interesting to note is that six of them have offices in Washington, D.C.

The *Corporate Crime Reporter* also compiled a list of the top 10 white-collar and corporate prosecutors who were named for consistently pursuing prosecution of high-profile corporate cases. They are listed in Table 6.14.

The *Corporate Crime Reporter*'s list of the top 10 corporate violators of the 1990s, their crimes, and the criminal fines they were required to pay appear in Table 6.15.

TABLE 6.12
Dollar Amount of Fine Ordered in Organizational Cases

Fine in Dollars	Frequency	Percent
None	48	25.7
Less than 10,000	27	14.4
10,000 to 99,999	46	25.0
100,000 to 499,999	39	20.8
500,000 to 999,999	5	2.7
1,000,000 to 4,999,999	8	4.2
5,000,000 to 9,999,999	5	2.7
10,000,000 to 100,000,000	7	3.5
More than 100,000,000	2	1.0
Total	**187**	**100**

Source: Compiled by the author from U.S. Sentencing Commission data, 2005.

TABLE 6.13
Top 10 White-Collar Criminal Defense Attorneys in the United States

Attorney	Law Firm	City
Dan Webb	Winston & Strawn	Chicago, IL
John Keker	Keker & Van Nest	San Francisco, CA
Reid Weingarten	Steptoe & Johnson	Washington, DC
Brendan Sullivan	Williams & Connolly	Washington, DC
Robert Bennett	Skadden, Arps	Washington, DC
Thomas Green	Sifley & Austin	Washington, DC
Earl Silbert	Piper Rudnick	Washington, DC
Daniel Reidy	Jones, Day	Chicago, IL
Robert Fiske	Davis, Polk	New York City, NY
Theodore Wells	Paul, Weiss	New York City, NY
Plato Cacheris	Baker & McKenzie	Washington, DC

Source: Corporate Crime Reporter 2003.

TABLE 6.14
Top 10 White-collar Prosecutors in the United States

Prosecutor	Title	Jurisdiction
Christopher Christie	U.S. Attorney	New Jersey
James Comey	Deputy Attorney General	Washington, DC
Patrick Fitzgerald	U.S. Attorney	Chicago
David Kelley	U.S. Attorney	Manhattan
Alice Martin	U.S. Attorney	Birmingham
Patrick Meehan	U.S. Attorney	Philadelphia
Robert Morgenthau	District Attorney	Manhattan
Eliot Spitzer	Attorney General	New York
Michael Sullivan	U.S. Attorney	Boston
Debra Yang	U.S. Attorney	Los Angeles

Source: Corporate Crime Reporter 2004.

TABLE 6.15
Top 10 Corporate Violators in the 1990s

Corporation	Crime Type	Fine
F. Hoffmann—La Roche Ltd.	Antitrust	$500 million
Daiwa Bank Ltd.	Financial	$340 million
BASF Aktiengesellschaft	Antitrust	$225 million
SGL Carbon Aktiengesellschaft	Antitrust	$135 million
Exxon	Environmental	$125 million
UCAR International, Inc.	Antitrust	$110 million
Archer Daniels Midland	Antitrust	$100 million
Banker's Trust	Financial	$60 million
Sears Bankruptcy Recovery Management Services	Fraud	$60 million
Haarman & Reimer Corp.	Antitrust	$50 million

Source: Compiled by the author from www.corporatepredators.org/top100.html.

Government Documents and Reports

The U.S. government has, in recent years, enacted legislation aimed at holding corporations responsible for their wrongdoing. Governmental agencies have also begun to publish reports of corporate offending and require corporations to report information about their business practices in order to protect shareholders and investors from being harmed by corporate wrongdoing. Statistics reveal that white-collar crime costs the United States more every year than all of the FBI index crimes combined (Reiman 2007). Although estimates are hard to obtain, and those that have been conducted vary considerably, even conservative estimates place the costs in the hundreds of billions of dollars. The FBI (2007) has estimated that white-collar and corporate offending cost the United States over $300 billion a year. Reiman (2007), using U.S. Chamber of Commerce statistics, places the loss conservatively at $418 billion for 2003. This is roughly 24 times the cost of property crimes for the same year, according to the FBI's UCR total of $17 billion in losses. The Association of Certified Fraud Examiners in 2004 estimated $660 billion in fraud losses annually. Tax evasion alone has been projected to cost the United States anywhere from 5 to 7 percent of its gross national product every year (Reiman 2007). Using numbers from the U.S. Department of Commerce's Bureau of Economic Analysis for 2006, the cost of tax evasion is somewhere between $553 billion and $774 billion.

Also, if we look at the pay for corporate executives compared to other workers, we see huge differences. The ratio of CEO pay to regular worker pay was 431 to 1 in 2004, up from 301 to 1 in 2003, and 107 to 1 in 1990 (Anderson, Cavanagh, Klinger, and Stanton 2005). Yet, the minimum wage had not increased in 10 years until July 2007, when it went up to $5.85 an hour (Associated Press 2007). White-collar and corporate crimes continue to cost the United States hundreds of billions, and CEO pay continues to increase. But prosecution of corporate offenders is declining, not as a result of a decrease in offending but because of shifts in government priorities (Marks 2006). These statistics lead us to believe that Reiman (2007) is correct when he states that the rich get richer and the poor get prison. Despite these prosecutorial decreases, though, the government has made some attempts to get tougher on white-collar criminals.

Executive Order 13271

The following is an excerpt from Executive Order 13271, enacted on July 9, 2002, by George W. Bush. This executive order established the United States Corporate Fraud Task Force whose director is the Deputy Attorney General of the United States and whose duties are to improve enforcement of corporate laws and maximize cooperation of all federal agencies to this end.

By the authority vested in me as President by the Constitution and the laws of the United States of America, and in order to strengthen the efforts of the Department of Justice and Federal, State, and local agencies to investigate and prosecute significant financial crimes, recover the proceeds of such crimes, and ensure just and effective punishment of those who perpetrate financial crimes, it is hereby ordered as follows:

Section 1. Establishment. The Attorney General shall immediately establish within the Department of Justice a Corporate Fraud Task Force (Task Force). Without regard to any other provision of this order, the Task Force shall be subject to the authority of the Attorney General under applicable law.

Sec. 3. Functions. Consistent with the constitutional authority of the President, the authorities assigned to the Attorney General by law, and other applicable law, the Task Force shall:

(a) provide direction for the investigation and prosecution of cases of securities fraud, accounting fraud, mail and wire fraud, money laundering, tax fraud based on such predicate offenses, and other related financial crimes committed by commercial entities and directors, officers, professional advisers, and employees thereof (hereinafter "financial crimes"), when such cases are determined by the Deputy Attorney General, for purposes of this order, to be significant;

(b) provide recommendations to the Attorney General for allocation and reallocation of resources of the Department of Justice for investigation and prosecution of significant financial crimes, recovery of proceeds from such crimes to the extent permitted by law, and other matters determined by the Task Force from time to time to be of the highest priority in the investigation and prosecution of such crimes; and

(c) make recommendations to the President, through the Attorney General, from time to time for:

(i) action to enhance cooperation among departments, agencies, and entities of the Federal Government in the investigation and prosecution of significant financial crimes;

(ii) action to enhance cooperation among Federal, State, and local authorities responsible for the investigation and prosecution of significant financial crimes;

(iii) changes in rules, regulations, or policy to improve the effective investigation and prosecution of significant financial crimes; and

(iv) recommendations to the Congress regarding such measures as the President may judge necessary and expedient relating to significant financial crimes, or the investigation or prosecution thereof.

Sec. 5. Internal Management Purpose. This order is intended to improve the internal management of the Federal Government. This order is not intended to, and does not create any right or benefit, substantive or procedural, enforceable at law or equity or otherwise against the United States, its departments, agencies, entities, instrumentalities, officers, or employees, or any other person.

Sec. 6. Termination. The Task Force shall terminate when directed by the President or, with the approval of the President, by the Attorney General. (Presidential Documents 2002)

Legislation Pertaining to Corporate Offending

Some of the key statutes that have been enacted to fight corporate offending and impose penalties on those corporations that are found guilty of criminal activity are the Sherman Antitrust Act, the Clayton Antitrust Act, the Federal Trade Commission Act, and the Sarbanes-Oxley Act. What follows is a brief overview of each of these acts, as well as an excerpt from each act.

The Sherman Antitrust Act of 1890

The Sherman Act, 15 U.S.C. 1–7, was legislation enacted to prohibit the restraint of trade or commerce among the states or with foreign nations. It was also aimed at those who attempt to decrease economic competition. It set forth prohibitions against monopolies, including attempts or conspiracies. Violations can be prosecuted by the government in civil or criminal jurisdictions. The Sherman Act set forth penalties, including fines of up to $10 million for corporations, $350,000 for individuals, and imprisonment of up to three years. The following are excerpts from the act:

15 U.S.C. §1: Trusts, etc., in restraint of trade illegal; penalty
Every contract, combination in the form of trust or otherwise, or conspiracy, in restraint of trade or commerce among the several States, or

with foreign nations, is declared to be illegal. Every person who shall make any contract or engage in any combination or conspiracy hereby declared to be illegal shall be deemed guilty of a felony, and, on conviction thereof, shall be punished by fine not exceeding $10,000,000 if a corporation, or, if any other person, $350,000, or by imprisonment not exceeding three years, or by both said punishments, in the discretion of the court. (15, U.S.C. §1 1890)

15 U.S.C. §2: Monopolizing trade a felony; penalty

Every person who shall monopolize, or attempt to monopolize, or combine or conspire with any other person or persons, to monopolize any part of the trade or commerce among the several States, or with foreign nations, shall be deemed guilty of a felony, and, on conviction thereof, shall be punished by fine not exceeding $10,000,000 if a corporation, or, if any other person, $350,000, or by imprisonment not exceeding three years, or by both said punishments, in the discretion of the court. (15, U.S.C. §2 1890)

The Clayton Antitrust Act of 1914

The Clayton Antitrust Act expanded the Sherman Act in an attempt to remedy some of the deficiencies in the previous act relating to monopolies. It also further addressed economic competition regarding the sale, merger, or acquisition of corporate entities. It prohibits any one person from being in charge of more than one organization that is in competition with the others. The following are excerpts from sections 14 and 18:

15 U.S.C. §14: Sale, etc., on agreement not to use goods of competitor

It shall be unlawful for any person engaged in commerce, in the course of such commerce, to lease or make a sale or contract for sale of goods, wares, merchandise, machinery, supplies, or other commodities, whether patented or unpatented, for use, consumption, or resale within the United States or any Territory thereof or the District of Columbia or any insular possession or other place under the jurisdiction of the United States, or fix a price charged therefore, or discount from, or rebate upon, such price, on the condition, agreement, or understanding that the lessee or purchaser thereof shall not use or deal in the goods, wares, merchandise, machinery, supplies, or other commodities of a competitor or competitors of the lessor or seller, where the effect of such lease, sale, or contract for sale or such condition, agreement, or understanding may be to substantially lessen competition or tend to create a monopoly in any line of commerce. (15 U.S.C. §14 1914)

15 U.S.C. §18: Acquisition by one corporation of stock of another

No person engaged in commerce or in any activity affecting commerce shall acquire, directly or indirectly, the whole or any part of the stock or other share capital and no person subject to the jurisdiction of the Federal Trade Commission shall acquire the whole or any part of the assets of another person engaged also in commerce or in any activity affecting commerce, where in any line of commerce or in any activity affecting commerce in any section of the country, the effect of such acquisition may be substantially to lessen competition, or to tend to create a monopoly.

No person shall acquire, directly or indirectly, the whole or any part of the stock or other share capital and no person subject to the jurisdiction of the Federal Trade Commission shall acquire the whole or any part of the assets of one or more persons engaged in commerce or in any activity affecting commerce, where in any line of commerce or in any activity affecting commerce in any section of the country, the effect of such acquisition, of such stocks or assets, or of the use of such stock by the voting or granting of proxies or otherwise, may be substantially to lessen competition, or to tend to create a monopoly . . . (15 U.S.C. §18 1914)

The Federal Trade Commission Act of 1914

The Federal Trade Commission Act set up the Federal Trade Commission to oversee the activity of large corporations, to control trade, and to limit unfair trading practices. It made illegal several unfair methods of trading and competition that affect different areas of commerce. This act allowed the Federal Trade Commission to take action against any corporation that violated laws pertaining to the Sherman Act, the Clayton Act, and other violations not stated in those two acts. The Federal Trade Commission Act, Section 41:

15 U.S.C. §41: Federal Trade Commission established; membership; vacancies; seal

A commission is created and established, to be known as the Federal Trade Commission (hereinafter referred to as the Commission), which shall be composed of five Commissioners, who shall be appointed by the President, by and with the advice and consent of the Senate. Not more than three of the Commissioners shall be members of the same political party. The first Commissioners appointed shall continue in office for terms of three, four, five, six, and seven years, respectively, from September 26, 1914, the term of each to be designated by the President, but their successors shall be appointed for terms of seven years, except that any person chosen to fill a vacancy shall be appointed only for the unexpired term of the Commissioner whom he shall succeed: Provided, however, That upon the expiration of his term of office a Commissioner shall continue to serve until his successor shall have been appointed and shall have qualified. The President shall choose a chairman from the Commission's membership. No Commissioner shall engage in any other business, vocation, or employment. Any Commissioner may be removed by the President for inefficiency, neglect of duty, or malfeasance in office. A vacancy in the Commission shall not impair the right of the remaining Commissioners to exercise all the powers of the Commission. The Commission shall have an official seal, which shall be judicially noticed. (15 U.S.C. §41 1914)

The Sarbanes-Oxley Act of 2002

The Sarbanes-Oxley Act of 2002 was passed in response to major corporate and accounting scandals that resulted in numerous investors and shareholders losing their investments and retirement funds. The act established new standards for corporate entities, adding responsibilities to corporate boards for the actions of their companies as well as enhancing criminal penalties for violations. Under this act, board members are now responsible for disseminating their earning reports to shareholders. The act also established a new agency, the Public Company Accounting Oversight Board, whose duty is to oversee accounting firms' activities in auditing publicly traded companies. The following is an excerpt from the act:

15 U.S.C. §101 Establishment; administrative provisions

(a) Establishment of Board. There is established the Public Company Accounting Oversight Board, to oversee the audit of public companies that are subject to the securities laws, and related matters, in order to protect the interests of investors and further the public interest in the preparation of informative, accurate, and independent audit reports for companies the securities of which are sold to, and held by and for, public investors. The Board shall be a body corporate, operate as a non-profit corporation, and have succession until dissolved by an Act of Congress.

(b) Status. The Board shall not be an agency or establishment of the United States Government, and, except as otherwise provided in this Act, shall be subject to, and have all the powers conferred upon a nonprofit corporation by, the District of Columbia Nonprofit Corporation Act. No member or person employed by, or agent for, the Board shall be deemed to be an officer or employee of or agent for the Federal Government by reason of such service.

15 U.S.C. §103 Auditing, quality control, and independence standards and rules

(a) Auditing, Quality Control, and Ethics Standards.

(1) In General. The Board shall, by rule, establish, including, to the extent it determines appropriate, through adoption of standards proposed by 1 or more professional groups of accountants designated pursuant to paragraph (3)(A) or advisory groups convened pursuant to paragraph (4), and amend or otherwise modify or alter, such auditing and related attestation standards, such quality control standards, and such ethics standards to be used by registered public accounting firms in the preparation and issuance of audit reports, as required by this Act or the rules of the Commission, or as may be necessary or appropriate in the public interest or for the protection of investors.

(2) Rule Requirements. In carrying out paragraph (1), the Board

(a) shall include in the auditing standards that it adopts, requirements that each registered public accounting firm shall

(i) prepare, and maintain for a period of not less than 7 years, audit work papers, and other information related to any audit report, in sufficient detail to support the conclusions reached in such report;

(ii) provide a concurring or second partner review and approval of such audit report (and other related information), and concurring approval in its issuance, by a qualified person (as prescribed by the Board) associated with the public accounting firm, other than the person in charge of the audit, or by an independent reviewer (as prescribed by the Board); and

(iii) describe in each audit report the scope of the auditor's testing of the internal control structure and procedures of the issuer, required by section 404(b).

Governmental Commentary on Corporate Offending

Deputy Attorney General Larry D. Thompson, 2002

Several governmental officials have made speeches, composed memorandums, or otherwise commented on corporate wrongdoing and law enforcement actions with regard to prevention, apprehension, and prosecution of corporate offenders. Critics have charged that most of these efforts have been largely symbolic in nature, as they have not greatly affected official application of the laws. The following is an excerpt from a speech made by then-Deputy Attorney General Larry D. Thompson in Washington, D.C., on October 28, 2002.

I will say a few words about a subject near to my heart as both a prosecutor and a former white-collar defense lawyer of many years: and that is our efforts to combat the culture of greed and deceit that tolerates and propagates fraud within some of our corporations—and I would like to emphasize SOME. This aberrant corporate behavior exists in, I believe, a tiny minority of American businesses. Nevertheless, the problem is serious—and is certainly worth bringing to the attention of this distinguished group of business leaders . . .

Now, as we all are so painfully aware, our financial markets have been shaken by a wave of criminal conduct at the highest levels in some American corporations. While this conduct is shocking, it is not without precedent and the administration is taking swift and certain action to punish the wrongdoers and restore confidence to investors . . .

As noted, in discussing these crimes, it is important not to tar with too broad a brush the overwhelming majority of corporations that operate morally and productively in the best and highest interest of their shareholders and the country. Yet, I believe you will agree the breadth and extent of these recent scandals do demonstrate intolerable legal and ethical misdeeds that require a comprehensive response.

While we have focused the brunt of our actions on individual corporate criminals, there is a significant category of wrongdoers who cannot be imprisoned, but are nonetheless crucial targets of our efforts. Although it should be done sparingly, we will not hesitate to prosecute corporations themselves when the circumstances warrant it.

In making the decision to seek an indictment against a corporation, we consider a number of factors:

(1) The company's history of wrongdoing,

(2) Its response to regulatory actions,

(3) Its reaction to the criminal conduct committed by its employees, including the cooperation with the Government's investigation;

(4) The level within the corporation at which the crimes were committed or condoned, and

(5) The pervasiveness of the criminal behavior within the organization.

. . . Civil sanctions simply do not have the power of criminal penalties to concentrate the corporate mind and change corporate culture. Large business organizations, particularly public companies that are already regulated in myriad ways, sometimes have the disappointing tendency to view civil sanctions as merely the "cost of doing business"—a cost that can be passed on to customers and shareholders without lingering effect in the management suite and the board room.

Indeed, without corporate criminal liability, there would be no effective deterrent to a corporate culture that—expressly or tacitly—condones criminal conduct. Instead, corporations could merely appoint a "vice-president in charge of going to jail" who would serve as a whipping boy for the collective acts of the organization . . .

We will press ahead in these efforts and look forward to your continued cooperation and support. Our goal is to separate the offenders from law-abiding companies. In many cases, that separation will be physical and for an extended term of years. My hope is that comprehensive enforcement efforts will restore investor confidence in the integrity of the market by demonstrating that financial criminals will pay—and they will pay with more than financial penalties. (Thompson 2002)

Deputy Attorney General Paul J. McNulty, 2006

Almost four years later, Deputy Attorney General Paul J. McNulty tempered the Thompson memo and issued new charging guidelines in corporate fraud prosecutions. This is an excerpt from those remarks at the Lawyers for Civil Justice Membership Conference held in New York on December 12, 2006.

Those who investigate and prosecute corporate fraud should share in this sense of satisfaction. When we look back to the corporate scandals of 2000 and 2001, we remember that it was a time of great concern for the American investor and all those whose hopes and dreams were connected to investments. Public trust in our financial markets and corporate America was at an all-time low with the large-scale bankruptcies of companies like WorldCom and Enron . . .

Our response to this outcry reflected the duty we owe to the American public. As prosecutors, we are committed to the fair administration of justice and equal treatment under the law. Our duty is to enforce the law—duties not all that different from the duties of a corporate officer or director. Or at least they should not be. Directors and officers owe a fiduciary duty to a corporation's shareholders, the corporation's true owners, and they owe duties of honest dealing to the investing public when releasing regulatory filings and making public statements.

The faithful execution of these duties by corporate leadership serves the same values in promoting public trust and confidence that our criminal prosecutions are designed to serve.

In fact, the best corporate prosecution is the one that never occurs. Through successful corporate compliance efforts, investor harm can be avoided. Corporate officials must be encouraged to seek legal advice if they are in doubt about the requirements of the law. The attorney-client privilege is an important part of the legal framework supporting this compliance and accountability. The privilege promotes thorough and complete disclosure from a corporate employee to his attorney and candid advice from legal counsel. It is one of the oldest and most sacrosanct privileges in American law. In a government investigation, the corporation and its employees must have the ability to retain and communicate with a lawyer. If that relationship is interfered with, if those communications are unfairly breached, it makes it harder for companies to detect and remedy wrongdoing. And the reality is that the use and preservation of the attorney-client privilege is often not an issue.

Many have argued that the Department's corporate charging guidance, also known as the Thompson Memorandum, has discouraged seeking legal advice and full and candid communication between lawyer and client. Counsel have complained that we are demanding blanket waivers and making waivers a prerequisite for cooperation. This perception, well founded or not, is said to be discouraging corporate compliance by chilling attorney-client communications.

First, my policy now makes clear that attorney-client communications should only be sought in rare cases; that is, that legal advice, mental impressions and conclusions and legal determinations by counsel are protected. Before they are requested, the United States Attorney must seek approval directly from me. I must personally approve each waiver request for attorney-client communications. Both the request for approval and my authorization will be in writing.

Second, to support the request, prosecutors must show a "legitimate need" for the information. If they cannot meet that test, I will not authorize their seeking privileged information. To meet this test, prosecutors must show:

(1) the likelihood and degree to which the privileged information will benefit the government's investigation;

(2) Whether the information sought can be obtained in a timely and complete fashion by using alternative means that do not require waiver;

(3) The completeness of the voluntary disclosure already provided; and

(4) The collateral consequences to the corporation in requesting a waiver.

The American public cannot afford another round of corporate scandals. We rely on you to help us ensure it does not happen again.

Sustaining the achievements of the past five years will require devotion to duty by prosecutors, defense lawyers and corporate counsel. If we are faithful to these duties, America's financial markets will continue to support the hopes and dreams of all its citizens. (McNulty 2006)

Attorney General Alberto R. Gonzales, 2007

Attorney General Alberto R. Gonzales made a speech to the Corporate Fraud Task Force on its fifth anniversary, July 17, 2007, in Washington, D.C. The following is an excerpt from that speech.

We will never know how many investors were spared thanks to the work of the Task Force. In just five years, you've cleaned up a lot of fraud, from New York to New Hampshire to Colorado. And as a result you've helped to create an environment where honest businesses can compete and thrive . . .

But perhaps the most important accomplishment is the criminal conduct that never occurred because of the wide-spread deterrent effect triggered by the tireless and thorough efforts of the Task Force and everyone in this room . . .

As this is a recognition of your success, I thought that it would be worthwhile to look back. . . . By May of 2007, we'd obtained more than 1,200 convictions, including 214 corporate chief executives or presidents. And we've won hundreds of millions of dollars in fines and in restitution to investors, who are the ultimate victims of corporate fraud . . .

Through criminal trials and other methods—like deferred prosecution agreements—the Department of Justice and its partners on the Task Force have made clear that we expect private industry to help ferret out fraud and to work with us. For example, an important part of many of the agreements is the company's commitment to improved internal, corporate compliance. We are not only looking to punish past bad behavior, but are also interested in future good conduct. That is why we encourage corporations to be more responsible for ensuring that good conduct . . .

The actions we have taken together—and the actions we will take together in the future—will produce lasting benefits for the American people and the American economy. Each one of you has been a part of making our economic system stronger, and each one of you should feel immense pride at being a part of this historic effort. (Gonzales 2007)

Quotes

The dull, purblind folly of the very rich men; their greed and arrogance . . . and the corruption in business and politics, have tended to produce a very unhealthy condition of excitement and irritation in the popular mind, which shows itself in the great increase in the socialistic propaganda.

—Theodore Roosevelt, 1906

I think we are in a position, after the experience of the last 20 years, to state two things: in the first place, that a corporation may well be too large to be the most efficient instrument of production and distribution, and, in the second place, whether it has exceeded the point of greatest economic efficiency or not, it may be too large to be tolerated among the people who desire to be free.

—Louis Brandeis, 1911

White-collar crime is real crime. It is not ordinarily called crime, and calling it by this name does not make it worse, just as refraining from calling it crime does not make it better than it otherwise would be. It is called crime here in order to bring it within the scope of criminology, which is justified because it is in violation of the criminal law.

—Edwin Sutherland, 1939

It is time to reaffirm the basic principles and rules that make capitalism work: truthful books, and honest people, and well-enforced laws against fraud and corruption.

—President George W. Bush, July 9, 2002

The President's initiative will bring a new measure of accountability to American businesses. The President's proposal will help deter corporate crimes by making it clear that executives and companies will face tough penalties including longer jail sentences for individuals. The Department of Justice has been and will continue to investigate fully the reports of corporate fraud, and hold the guilty parties accountable for misleading shareholders and employees. With the added weight of the Corporate Fraud Task Force, we will continue to hold accountable those individuals and entities who violate the public trust, undermine our free enterprise system and put at risk the retirement savings of American workers.

—Attorney General John Ashcroft, July 9, 2002

By our concentrated efforts, the Department and our colleagues on the Corporate Fraud Task Force are moving decisively to combat corporate fraud and restore investor confidence in the marketplace.

—**Deputy Attorney General Larry Thompson, March 26, 2003**

Other Relevant Documents

The following is an excerpt from a November 6, 2003, letter written to then-Attorney General of the United States John Ashcroft from Ralph Nader on corporate crime data (Citizen Works 2003).

Recently, your Federal Bureau of Investigations released its annual "Crime in the United States" report, which pulls together comprehensive data on eight crime indexes: murder and manslaughter; forcible rape; robbery; aggravated assault; burglary; larceny-theft; motor vehicle theft; and arson. The report is obviously useful in empowering law enforcement professionals and the public; it helps them to better understand and respond to criminal trends.

Conspicuously absent from this report, however, is an assessment of corporate crime. The report contains no statistics on the accounting, securities, and financial services crimes that have rocked the economy in the last two years. It does not list details on the litany of food safety violations, product safety violations, workplace safety violations, environmental pollution and countless other crimes that kill, injure and sicken millions of Americans each year . . . Because the FBI does not collect data on corporate crime, both the American public and the law enforcement community lack good information on what has become a pressing national problem—a corporate crime wave. Comprehensive data on corporate crime would help law enforcement officials to better analyze patterns and better direct resources. Information is also a powerful tool for public support of strong law enforcement, and the lack of it hampers your efforts to stay true to your tough words on corporate crime . . .

There is now a growing consensus that corporate crime is a mammoth problem threatening the stability of our economy and the security of millions of Americans. But how mammoth, exactly? This is what millions of Americans would like to know through official and authoritative sources from a government that should be acting to diminish such public dangers, not ignore them.

Mr. Ashcroft, if you are indeed serious about enforcing the rule of law fairly and justly in this country, we urge you to direct the FBI to expand its annual "Crime in the United States Report" to actually describe all the crime in the United States, not just street-level criminal activity. Corporate crime is a huge problem, with far more impact on society than street crime. The major media has recognized this point more and more in the past three years in headlines and cover stories and editorials. And with the help of more comprehensive data, we could gain an even better understanding of the problem, which is essential to solving it.

References

Anderson, Sarah, John Cavanagh, Scott Klinger, and Liz Stanton. 2005. "Executive Excess 2005: Defense Contractors Get More Bucks for the Bang." Washington, DC, and Boston: Institute for Policy Studies and United for a Fair Economy. August 30.

Associated Press. 2007. "Hard Times for U.S. Workers." *Forbes.* www.forbes.com/business/2007/07/25/labor-wage-bush-biz-cx_0726oxford.html

Barnett, Cynthia. n.d. "The Measurement of White-Collar Crime Using Uniform Crime Reporting (UCR) Data." Washington, DC: U.S. Department of Justice, Federal Bureau of Investigation. www.fbi.gov/ucr/whitecollarforweb.pdf.

Citizen Works. 2003. "A Letter to Attorney General Ashcroft on Corporate Crime Data." November 6. www.citizenworks.org/corp/ashcroft-letter.php.

Clayton Antitrust Act of 1914, Ch. 323, 38 Stat. 730, codified at 15 U.S.C. §12–27, 29 U.S.C. §52–53.

FBI. 2007. "White Collar Crime Program." www.columbia.fbi.gov/invest.htm.

The Federal Trade Commission Act of 1914. Title 15 U.S.C. §41–51.

Gonzales, Alberto R. 2007. Prepared Remarks of Attorney General Alberto R. Gonzales at the Corporate Fraud Task Force Fifth Anniversary Event. Washington, DC: U.S. Department of Justice. July 17. www.usdoj.gov/ag/speeches/2007/ag_speech_070717.html.

Inter-university Consortium for Political and Social Research. 2007a. "Monitoring of Federal Criminal Sentences, 2005: United States Sentencing Commission." Ann Arbor, MI: ICPSR. Study No. 4630.

Inter-university Consortium for Political and Social Research. 2007b. *National Incident-Based Reporting System, 2005.* Ann Arbor, MI: ICPSR. Study No. 4720.

Inter-university Consortium for Political and Social Research. 2007c. "Organizations Convicted in Federal Criminal Courts, 2005." Ann Arbor, MI: ICPSR. Study No. 4609.

Marks, Alexandra. 2006. "Prosecutions Drop for U.S. White-Collar Crime." *The Christian Science Monitor.* August 31.

McNulty, Paul J. 2006. Prepared Remarks of Deputy Attorney General Paul J. McNulty at the Lawyers for Civil Justice Membership Conference Regarding the Department's Charging Guidelines in Corporate Fraud Prosecutions. December 12. www.usdoj.gov/archive/dag/speeches/2006/dag_speech_061212.htm.

Mokhiber, Russell. 2004. "Top Ten Corporate and White Collar Crime Prosecutors List Released." *Corporate Crime Reporter,* August 13.

Mokhiber, Russell. 2003. "Webb, Keker, Weingarten, Sullivan, Bennett, Green Are Top White-Collar Criminal Defense Attorneys, Survey Shows." *Corporate Crime Reporter,* May 27.

Pastore, Ann L., and Kathleen Maguire, eds. *Sourcebook of Criminal Justice Statistics 2003.* www.albany.edu/sourcebook/.

Presidential Documents. 2002. Executive Order no. 13271. *Federal Register* 67, no. 133: July 11.

Reiman, Jeffrey. 2007. *The Rich Get Richer and the Poor Get Prison: Ideology, Class, and Criminal Justice.* 8th ed. Boston: Allyn and Bacon

Sarbanes-Oxley Act of 2002, Public Law 107–204, 116 Stat. 804.

The Sherman Antitrust Act of 1890.Ch. 647, 26 Stat. 209, codified at 15 U.S.C. §1–7.

Sutherland, Edwin, H. 1940. "White-Collar Criminality." *American Sociological Review* 5: 12.

Thompson, Larry D. 2002. "A Day with Justice." Speech of Deputy Attorney General Larry D. Thompson. Washington, DC: U.S. Department of Justice. October 28. www.usdoj.gov/archive/dag/speeches/2002/102802daywithjustice.htm.

Transactional Records Access Clearinghouse. 2007a. "Federal Judicial District: U.S. Number Prosecuted by Selected Major Crime Category." trac.syr.edu/tracreports/crim/136/include/table_4.html.

Transactional Records Access Clearinghouse. 2007b. "White Collar Crime Convictions for March 2007." trac.syr.edu/tracreports/bulletins/white_collar_crime/monthlymar07/gui/.

Transactional Records Access Clearinghouse. 2007c. "White Collar Crime Prosecutions for March 2007." trac.syr.edu/tracreports/bulletins/white_collar_crime/monthlymar07/fil/.

Uniform Crime Reports. 2006. *Crime in the United States, 2005.* Washington, DC: U.S. Department of Justice, Federal Bureau of Investigation.

United States Sentencing Guidelines Manual. 2005. Chapter 8. www.ussc.gov/.

U.S. Department of Commerce. 2007. "Gross Domestic Product: Fourth Quarter 2006 (Advance)." Washington, DC: Bureau of Economic Analysis. www.bea.gov/bea/newsrelarchive/2007/gdp406a.pdf.

7

Directory of Organizations

Corporate and white-collar offending have become increasingly significant in the minds of justice officials and the general public alike. With investors and shareholders losing life savings and retirement funds from such corporate scandals as those involving Enron, WorldCom, and their accounting firms, the public has demanded that more attention and resources be put in place to regulate and govern the economic interests of the American marketplace. Many nonprofit and public watchdog organizations have sprung up as a result of corporate malfeasance and government misconduct. The mass media is also backing this movement and has lobbied for the government to keep better records and statistics on offenders and offending in order to increase violators' accountability. Many Web sites report daily news on corruption, consumer fraud, securities fraud, embezzlement, tax evasion, environment-related crimes, and workforce and product-related safety issues. These online news organizations help publicize the frequency with which these events occur as well as the monetary loss associated with the offenses. Heightened awareness has, in turn, spurred the creation and implementation of a number of agencies charged with the apprehension of corporate wrongdoers and the prosecution of their acts.

This chapter presents descriptions of and contact information for a number of public and private organizations that deal with corporate offending. Some educate the public about the topic; others are in charge of investigation, apprehension, and prosecution of corporate offenders. Many of them have similar goals, objectives, and mission statements, although they are not likely to be working together or sharing information. An attempt has been made here to provide the most recent and up-to-date information available on these organizations. Some are relatively new while others have been around for decades.

American Antitrust Institute (AAI)
www.antitrustinstitute.org

The American Antitrust Institute is a nonprofit research organization based in Washington, D.C. Its mission is to oversee competition in the economic sphere, to be sure that corporations are working with the best interests of consumers in mind, and to dispute instances of abuse in both the American and world economies. AAI began in 1998 primarily because there were no public interest organizations dedicated to the antitrust arena. The institute believes that—due to ever-growing abuses of corporate power and the new global economy—there is an increased need for organizations that support more balanced and fair competitive economic policies. AAI is a champion of the competitive economic marketplace and a strong advocate for increased enforcement of laws relating to antitrust abuses. Public resources devoted to antitrust issues have diminished since the mid-1980s. One role of the AAI is to act as a notification system for any efforts designed to reduce the role of antitrust issues. The AAI Web site provides useful information about antitrust for professionals with an interest in the field, whether journalists, researchers, businesspeople, or government officials. It also features links to resources available for the general public and students interested in learning about anticompetitive practices and a working paper series that contains scholarly papers on antitrust topics.

Antitrust Modernization Commission (AMC)
www.amc.gov

The Antitrust Modernization Commission no longer exists, but its Web site serves as an archive for important information on antitrust laws. The bipartisan commission was originally created as a part of the Antitrust Modernization Commission Act of 2002 and consisted of four appointees each chosen by the president, the Senate, and the House of Representatives. Its goals were to study current antitrust laws with an eye toward modernizing them, to assess suggestions and planning of issues surrounding antitrust laws, and to draft and present reports to Congress and the president. Reports of the commission are available on its Web site.

Center for Corporate Policy
www.corporatepolicy.org

According to its Web site, the Center for Corporate Policy is "a non-profit, non-partisan public interest organization working to curb corporate abuses and make corporations publicly accountable." The center's Web site provides ample information on current corporate crime issues, stories in the news regarding corporate crime, as well as information on how the public can become involved in the fight against corporate crime and political corruption. Links to related stories and papers are also included, and the site has a virtual library containing lists of recommended readings.

Corporate Fraud Task Force (CFTF)
www.usdoj.gov/dag/cftf

The Corporate Fraud Task Force is led by the deputy attorney general of the United States and is made up of U.S. attorneys, FBI agents, and representatives of the Securities and Exchange Commission (SEC). It focuses its efforts on investigating and prosecuting corporate criminal activity. The task force was established by President George W. Bush on July 9, 2002, in the wake of numerous corporate fraud and accounting scandals in which investors and shareholders lost billions. It is made up of two groups: one from the U.S. Department of Justice, which concentrates its efforts on enhancing criminal enforcement and prevention activities regarding corporate wrongdoing, and the other from representatives of many agencies to maximize cooperation among enforcement and regulatory agencies working on cases of corporate crime. The task force has issued annual reports to the president and to Congress each year since its inception; results indicate that there has been increased prosecution and punishment of corporate offenders. The Corporate Fraud Task Force Web page, a part of the U.S. Department of Justice's Web site, provides information on any legislation, speeches, testimony, or documents related to corporate offending. The site also provides links to internship opportunities, information about the Freedom of Information Act, and background on the No FEAR Act, a federal antidiscrimination and whistleblower law.

The Council of Europe
www.coe.int

The Council of Europe was founded in 1949 as an organization of European states, and a few nations outside of Europe, seeking to develop universal and democratic principles throughout Europe. The council aims to protect human rights, pluralist democracies and the rule of law, as well as advance awareness, and encouragement, of cultural identity and diversity in Europe. Its member states work together to find solutions to the problems plaguing European society. Some of the issues worked on thus far include: intolerance of difference, discrimination against minorities, human trafficking, terrorism, bioethics, violence against children, and organized crime and corruption. The council also supports political, legislative, and constitutional reform. The Council of Europe's current political mandate was defined in 2005, in Warsaw, Poland. The Council of Europe is made up of the Committee of Ministers (the decision-making body), the Parliamentary Assembly (a group of 636 members facilitating European co-operation), and the Congress of Local and Regional Authorities (the voice of the regions and municipalities). In 2007, the budget of the Council of Europe was 197,214,000 euros. The Council of Europe makes many of its publications available on its Web site, which also contains a list of the council's newsletters. Recent work by the Council of Europe includes overseeing the European Court of Human Rights' judgments concerning rights to fair trial, fair treatment, self-expression, and religion in countries throughout Europe.

Department of Justice Antitrust Division
www.usdoj.gov/atr

The Antitrust Division of the U.S. Department of Justice is a governmental agency whose mission is to advance the American economy and safeguard competition in a free market by enforcing the nation's antitrust laws. The division is responsible for the prosecution of those who violate antitrust laws, some of which include: conspiracy, price fixing, monopolistic practices, and any other acts that restrain trade or competition. Antitrust laws apply to most sectors of business in the United States, and as trade and business mergers increase, the Antitrust Division sees an increased number of cases for investigation. The division works closely with other agencies like the Federal Trade Commission and foreign antitrust agencies in both investigative and prosecutorial efforts. Its Web site includes links to press releases regarding antitrust offenses, alerts for the public of any fraudulent or deceptive practices by organizations, resources on the rights of businesses and victims, and a citizen complaint center where the public can report possible antitrust violations or file complaints against businesses.

Federal Trade Commission (FTC)
www.ftc.gov

The Federal Trade Commission is the federal agency responsible for upholding competition and consumer protection in the United States. The FTC was created in 1914 as an agency charged with maintenance of a fair and competitive marketplace for businesses and consumers. Labels on everything we buy—from washing instructions on items of clothing to energy consumption rates on new household appliances—are regulated by the FTC. The commission's duties range from guarding against price fixing to ensuring equal credit opportunity to enforcing telemarketing rules. The FTC is the only federal agency responsible for both effective law enforcement and the advancement of the interests of consumers. The commission cooperates and shares knowledge with many federal, state, and international government agencies; it also develops policy and tools for research. In 1975, the FTC was given authority by Congress to adopt trade regulation rules for industry. The FTC reports to Congress about its work and is headed by five commissioners who serve for terms of seven years. These commissioners are nominated by the president and confirmed by the Senate. The FTC is divided into three key bureaus: the Bureau of Competition, the Bureau of Economics, and the Bureau of Consumer Protection. The Bureau of Consumer Protection's mandate is to educate and protect consumers against unfair, deceptive, or fraudulent practices, including false advertising claims. It investigates individual companies as well as entire industries and is responsible for administrative rule enforcement and federal court litigation. The FTC has produced award-winning print and online publications and maintains the

Web site www.consumer.gov. This site provides consumer information on electronic banking, online shopping, identity theft, and dozens of other topics with the help of four other agencies: the Food and Drug Administration, the Securities and Exchange Commission, the Consumer Product Safety Commission, and the National Highway Traffic Safety Administration.

The International Monetary Fund (IMF)
www.imf.org

The International Monetary Fund is a multinational organization headquartered in Washington, D.C., consisting of 185 member countries. It supports monetary cooperation on a global scale to facilitate economic growth and increase employment around the world. The IMF has three main duties that include: (1) surveillance of economic and financial development, (2) lending of money to countries to help relieve debt and reduce poverty, and (3) providing technical assistance and training to those countries needing advice and expertise in the areas of finance and development. The IMF has also set forth standards and codes of conduct for prevention of financial crises and for strengthening world financial systems. As such, the IMF supports the compilation of research and statistics concerning world financial problems. The organization issues annual reports on its projects and publishes the *World Economic Outlook* and the *Global Financial Stability Report*. Additionally, the IMF Web site is a warehouse that maintains data and statistics about lending and development activities throughout the world.

Internet Crime Complaint Center (IC3)
www.ic3.gov

The Internet Crime Complaint Center, formerly called the Internet Fraud Complaint Center, is a service center set up for victims of cybercrime. The center was established as a partnership between the National White Collar Crime Center and the Federal Bureau of Investigation in order to receive and refer complaints to the appropriate agencies regarding violations of the law. IC3 has received numerous cybercrime complaints, including reports of identity theft, hacking, intellectual property rights violations, economic espionage, and international money laundering. The center also issues annual reports of information on complaints received through their Web site.

INTERPOL
www.interpol.int

INTERPOL—the International Criminal Police Organization—is the largest police organization in the world. Comprised of 186 member countries, it was established in 1923 to foster cooperation between police agencies around the world. INTERPOL uses the Universal Declaration of Human Rights as its foundation for law enforcement support, but it also respects the limits of existing laws in its various member countries. The constitution of the organization does not allow interventions of a political, religious, military, or racial character. INTERPOL's organizational structure includes a general assembly, an executive committee, a general secretariat, national census bureaus, and advisers. The organization focuses its efforts on securing communication services for police around the world, maintaining databases for police, and overseeing support services for police. Its communications system, called I-24/7, gives police agencies throughout the world a platform to share information about crime and criminals. INTERPOL's numerous databases link police agencies to global information on stolen goods and to profiles of known criminals. A 24-hour command and coordination center is also run by the organization to support police agencies.

The Latin American Centre for Development Administration
www.clad.org.ve

The Latin American Centre for Development Administration (CLAD) was established in 1972 by the governments of Mexico, Peru, and Venezuela. CLAD acts as an agency of intergovernmental collaboration. It is recognized as a regional agency that promotes the modernization of public administration throughout Latin America. CLAD links member countries with the research and teaching institutions of Europe, the United States, and Canada. The organization supports many missions, including the promotion of knowledge exchange between countries about state reform. Many nations have joined CLAD since its founding. The heads of government of CLAD have expressed their commitment to progress in the civil service arena and have signed treaties with other multilateral and bilateral organizations with the goal of creating global cooperation.

National Association of Criminal Defense Lawyers (NACDL)
nacdl.org

The mission of the National Association of Criminal Defense Lawyers (NACDL) is to ensure justice and due process for persons accused of crime; to foster the integrity, independence, and expertise of the criminal defense profession; and to promote the proper and fair administration of criminal justice. The NACDL is a professional bar association that was founded in 1958. It has roughly 12,800 members and 94 state, local, and international organizations with an additional 35,000 members. Members include public defenders, private criminal defense attorneys, active U.S. military defense counsel, judges, and law professors. According to its Web site, the association promotes a "rational and humane criminal justice policy" at all levels of federal, state, and local government—specifically, a criminal justice system that encourages fairness for everyone, due process for those accused of violations of law, concern for both victims and witnesses of crime, and just punishment for those found guilty. The NACDL's mission gives reverence to the civil rights and liberties that are a fundamental part of the democracy of the United States. Members of the NACDL direct society to avoid simple crime prevention solutions such as inflexible mandatory sentencing, punishment of juveniles as adults, and the trampling of the constitutional rights of all because of the actions of a few. The Web site of the NACDL acts as an open forum to discuss criminal justice practice and policy. The organization has recently appointed a director of its White Collar Crime Project whose main duties are to oversee the over-criminalization and over-federalization of white-collar offending.

National White Collar Crime Center (NW3C)
www.nw3c.org

The mission of National White Collar Crime Center is to provide a nationwide support system for agencies involved in preventing, investigating, and prosecuting economic and high-tech crimes and to support and partner with other appropriate entities in addressing homeland security initiatives as they relate to economic and high-tech crimes. The center is a congressionally funded, nonprofit corporation that equips state and local law enforcement agencies with the skills and resources they need to undertake emerging economic and cybercrime problems. It also provides information to the general public so that citizens can become proactive in the prevention of these types of crimes. Victims can visit the center's Web site for information on registering Internet crime complaints and notifying the appropriate authorities at local, state, and federal levels promptly, accurately, and securely of the offenses committed against them. NW3C also provides global, national, and regional conferences and workshops on the latest techniques and information for investigation and prosecution of white-collar crimes. NW3C believes that through conferences, beneficial networks can be set up consisting of law enforcement, prosecutors, regulators, and other professionals, as well as researchers, educators, and advocates, in order to receive information on programs and disseminate best practices that address all facets of white-collar crime.

Organization for Competitive Markets (OCM)
www.competitivemarkets.com

The Organization for Competitive Markets is a nonprofit, nationally based public policy research organization. The main office is in Lincoln, Nebraska, and its purpose is to reinforce competitive markets for rural America and farmers and ranchers. Focusing mainly on trade policies and antitrust issues in the agricultural sector, the organization wishes to carry on the legacy of Theodore Roosevelt by upholding antitrust laws and supporting true competition and entrepreneurship. The organization also campaigns for government to take a proper role in regulating the market and enforcing the rules when necessary in order to make markets fair and accessible to all citizens. OCM is especially concerned about antitrust issues, fair trade, and competition in today's increasingly global marketplace, which threatens national sovereignty and increases the strength of global agribusinesses. OCM believes that the goal for America is to regain competitive markets in agriculture for farmers, ranchers, and rural communities. The organization has undertaken an extensive program of disseminating information and knowledge about the American tradition of free market principles. The organization maintains a monthly newsletter of important events and ideas regarding competition and trade. Members of the staff of OCM discuss and comment on current issues in annual meetings and on weekly radio programs broadcast in agricultural communities.

The Organization of American States (OAS)
www.oas.org

The Organization of American States is made up of Western Hemisphere nations that seek to strengthen cooperation, debate some of the major concerns of the region and the world, and defend common interests. OAS objectives include promoting human rights, strengthening democracies, and combating problems such as poverty, terrorism, narcotics, and corruption. OAS recognizes four official languages—English, Spanish, Portuguese, and French—and is made up of 35 member states, including the independent nations of North, Central, and South America and the Caribbean. Cuba, however, has been banned from participation since 1962. The OAS member countries establish policies and goals through their General Assembly, which gathers once every year.

The United States Securities and Exchange Commission
www.sec.gov

The SEC's mission is to protect investors and promote fair and efficient markets through market regulation. The SEC was established by Congress in 1934 to enforce securities laws and protect investors. One of the SEC's mandates is to ensure that public companies make their financial records public. The U.S. laws and rules governing the securities industry were designed to make sure that all investors have access to facts about investments before going ahead with them. The SEC works with many agencies to see that this mandate is met.

The SEC provides oversight of many areas of the securities market: securities exchanges, mutual funds, brokers and dealers, and investment advisors. Every year, the SEC brings civil enforcements against companies and individuals for violations such as insider trading, providing false information, and accounting fraud. The SEC maintains a Web site where the public can access important information assisting them in navigating the investment market. The SEC has five commissioners who are appointed by the president, four divisions, and 18 offices. It is headquartered in Washington, D.C., with 11 regional offices and approximately 3,100 staff.

White Collar Crime Research Consortium (WCCRC)

www.nw3c.org/research/white_collar_crime_consortium.cfm

The White Collar Crime Research Consortium is the research arm of the National White Collar Crime Center. This group uses research and studies to promote increased public awareness about the effects of white-collar and corporate offending for society. Specifically, it encourages the membership of individuals interested in developing and enhancing research on white-collar and corporate offending. Its mission is to highlight the importance and need for increased research as well as funding sources to support this research.

World Bank

worldbank.org

The World Bank is an institution devoted to assisting developing countries with financial and technical issues with the objective of reducing poverty around the globe. Another goal is to improve living standards for those in many of the poorest countries. The bank provides grants, low-interest loans, and interest-free credit for infrastructure, education, health, and other uses to developing countries. The World Bank is actually comprised of two development institutions: the International Bank for Reconstruction and Development (IBRD) and the International Development Association (IDA). The former focuses on middle-income countries and the latter focuses on the poorest of countries. The World Bank is headquartered in Washington, D.C., but it has over 100 offices in countries around the globe. It was established on July 1, 1944, and now employs roughly 10,000 people worldwide. Generally, the governors of the member states are ministers of finance or ministers of development in each country. They convene annually at the meetings of the boards of governors of the World Bank Group and the International Monetary Fund. On July 1, 2007, Robert B. Zoellick became president of the World Bank; it is his duty to chair the meetings and manage the bank. Traditionally, the bank president is a U.S. citizen, nominated by the United States because it is the World Bank's largest shareholder. In 2006, the World Bank provided $23.6 billion for 279 projects.

World Trade Organization (WTO)
www.wto.org

The World Trade Organization is a global organization head-quartered in Geneva, Switzerland. It is made up of 150 member nations and oversees global trade. First and foremost, the WTO deals with the rules surrounding trade on a global scale. It is also an advocate for the liberalization of trade, a negotiator for governments wishing to do trade with one another, and a forum where trade disputes can be settled. The WTO began in 1995; before its inception, the General Agreement on Tariffs and Trade (GATT) laid forth the rule dealing with trade. The WTO is run by its member governments and decisions are made by consensus. The WTO negotiates, makes decisions, and even imposes sanctions regarding trade through its member delegates. In this way, the power of the organization is not entrusted to one head official or board of directors. The WTO's chief objective is to ensure that trade flows smoothly, freely, and fairly. The WTO is headed by a director general and has roughly 637 staff. It has no branch offices outside of Switzerland. The WTO's annual budget is approximately 182 million Swiss francs.

Member countries can raise disputes at the WTO if they believe their rights have been infringed upon under current trade agreements. Settlements are made by independent experts who are appointed to interpret the correct action under the agreements. This method pushes countries to consult with each other first to attempt a settlement, and then seek the help of the WTO. The WTO has settled over 300 cases in the last decade. The WTO also holds hundreds of training sessions and conferences every year to help developing countries with issues and technical assistance, and it holds trade policy courses for government officials every year in Geneva. The organization has set up over 100 reference centers in the capital cities of the least developed and developing countries, giving them access to the resources and latest developments of the WTO.

8

Resources

Resource materials in print about corporate crime are slowly becoming more widely published and available, although compared to other criminal justice topics, resources about corporate and white-collar crime are limited. This chapter lists key resources devoted to the topic: books, journal articles, dissertations, magazines, newsletters, government documents, and agency publications. Books include texts and scholarly pieces that feature topics related to corporate and white-collar crime. Journal articles are usually research studies on various aspects of white-collar and corporate offending written to enhance our knowledge of current issues. Doctoral dissertations or theses are also important sources of information because they are usually empirical studies that are eventually converted to books or journal articles. The end of the list offers some nonprint resources as well, including videos, DVDs, and Web site URLs.

Many agencies, most of which were mentioned in the previous chapter, also collect information about topics related to white-collar and corporate criminal offending. Governmental and nonprofit organizations often publish reports and information sheets on statistics they have collected and trends they have observed. These reports keep administration officials informed of progress and problems related to prevention, enforcement, and prosecution of corporate offending and governmental fraud, waste, or abuse. They are usually available at the organizations' Web sites, or they can be requested from governmental offices (sometimes a small fee may be required to purchase the document). Finally, there are also various resources that are available on DVD or in VHS format. These are most often advertised to academic institutions for the purpose of classroom instruction.

Print Resources

Books

Albanese, Jay S. *White Collar Crime in America*. 1995. Upper Saddle River, NJ: Prentice Hall. 320 pages.

This textbook presents material on white-collar crime in a very clear and precise manner. The book defines white-collar crime and divides different crime types into three categories: crimes of fraud, regulatory offenses, and crimes against public administration. It also cites statistics on the nature and extent of white-collar offending, as well as data on enforcement, prosecution, and sentencing of white-collar criminal offenders. This text is unique in that it deals with white-collar offending in the same manner that other criminal justice texts portray street offending.

Blankenship, Michael B., ed. *Understanding Corporate Criminality*. 1995. New York: Garland. 266 pages.

This book is a collection of original works by a number of white-collar and corporate crime scholars. Articles range from problems with understanding corporate crime to measurement issues surrounding corporate crime to the regulation and punishment of corporate criminal behavior. It covers a wide range of the most important issues in this field.

Brickley, Kathleen F. *Corporate and White Collar Crime: Cases and Materials*. 2006. New York: Aspen Publishers. 755 pages.

This book deals with corporate criminal liability, intent, organizations, definitions of participation and management, as well as white-collar and corporate offenses themselves. It also gives information regarding different types of corporate and white-collar offending from fraud to the environment. In addition, it outlines material and cases on investigation, governance, and sentencing and punishment of white-collar and corporate wrongdoing.

Coleman, James W. *The Criminal Elite: Understanding White-Collar Crime*. 2005. New York: Worth Publishers. 352 pages.

This book takes advantage of the fact that white-collar and corporate offending are receiving greater attention from the media and the public. It provides a look into the most prevalent forms and causes of white-collar offending, as well as the repercussions for American society. It also provides readers with updated statistics, research, and information on new laws.

Fisse, Brent, and John Braithwaite. *Corporations, Crime, and Accountability.* **1993. New York: Cambridge University Press. 289 pages.**

This book looks at various corporate behaviors and the harm they cause. The authors pose thought-provoking questions such as: Who should be held responsible in these cases? Should it be the individual actor? Or should the corporation also be held accountable? The writers also note that accountability is seldom enforced by the law and proffer remedies that would include imputing accountability to a wider range of persons.

Fraser, Jill A. *White Collar Sweat-Shop: The Deterioration of Work and Its Rewards in Corporate America.* **2001. New York: W. W. Norton. 279 pages.**

This book provides insight into how corporate mergers, takeovers, and buyouts have made financial goals more important than any other aspect of doing business. The author outlines what this means for the workforce in corporate America: benefit reduction, layoffs, and cutting of costs. Specifically, Fraser looks at the banking, technology, and communications industries and at sector trends within power structures. She says that management and CEOs are getting more powerful, while the workforce has been left with little influence and a lot of stress. The book shows that many of our so-called "white-collar" employees do not have the high salaries or good benefits that we believe they do. This book is similar to others in the past that have attempted to show how changes in industry affect each section of the workforce.

Friedrichs, David O. *Trusted Criminals: White Collar Crime in Contemporary Society.* **2006. Belmont, CA: Wadsworth. 464 pages.**

This book clearly and comprehensively explains the key issues involved in the study of white-collar crime. These include: theories for explaining offending, the role of the media, whistleblowers' and news reporters' responsibilities, policing and prosecuting, and policy responses to white-collar crimes and criminals.

Gaines, Larry K., Richard Ball, and David Shichor, eds. *Readings in White-Collar Crime.* 2001. Long Grove, IL: Waveland Press. 400 pages.

This book is an edited work of 18 articles published together to give readers an increased understanding of the issues surrounding white-collar crime, the consequences it has for society, and what can be done by way of deterrence and prevention. These articles deal with issues such as: How is white-collar crime defined? What does white-collar offending say about the society in which it exists? What has the criminal justice system done in response to white-collar offending and offenders? And is there a difference between white-collar and street-level offending?

Geis, Gilbert. *White-Collar and Corporate Crime.* 2007. Upper Saddle River, NJ: Prentice Hall. 100 pages.

This book is part of Prentice Hall's Masters Series in Criminology and presents a brief and easily understandable introduction to topics in criminology, in this case, white-collar and corporate crime. The authors in this series have forged the way to a better understanding of issues that provide the foundations for modern criminology.

Gerber, Jurg, and Eric Jensen, eds. *Encyclopedia of White-Collar Crime.* 2006. Portsmouth, NH: Greenwood Press. 336 pages.

This encyclopedia covers currents events such as recent corporate scandals and their players, and it also highlights important incidents that helped shape the history of white-collar crime. It features descriptions of 200 persons, places, events, corporations, and laws relating to various facets of white-collar crime.

Gray, Kenneth R., Larry A. Freider, and George W. Clark. *Corporate Scandals: The Many Faces of Greed.* St. Paul, MN: Paragon House. 307 pages.

This book focuses on the nature of corporate scandals. It looks at the history of corporate offending in various realms as well as the attempts by government to respond to corporate criminal activity. It reveals the extent of business impropriety and unethical behavior, offers advice for what the government can do to address future corporate criminal activity, and looks at the impact these issues have for the business community. This book is an excellent source for how businesses in the United States should be functioning. The authors provide insight into what corporate America needs to do in order to regain trust lost by scandals throughout history.

Green, Gary S. *Occupational Crime.* **1997. Chicago: Nelson-Hall. 329 pages.**

This book focuses on crime in the workplace and takes a different stance than most other white-collar crime books by showing that occupational crime is committed by employees of all different types, not just the elite. The author presents a definition of occupational crime and discusses four different categories: individual occupational crime, organizational occupational crime, professional occupational crime, and state authority crime. The book also discusses theories behind this type of deviance as well as research, policy, legal issues, and case studies.

Green, Stuart P. *Lying, Cheating, and Stealing: A Moral Theory of White-Collar Crime.* **2007. New York: Oxford University Press. 306 pages.**

The premise of this book is that our ideas of white-collar versus conventional offenders and offending provide two very divergent pictures. It can be difficult to differentiate between lawful and unlawful behaviors and between criminal and civil matters. What is the difference between criminal fraud and tax evasion? What is the difference between obstruction of justice and zealously defending a client? These are some of the questions this book brings to the fore in an attempt to show that uncertainty still permeates the idea of what constitutes white-collar offending. The author tries to ameliorate some of the confusion by examining what types of behavior warrant criminal sanction.

Leap, Terry L. *Dishonest Dollars: The Dynamics of White-Collar Crime.* **2007. Ithaca, NY: Cornell University Press. 243 pages.**

This book looks at various aspects of corporate behavior and offending and takes a more integrated approach to explaining it. The author believes that by using various disciplines from business and public policy to psychology and sociology, we can gain a better understanding of criminal behavior within the business sector. He includes many examples of different types of offending and concludes that there are many similarities between white-collar and conventional criminal offending.

Lewis, Roy V. *White Collar Crime and Offenders: A 20-Year Longitudinal Cohort Study.* **2002. Lincoln, NE: Writers Club Press. 232 pages.**

This book is based on a longitudinal study conducted over 20 years involving a cohort of both street offenders and white-collar criminal offenders. It analyzes data from more than 17,000 offenders followed from 1973 to 1993. Results of the study shed light on patterns of behavior, frequency of arrest and charging, and specialization of offenders in certain types of offenses.

Lynch, Nancy K., and Michael J. Lynch. *Corporate Crime, Corporate Violence: A Primer.* **1992. Albany, NY: Harrow and Heston. 176 pages.**

This is a revised edition of an earlier book called *Crimes against Health and Safety.* It breaks down popular myths associated with traditional reporting of crime in the country, revealing that corporate crime costs more in monetary loss and lives lost than street-level offenses. The actions of corporations often harm America's workforce, consumers, and the public in general. Sometimes what we have labeled an accident should have been prosecuted as a criminal offense. The authors analyze numerous cases of corporate wrongdoing (crime and violence), offer possible reasons for why they occurred, describe the impact of prosecution, and suggest what might be done to avoid future episodes of these crimes.

Michalowski, Raymond J., and Ronald C. Kramer, eds. *State-Corporate Crime: Wrongdoing at the Intersection of Business and Government.* **2006. Piscataway, NJ: Rutgers University Press. 298 pages.**

This book features 15 different articles relating to state corporate crime. The main theme is that those persons in positions of power, whether political or economic, often work in concert and collaborate in the name of profit and political advantage— typically at the expense of the general public. The essays recount incidents of wrongdoing that resulted in harmful and deleterious consequences. The book reminds readers that the greatest threat to the public comes not from conventional crimes but from the corrupt practices of those most powerful and those in the upper echelon of society.

Pontell, Henry N., and Gilbert Geis, eds. *International Handbook of White-Collar and Corporate Crime.* **2007. New York: Springer. 702 pages.**

This handbook includes 34 articles written on various topics related to white-collar and corporate crime. The contributors come from nine different countries, and each one adds a different dynamic to the literature on white-collar and corporate offending. Some of the articles are case studies, others are historical analyses, others still report on legal perspectives or theoretical underpinnings in explaining this type of crime. Many of the pieces discuss enforcement issues, including the roles of the government, the criminal justice system, the media, and corporations themselves.

Poveda, Tony G. *Rethinking White-Collar Crime.* **1994. Westport, CT: Praeger. 184 pages.**

This book acts as an overview and synthesis of some of the research on white-collar crime. The author contends that learning about white-collar crime also lends insight into issues about crime and criminal justice at the conventional level. He also provides a new definition of white-collar offending and encourages critical thought about our current system of justice and the nature of criminal offending.

Rosoff, Stephen, Henry Pontell, and Robert Tillman. *Profit without Honor: White Collar Crime and the Looting of America.* **2007. Upper Saddle River, NJ: Prentice Hall. 624 pages.**

This book examines the conflict between personal gain and individual integrity and the consequences for white-collar criminal offending in the United States. It looks at several high-profile cases and analyzes trends regarding offending, victimization, and corollary consequences for society.

Salinger, Lawrence M., ed. *Encyclopedia of White-Collar and Corporate Crime*. 2004. Thousand Oaks, CA: Sage. 1,016 pages.

This encyclopedia includes nearly 500 entries on individuals, places, events, corporations, crimes, and scandals related to white-collar and corporate offending. It also has entries on different types of immoral behavior as well as coverage of suspicious events that were not investigated by law enforcement officials, such as the Space Shuttle *Challenger* disaster.

Shover, Neal, and Andrew Hochstetler. *Choosing White-Collar Crime*. 2006. New York: Cambridge University Press. 272 pages.

The authors state that rational choice theory has been widely used to explain traditional street offending and has been the impetus behind increased crime control efforts as well as the implementation of sanctions that are more harsh. They report, however, that this theory has not been applied as broadly in explanations of white-collar offending and crimes of the upper class. The authors purport that if the same stance were taken against white-collar crime as has been taken against more conventional criminal behaviors, we might see increased progress toward deterrence. They believe that policy on corporate criminal wrongdoing will be of the utmost importance in the coming years with increases in the global economy. They call for increased oversight as well as harder lines taken by citizens' rights groups to thwart white-collar offending.

Simon, David R. *Elite Deviance*. 2006. Boston: Allyn and Bacon. 372 pages.

This book explains elite deviance as a product of the power structure and wealth distribution in the United States. It contains information on both criminal and noncriminal actions that are damaging to society. The authors cite public opinion polls that reveal the extent to which the American populace lacks confidence in business and governmental practices. They also examine serious malfeasance, analyze the recent wave of corporate scandals, and propose some remedies to help alleviate the social suffering caused by these events.

Simpson, Sally, S. *Corporate Crime, Law, and Social Control.* **2002. Cambridge, UK: Cambridge University Press. 192 pages.**

This book asks whether a change in the criminal law emphasizing punishment and shame would work as a way to curb and control corporate crime. The author examines whether our current system of dealing with corporate offending—whether criminal, civil, or regulatory—is really a deterrent to this behavior. She concludes that strict criminalization will not lead to compliance, and that cooperative models probably work best. She does, however, stress that punishment must be used jointly with cooperative prosecution models.

Sutherland, Edwin, H. *White Collar Crime.* **1949. New York: Holt, Rinehart and Winston.**

This is Sutherland's seminal work on white-collar crime, in which he attempts to define and explain this type of criminal behavior. In it, he touts his own differential association theory as an explanation for the causes of white-collar offending. He focuses on the social position of the persons involved in these activities, emphasizing the actor rather than the act. This is the first book devoted solely to white-collar crime and has been the impetus for numerous books, articles, and other works that followed it.

Williams, Howard F. *Investigating White-Collar Crime: Embezzlement and Financial Fraud.* **2006. Springfield, IL: Charles C. Thomas. 346 pages.**

This book begins with a definition of white-collar offending and discusses the varying types of behaviors included under that heading. It then gives examples of offenses such as fraud and embezzlement and discusses problems with the investigation of them. The author integrates accounting and auditing theory in a discussion of techniques for the investigation of financial crimes. A portion of the book is devoted to interviewing strategies for investigators to help uncover any wrongdoing. It finishes with a discussion of documented evidence as well as strategies for proving illicit transactions and methods for preparing reports and cases for court.

Journal Articles

Boss, Barry. "Sentencing in White Collar Cases: Time Does Not Heal All Wounds." 2000. *Federal Sentencing Reporter* 13: 15–18. This article uses 1997 data from the United States Sentencing Commission to examine sentencing practices for white-collar offenders. It discusses issues related to sentencing guidelines for federal offenders.

Holtfreter, Kristy. "Is Occupational Fraud 'Typical' White-Collar Crime? A Comparison of Individual and Organizational Characteristics." 2005. *Journal of Criminal Justice* 33: 353–65.

This study used 1,142 occupational fraud cases and compared organizational victim characteristics and offender characteristics for three types of fraud: corruption, asset misappropriation, and fraudulent statements. The results show that there were characteristic differences between persons committing corruption and asset misappropriation compared to those who committed fraudulent statements. Furthermore, organizations victimized by corruption fit the traditional literature's view of a large, for-profit company, whereas those victimized by the other two offenses had different characteristics.

Lynch, Michael, Danielle McGurrin, and Melissa Fenwick. "Disappearing Act: The Representation of Corporate Crime Research in Criminological Literature." 2004. *Journal of Criminal Justice* 32: 389–98.

This article looks at the two divergent assumptions among criminologists regarding the frequency with which articles on white-collar and corporate offenses appear in the literature. The argument is that criminologists in general believe that the subject is adequately represented; however, those conducting research on corporate and white-collar offending believe that their topics still lack sufficient coverage in the criminological literature. These authors utilized three methods to gauge the prevalence of corporate crime research: interviews with criminology departments to determine whether they offer courses in these topics, analyses of textbooks to gauge coverage of the topic, and content analysis of journals in criminal justice for five years. The authors then compared the coverage on this topic to article and textbook coverage on other issues in criminology.

**Passas, Nikos. "Lawful but Awful: 'Legal Corporate Crime.'"
2005. *Journal of Socio-Economics* 34: 771–86.**

In this article, the author purports that serious threats to society are not given priority when authorities focus on behaviors that are only officially criminal or illegal. Basically, the author notes that there is some corporate behavior that is not illegal yet has serious consequences for society. This article also looks at the role of the state and deregulation in perpetuating misconduct by corporations.

Piquero, Nicole Leeper, Stephen G. Tibbetts, and Michael B. Blankenship. "Examining the Role of Differential Association and Techniques of Neutralization in Explaining Corporate Crime." 2005. *Deviant Behavior* 26: 159–88.

This article examines the extent to which differential association theory and techniques of neutralization theory can explain corporate crime etiology. The authors studied 133 MBA students' attitudes toward offending behaviors related to the marketing and sale of a pharmaceutical drug. Findings revealed that agreement to wrongdoing by other employees and management in a company makes it more likely that students may engage in inappropriate corporate behavior. Findings counter to a differential association explanation, however, were also found. Results also show that neutralization techniques play an important role in offending, especially for older persons and if profit is involved.

Recine, Jennifer S. "Examination of the White Collar Crime Penalty Enhancements in the Sarbanes-Oxley Act." 2002. *American Criminal Law Review* 39: 1535–70.

This study looks at whether giving white-collar criminals longer sentences will remedy some of the corporate criminal offending the United States is experiencing. It looks at the business events that occurred in 2001 and 2002 with a description of the Sarbanes-Oxley Act and the political processes that led to its passage. The author concludes that white-collar offenders rarely pay penalties that are proportional to the losses involved in their acts, and that longer punishment may not deter them, but it is necessary for the criminal justice system to have options to hold culpable individuals responsible for their actions.

Rosenmerkel, Sean P. 2001. "Wrongfulness and Harmfulness as Components of Seriousness of White-Collar Offenses." *Journal of Contemporary Criminal Justice* 17: 308–27.

This article examines perceptions of crime seriousness by comparing rankings for white-collar offenses with rankings for traditional street crimes. The author contends that white-collar offenses will be rated as less serious.

Schanzenback, Max, and Michael L. Yeager. 2006. "Prison Time, Fines, and Federal White-Collar Criminals: The Anatomy of a Racial Disparity." *Journal of Criminal Law and Criminology* 96: 757–93.

This article looks at race and sex disparities for white-collar criminal sentences. Data come from the United States Sentencing Commission. The authors focus on the fact that white-collar offenses are typically nonviolent and economic in nature and that alternative punishments such as fines can open the door for increased judicial discretion. Controlling for all other characteristics, the authors find large racial and ethnic disparity where blacks and Hispanics are punished more harshly than whites. They attribute some of this disparity to the ability of whites to pay fines. Disparities regarding sex are present as well and results show that males are punished more harshly than females, all else being equal.

Schoepfer, Andrea, Stephanie Carmichael, and Nicole Leeper Piquero. 2007. "Do Perceptions of Punishment Vary Between White-Collar and Street Crimes?" *Journal of Criminal Justice* 35: 151–63.

This study uses data from a national probability sample to look at whether the perceptions of the certainty and severity of sanctions are the same for white-collar crime as for street crime. The authors studied robbery and fraud as the street level and white-collar offenses and found that although street-level offenders are perceived as being more likely to get caught and punished, respondents did not feel that one type of crime deserved harsher punishment than the other.

Dissertations

Chopra, Parveen C. "Organizational and Environmental Correlates of OSHA Violations in Selected Industries: An Exploratory Study." 1997. Ann Arbor, MI: University Microfilms International. 222 pages.

This dissertation explores both the organizational and environmental factors that may contribute to corporate violation of OSHA laws. The study was conducted on both large and small, public and private companies and their compliance with industry standards. Among the variables that had significant influence were corporate negative growth rate, number of OSHA inspections and long term debt ratio, all of which had positive effects, on likelihood to offend.

Gibbs, Carole E. "Corporate Citizenship, Sanctions, and Environmental Crime." 2006. Ann Arbor, MI: University Microfilms International. 280 pages.

This dissertation looks at three different subject areas: corporate citizenship, the environment, and corporate crime. It points out that traditional research on corporate crime leaves out measures of environmental crime. It looks at environmental performances of businesses to explain engagement in environmental criminal activity. The study concludes that the addition of corporate citizenship is negligible in an understanding of the environmental practices of a business.

Jamieson, Katherine Marie. "Corporate Crime and Organizational Processes." 1989. Ann Arbor, MI: University Microfilms International. 241 pages.

This dissertation examines violations of antitrust for Fortune 500 companies over a five-year period. Data are from 1981–1985 and include 166 violators. Findings from the analysis include that violators tend to be larger companies, those companies with greater profit and high levels of industry production intensity. The study provides several explanations for corporate offending and includes dialogue from interviews with regulatory enforcement agents.

Mullen, Linda Greef. "An Examination of the Antecedents of White-Collar Criminal Behavior in Marketing." 2005. Ann Arbor, MI: University Microfilms International. 159 pages.

This dissertation examines which theories are relevant to white collar offending. It is an interdisciplinary study that uses data from convicted white-collar criminals. It assesses the extent to which various factors—corporate culture, personality character-istics, and social variables—contributed to their engaging in white-collar offending. Specifically, it attempts to answer three questions: which corporate cultures increase or decrease the like-lihood for a marketer to commit a white-collar offense, what per-sonality characteristics increase or decrease this likelihood, and what social variables are related. The data for this study come from three federal institutions.

Reifert, Steven Edward. "State-Corporate Crime in Kalamazoo Department of Public Safety: A Case Study of Deviant Activity between the Police and Computer Vendors." 2006. Ann Arbor, MI: University Microfilms International. 251 pages.

This dissertation examines the state corporate crimes that took place in Kalamazoo, Michigan, and the resultant injury, death, and monetary loss that occurred because of it. An integration of theories is used in an explanation of wrongful behavior among public departments, private vendors, and the government. Pol-icy recommendations are given as well as directions for future replication and research.

Magazines and Newsletters

Corporate Crime Reporter
1209 National Press Building
Washington, DC 20045
(202) 737–1680
www.corporatecrimereporter.com

The *Corporate Crime Reporter* is a legal print newsletter published 48 times a year. It contains various reports and news about cur-rents events each week. It is aimed at federal and state prosecu-tors, corporations, law schools, media outlets, and white-collar and corporate criminal defense firms.

FTC: Watch
P.O. Box 356
Basye, VA 22810–0356
(202) 639–0581
www.ftcwatch.com

This is a newsletter that is published 22 times a year and was started in 1976 by former Federal Trade Commission employees. It specializes in covering information about the FTC, states' attorneys general, U.S. Congress, and the Department of Justice's Antitrust Division. Topics covered include trade regulation, consumer protection, the latest corporate mergers and acquisitions, and issues surrounding trade at the national and global level.

Multinational Monitor
Essential Information
P.O. Box 19405
Washington, DC 20036
(202) 387–8034
multinationalmonitor.org

This is a monthly journal published by Essential Information, a nonprofit organization started by Ralph Nader that tracks corporate activity around the globe. It spotlights Third World development by publishing information on the environment, worker health and safety, labor union issues, and the politics of business. Each year, this journal compiles a list of the 10 worst corporations based on their involvement in corporate criminal behavior.

White Collar Crime Fighter
213 Ramapoo Rd.
Ridgefield, CT 06877
(202) 440–2261
www.wccfighter.com

This magazine is published monthly and offers strategies to combat fraud for organizations and corporations. The magazine's purpose is to give information on detection, prevention, and investigation of fraud-related activity and how best to deal with it. It also discusses the latest technologies, software, tools, and techniques available to protect businesses.

White Collar Crime Report
The Bureau of National Affairs
1231 25th St. NW
Washington, DC 20037
(202) 372–1033
www.bna.com/products/lit/wcln.htm

This is a biweekly magazine that focuses on legal developments concerning the prosecution and defense of white-collar crime. It keeps subscribers up to date on any policy changes or action taken by the United States Sentencing Commission and the Justice Department. It also tracks litigation pertaining to white-collar and fraud-related cases from federal courts and significant state court cases.

Government Documents and Agency Publications

Corporate Fraud Task Force. *First Year Report to the President.* Washington, DC: U.S. Department of Justice, Office of the Deputy Attorney General, 2003. 76 pages.

This is the first report of the Corporate Fraud Task Force to the president. It outlines the task force's mission and provides a summary of first-year highlights regarding criminal prosecutions and civil and regulatory enforcement efforts. It also discusses the role and contributions of various members of the task force, including the FBI, U.S. attorneys, the Securities and Exchange Commission, the Department of Labor, and the Department of Treasury.

Corporate Fraud Task Force. *Second Year Report to the President.* Washington, DC: U.S. Department of Justice, Office of the Deputy Attorney General, 2004. 45 pages.

This report provides facts and statistics from the task force's second year of combating corporate criminal activity and enforcing the nation's laws, both criminal and civil. This is a summary of the efforts of each contributing member toward apprehension, prosecution, and punishment of corporate wrongdoers.

Department of Health and Human Services. *The Health Care Fraud and Abuse Control Program FY 2005.* **Washington, DC: U.S. Department of Justice, Health Care Fraud and Abuse Control Program, 2005. 44 pages.**

This publication is an annual report of the Health Care Fraud and Abuse Control Program, which is under the direction of the secretary of the Department of Health and Human Services and the U.S. attorney general. The program was set up to coordinate health care fraud enforcement activities at the federal, state, and local levels. This report is a summary of the results of cooperated efforts to investigate and prosecute the most harmful health care fraud cases for the past year.

Helmcamp, James, Richard Ball, and Kitty Townsend, eds. *Definitional Dilemma: Can and Should There Be a Universal Definition of White Collar Crime?* **Morgantown, WV: Training and Research Institute of the National White Collar Crime Center, 1996. 343 pages.**

This publication is based on the proceedings of a white-collar crime workshop cosponsored by the National White Collar Crime Center and West Virginia University. The workshop centered on the many definitions of white-collar crime. This document brings together the ideas of prominent white-collar crime scholars to form a working definition of the term for the National White Collar Crime Center and its membership. A definition that is common and can be operationalized will help to support and expand research efforts on white-collar criminal offending.

Kane, John, and April D. Wall. *Identifying the Links Between White-Collar Crime and Terrorism: For the Enhancement of Local and State Law Enforcement Investigation and Prosecution.* **Morgantown, WV: National White Collar Crime Center, 2005. 94 pages.**

This report identifies and discusses the relationship between white-collar crime and terrorism and presents the issues and problems involved in investigating and prosecuting these types of cases. It gives detailed information on cases investigated in Colorado that involved insurance fraud, identity theft, money laundering, and tax evasion by a terrorist group for the purposes of raising money to fund terrorism.

Kane, John, and April D. W6all. *The 2005 National Public Survey on White Collar Crime.* **Morgantown, WV: National White Collar Crime Center, 2006. 54 pages.**

This is a report of the National Public Survey on White Collar Crime conducted in 2005, which is a follow-up to the original survey conducted in 1999. The survey utilizes individual and household measures in a nationally representative survey. This report highlights the findings from the survey on such topics as public experience with white-collar offending. Questions were asked about victimization, perceptions of crime seriousness, and reporting behavior of those victimized.

McNulty, Paul J. *Principles of Federal Prosecution of Business Organizations.* **Washington, DC: U.S. Department of Justice, Office of the Deputy Attorney General. 2006. 21 pages.**

This memorandum from Deputy Attorney General Paul McNulty emphasizes the importance of protecting the integrity of the U.S. economy and marketplace. It informs the U.S. attorneys of changes to policy that support corporate crime prevention and makes clear the goals of the department. McNulty's memo replaces an earlier memorandum from Larry D. Thompson, the previous deputy attorney general.

National White Collar Crime Center. *Annual Report.* **Morgantown, WV: Training and Research Institute of the National White Collar Crime Center, 2007. 40 pages.**

This report is a summary of the yearly activities of the National White Collar Crime Center and is intended to be used for informational purposes by the agencies that provide funding for the center. It summarizes the accomplishments and work conducted by each of the departments and divisions and includes updates of future goals and a list of objectives for each section.

Office of the Inspector General. *Quarterly Report to Congress.* **Baghdad, Iraq: Coalition Provisional Authority, 2004. 87 pages.**

This is a quarterly report to Congress by the Special Inspector General for Iraq Reconstruction, who oversees the Iraq Relief and Reconstruction Fund. The publication summarizes the progress of efforts in Iraq regarding reconstruction. It reports on the effectiveness of the administration of program efforts as well as any detection of waste, fraud, or abuse in the operations of the program. These quarterly reports were designed to keep Congress, the American taxpayers, the secretary of defense, and the secretary of state informed of deficiencies or issues relating to program goals.

Transparency International. *Global Corruption Report 2007.* **Cambridge, UK: Cambridge University Press, 2007. 429 pages.**

Transparency International's annual corruption report examines wrongdoing in the judicial process around the globe. It brings together legal professionals, scholars, and activists to discuss remedies for systems that are corrupt. The report focuses on two main issues: the pressure on judges from politicians to make rulings in favor of certain legislative or economic interests, and smaller incidents of bribes from court officials. It analyzes how judicial integrity and accountability can be strengthened in order to combat corruption worldwide. It also includes case studies from different countries around the world.

U.S. Department of Justice. *Financial Crimes Report to the Public.* **Washington, DC: U.S. Department of Justice, Federal Bureau of Investigation, 2006. 48 pages.**

The FBI investigates crimes of fraud, embezzlement, and theft and characterizes these as crimes of deceit, violation of trust, or concealment. The financial crime investigations by the FBI focus on health care fraud, corporate fraud, identity theft, mortgage fraud, insurance fraud, and money laundering to name a few. This report is an annual summary of the extent and nature of the crimes that have come to the attention of the FBI and that they have investigated. These statistics are released by the FBI to inform the public, to gauge trends, and to analyze the effectiveness of the Department of Justice's efforts.

Nonprint Resources

Videos

Crime in the Suites
Type: VHS
Date: 1987

This video discusses the extent of white-collar offending in the United States and looks at how these individuals use their positions of power to embezzle billions of dollars. It includes personal stories of white-collar criminals and victims.

Cyber Crime Fighting II
Type: DVD
Date: 2005

This video was produced by the National White Collar Crime Center and contains information for law enforcement agencies on investigative tools designed to fight cybercrime. It features tactics and techniques for searching for digital evidence and how to maintain and preserve it. The disc is divided into four sections: First Responders, Detectives and Investigators, Computer Forensics, and Case Files.

Organized Crime: A World History
Type: VHS, 4 tapes
Date: 2001

This video series looks at organized crime in Sicily, Russia, Colombia, and China/India. Together, they give a comprehensive review of the most infamous crime organizations in the world. The video includes interviews with gangsters and law enforcement officials in these five different countries.

Theories of Crime: Crooks in White Collars
Type: VHS
Date: 1985

This video discusses white-collar crime and group conflict theory. It debates the theories of Ralph Dahrendorf, George Vold, Austin Turk, and Richard Quinney.

Web Sites

American Antitrust Institute
www.antitrustinstitute.org

Center for Corporate Policy
www.corporatepolicy.org

Council of Europe
www.coe.int

Environmental Protection Agency
www.epa.gov

Federal Bureau of Investigation
www.fbi.gov

Federal Trade Commission
www.ftc.gov

Financial Crimes Enforcement Network
www.fincen.gov

FTC Watch
www.ftcwatch.com

International Monetary Fund
www.imf.org

Internet Crime Complaint Center
www.ic3.gov

Interpol
www.interpol.int

Multinational Monitor
multinationalmonitor.org

National Association of Criminal Defense Lawyers
nacdl.org

National White Collar Crime Center
www.nw3c.org

Organization for Competitive Markets
www.competitivemarkets.com

Organization of American States
www.oas.org

Transactional Records Access Clearinghouse
trac.syr.edu

Transparency International
www.transparency.org

United States Computer Emergency Response Team (US-CERT)
www.us-cert.gov

United States Department of Justice
www.usdoj.gov

United States Secret Service
www.treas.gov/usss

United States Securities and Exchange Commission
www.sec.gov

White Collar Crime Fighter
www.wccfighter.com

World Bank
worldbank.org

World Trade Organization
www.wto.org

Glossary

Actus reus   An actual physical criminal act. Actus reus is necessary to prove that a crime actually occurred, except in instances of conspiracy or attempts at wrongdoing.

Antitrust legislation   Laws prohibiting businesses from engaging in practices or acts that deprive consumers of the benefits of competition, resulting in higher prices for inferior products and services.

Bribery   Offering or taking something of value, usually money or monetary instruments, to influence persons or gain an unfair advantage.

Clayton Antitrust Act of 1914   Expanded the Sherman Antitrust Act in an attempt to remedy some deficiencies relating to monopolies. The Clayton Antitrust Act addresses the issues of economic competition involving the sale, merger, or acquisition of corporate entities. It prohibits any one person from being in charge of more than one competing organization.

Compliance programs   Programs implemented by corporations and businesses to ensure conformity with laws or legal rules. Compliance programs can be mandated for corporations by law enforcement authorities as part of punishment for legal wrongdoing.

Corporate charter   A document, filed with authorities by the founders of a corporation, which states or proves the existence of a corporation as well as its purposes. Corporate charters include important information about a corporation and are sometimes referred to as articles of incorporation.

Corporate crime   Any criminal behaviors engaged in by a corporation for its own benefit or for the benefit of its employees.

Corporate death penalty   Revoking the licenses (corporate charter) of a corporation for criminal wrongdoing and forcing the corporation out of business.

Corporate Fraud Task Force (CFTF)   A task force created by President George W. Bush and led by the deputy attorney general of the United States. It was created to vigorously enforce laws against corporate criminal violations and restore investor confidence in corporations. The CFTF is made up of two groups: the Department of Justice group, which focuses on the enforcement of the corporate criminal law, and an inter-agency group, whose purpose is to assist in maintaining cooperation between legal and regulatory enforcement authorities.

Corporation An organization composed of a group of individuals organized by law for some purpose and having powers and existence apart from its members.

Corruption Among organizations, corruption occurs when part of an organization is not performing actions that are intended by law or performs actions in an improper manner. Among individuals, corruption refers to any dishonest practice or abuse of a position of power for personal gain.

Criminal forfeiture The taking of property by the government as punishment for criminal violations. Property can typically be seized if it was used in committing a criminal offense or was acquired by criminal activity.

Criminal liability Responsibility for actions or behaviors under criminal law.

Elite crime Violations of the law that occur while carrying out the duties of an occupation or through any financial transactions.

Embezzlement Taking or using money entrusted by another to someone's care.

Extortion Acquiring money or property by force, intimidation, harm to reputation, damage of property, or other unfavorable outcome rather than by threat of imminent bodily harm.

False advertising Using deceptive or misleading statements in advertising to gain an advantage in the market.

False pretenses Obtaining the personal property of another by misrepresentation of a past or present fact, swindling, and/or confidence game. The confidence game is an attempt to cheat someone out of money or some other assets by gaining their confidence.

Forgery Falsifying documents with the intent to deceive.

Federal Trade Commission Act of 1914 Set up the Federal Trade Commission (FTC) to control trade, oversee the activity of large corporations, and limit unfair trading practices. It made illegal several unfair methods of trading and competition that affect different areas of commerce. This act made it possible for the FTC to take action against any corporation that violated laws pertaining to the Sherman Act, the Clayton Act, and other violations not stated in those two acts.

For-profit corporation   An organization that functions to increase the wealth of investors through some commercial purpose.

Fraud   Deliberate deception for personal gain or an unfair advantage.

Free-market economy   Economic system where the production and distribution of goods or services are directed by supply, demand, and competition; a system in which the government has no part of any aspect of the production or distribution. In its purest sense, a free-market economy does not exist; most countries have some sort of mixed economic system.

Globalization   Process by which societies around the world increasingly use the same or similar practices, whether economic, social, technological, or cultural.

Limited liability   The features of a corporation which state that the owners cannot be responsible or liable for more than they have personally invested in the corporation.

Mala in se   Behaviors that are inherently criminal or wrong.

Mala prohibita   Behaviors that are criminal only because a legislature has defined them as such.

Mens rea   The criminal intent or guilty mind. Proving mens rea shows premeditation by the perpetrator.

Money laundering   Literally, the cleaning of money. Engagement in any financial transactions that are meant to hide the source or destination of money from legal and financial authorities; attempts to make money that was obtained illegally into money that comes from a legitimate source.

Monopoly   A corporation that has exclusive control over a service or a commodity; also, when a business has no competition for its goods, products, or services.

Multinational corporations   Corporations that operate in two or more countries.

National Incident-Based Reporting System (NIBRS)   A system of recording crimes and situational factors of crimes. For each criminal incident known by the police, the information recorded includes the nature and type of criminal offense, the characteristics of the offender and victim, and the nature and type of property taken.

Not-for-profit corporation   An organization with noncommercial goals; these corporations are not concerned with monetary profit; rather, they support matters of private or public interest. Examples include the environment, charities, education, health care, politics, religion, sports, and research.

Occupational crime Illegal activities committed during the course of employment in a legitimate occupation.

Organization According to the U.S. Sentencing Commission, an organization is a person other than an individual. An organization may be a corporation, association, partnership, union, joint-stock company, pension fund, unincorporated entity, trust, government, or nonprofit entity.

Organizational crime Acts in violation of the law performed to further an organization's goals.

Perpetual lifetime The idea that a corporation, its assets, and structure will continue to exist after the lifetimes of its members.

Political crime Crime committed by or for any agent of the government. Political crimes involve commissions or omissions that threaten any interests of the government or state.

Price fixing When companies act in collusion to fix the prices of a commodity or service at a high level in order to make a bigger profit at the expense of consumers.

Price gouging Pricing commodities or services over the expected market price when the supply is low or there is no other vendor.

Racketeering Engaging in illegal or criminal activities through a business enterprise.

Respondiat superior Doctrine enabling corporations to be held responsible for the wrongful behavior of their employees.

Sarbanes-Oxley Act of 2002 Passed into law in response to corporate and accounting scandals that caused numerous investors and shareholders to lose their investments and retirement funds. It established new guidelines for corporate entities, added responsibilities to corporate boards for the actions of their companies, and enhanced criminal penalties for violations. Under this act, board members must disseminate earnings reports to shareholders. The act also established a new agency, the Public Company Accounting Oversight Board, to oversee accounting firms' activities in auditing publicly traded companies.

Sherman Antitrust Act of 1890 Legislation enacted to prohibit the restraint of trade or commerce between the states or with foreign nations. Aimed at those who attempt to decrease economic competition, it prohibits monopolies, including attempts or conspiracies to form monopolies. Violations can be prosecuted by the government in civil or criminal jurisdictions, and penalties under the act include fines of up to $10 million for corporations, $350,000 dollars for individuals, and imprisonment of up to three years.

Sourcebook of Criminal Justice Statistics   A compilation of data and statistics from over 100 sources that gives information on various aspects of crime and criminal justice in the United States. Funded by the U.S. Department of Justice, Bureau of Justice Statistics.

Transparency   Accurate disclosure—in full and in a timely fashion—of information that is of a public nature.

Uniform Crime Reports (UCR)   Established in 1929 by the International Association of Chiefs of Police to provide a comprehensive list of annual crime statistics in the United States. Today, compiled by the FBI, the UCR provides information on eight index offenses and reflects information on criminal arrests by over 17,000 police agencies in the country.

Welfare fraud   The intentional misuse of welfare systems by providing inaccurate or false information. Involves obtaining benefits of the system that are not deserved because the recipient does not meet the qualifications or standards for receipt.

White-collar crime   According to Edwin H. Sutherland, this type of crime is "committed by a person of respectability and high social status in the course of his [or her] occupation." White-collar crime overlaps with corporate crime because opportunities to commit such crimes as fraud, embezzlement, or forgery occur more often among white-collar employees.

Index

About the Author

Richard D. Hartley is an assistant professor of criminal justice at Texas A&M International University in Laredo, Texas. He received his Ph.D. from the University of Nebraska at Omaha and his M.S. and B.S. degrees from Minot State University. Hartley is or has been a member of several professional organizations, including the American Society of Criminology, the Academy of Criminal Justice Sciences, the Midwestern Criminal Justice Association, and the Southwestern Association of Criminal Justice. He is the coauthor of *Criminal Courts: Structure, Process, and Issues* (2nd ed., Prentice Hall, 2008) as well as several peer-reviewed journal articles. His research interests include disparities in sentencing practices, especially at the federal level; prosecutorial and judicial discretion; sentencing for narcotics; white-collar violations; and race/ ethnicity and crime.